Andrew Carter

Proverse Hong Kong

2018

Andrew Carter is a man in his thirties with a wife and child, greying hair and a tendency to go to bed before 10pm. His second book, THE THING IS, is a collection of charming and hilarious tales about all that went on before. From a childhood where he cheated in chess tournaments and tough kids stole his SNES games, he grows into an adolescence including dalliances with drink and drugs, attempts at punk rock stardom and an overwhelming desire to look cool in front of girls. Wanderlust takes him across the globe where there's a spot of bother in Bolivia, Australia in a battered van, a police chase in the Greek mountains and a stint as a minor celebrity in Hong Kong. There are late nights and fistfights, Sunday league struggles, call centre hell, a campus love story and a whole lot more. Like a perfect conversation with your pals in the pub, you'll feel fuzzy with nostalgia, wince in recognition and laugh out loud.

ANDREW CARTER was born in Leeds in 1986 and grew up in the city. After graduating from Lancaster University in 2009, he spent three years in Hong Kong where he taught English and wrote his first novel, *Bright Lights and White Nights*, which was released in 2015 to critical acclaim. Andrew has since moved back to Leeds where he works as a probation officer and occasionally writes for local magazines. In his free time, he plays tennis and 6-aside football and enjoys hiking in the Yorkshire dales. He lives with his wife, Louise and son, Joshua.

The Thing Is

Andrew Carter

Proverse Hong Kong

The Thing Is
By Andrew Carter
Copyright © Proverse Hong Kong October 2018.
First published in Hong Kong by Proverse Hong Kong,
November 2018.
ISBN: 978-988-8491-40-7

Distribution and other enquiries to:
Proverse Hong Kong, P.O. Box 259,
Tung Chung Post Office,
Lantau, NT, Hong Kong SAR, China.
Email: proverse@netvigator.com;
Web: www.proversepublishing.com

The right of Andrew Carter to be identified as the author
of this work has been asserted by him
in accordance with
the Copyright, Designs and Patents Act 1988.
Cover created and designed by Marcus Fox.

British Library Cataloguing in Publication Data.
A catalogue record for this book is available
from the British Library.

For Louise and Joshua

The Thing Is by Andrew Carter

2006

Following three hours' sleep, we said our goodbyes to Rio de Janeiro and sat in silence on the minibus to the airport. As the Copacabana whizzed by for a final time, I caught my reflection in the window. I looked rough. Glassy eyes with bags under them, blotchy skin and greasy, sun-bleached hair. Eddie had a bad tattoo on his calf, Patrick's hair was receding and Rodney was sporting an impressive pot belly. It was time to go home. It was over.

The four of us were hungover having spent our final evening with a group of men from somewhere in the Midlands who were staying in our hostel, among them a bus driver, an accountant and a drug dealer. It had turned into a late night, dancing clumsily at a samba club and on arriving back in our dormitories, we'd angered a pair of amiable German ladies after I picked up a guitar and initiated a 4am singsong.

We arrived at the airport, clambered out of the minibus and trudged into the departures lounge.

"Have you got your passport, Andy?" Patrick asked.

"Of course. You don't need to patronise me."

I patted my right pocket. Empty. I patted my left. Same result. No problem, I told myself, reaching deep into my back pocket. I found a used tissue and a leaflet advertising a water park in Brisbane. My heart rate was increasing. Eddie, Patrick and Rodney, all holding their passports with assurance, were staring at me.

"Hurry up, Andy."

I rummaged through the top section of my filthy rucksack, unearthing a half empty pack of anti-malaria tablets which had sent me mental a few months earlier and a CD – the Top Gun soundtrack. Unhelpful. Not a passport. The feeling of dread exploded in my stomach and began to fill my body, seeping through my limbs.

The shorts.

With tears forming in my eyes I emptied my backpack on the floor with stinking clothes, toiletries and bad wooden souvenirs smashing onto the hard tiles. I knew it was in vain.

I'd left my passport in the pocket of my shorts.

Last night, I'd spilt red wine on the shorts and thrown them away.

"It was in my shorts."

"Are you joking?" Rodney asked.

"He must be," Eddie said, shaking his head.

I wished I was. I couldn't handle this. I put my face in my hands, crumpled to the floor and began to cry. Bystanders were looking on now. I punched my bag repeatedly, shouting obscenities in the gaps between sobs. I was, without a doubt, causing a scene.

An electronic voice sounded through the airport speakers: "Last call for flights to Heathrow." My friends looked at me, then at one another. I tried to compose myself.

"I don't want anyone to stay with me. You need to get on this flight."

"Really?" Eddie asked. "I don't mind staying."

"Please, just go. It'll cost hundreds to buy another flight. This is my fault. I'll sort it out."

"Are you sure?"

"Yes."

"To be honest, that's a relief," Eddie said, apologetically. "I do, kind of, need to get home,"

"I've got work on Monday," Patrick said.

Rodney nodded gloomily.

"What are you going to do, Andy? Are you going to be okay?"

"I'll be fine. It's always fine."

My pals conducted a whip round, which quashed their plans to buy gifts from duty-free for mothers who'd been worried sick for months. This provided me with enough cash for a bus back to Rio and one more night's accommodation in the hostel near Ipanema beach. I thanked my friends, we hugged and I watched as they turned their backs and walked away. At the gate, they looked over for a final time and waved with flat smiles. Was Eddie sobbing?

As soon as they'd disappeared I resumed my face in hands pose and began to cry again. There's only so long you can have a breakdown in an airport before the staff encourage you to move along and after being helped/dragged to my feet, I stuffed my meagre belongings back in the bag and stumbled off. I was on my own now, it was fight or flight. Well, not a flight. I'd missed that. I needed a new plan.

As I walked towards the sliding doors I felt a glimpse of light in my addled mind. There was a chance – a small one, but a chance – that my passport was retrievable. It was only 8am, the bin at the hostel might not have been emptied yet? Energised, I ran outside into a wall of oppressive heat and took the next bus to Ipanema beach. As we emerged from a tunnel to see views of Rio's stunning cityscape, I was indifferent to the panorama. The morning sun glinting off the turquoise sea surrounding Sugar Loaf Mountain was of no interest anymore. It was the most impressive city I'd ever been to but I'd had enough of it.

With my cheeks still tear-stained, I barrelled into the hostel foyer. The two German women were sat, having breakfast. I wiped my face.

"Hi, sorry about last night."

"It's okay," one of them said, smiling. "Don't worry about it."

"Thanks."

"I thought you were going home though?" she asked. "What happened?"

I explained my quandary and the ladies each gave me a hug, telling me everything would be okay. Given that the last time I'd seen them, they'd called me a selfish *schuft* who was *scheisse* on the guitar, this was a marked improvement. Their kindness was indicative of a maternal instinct and it comforted me. I couldn't, however, talk for long. I needed to check the bins.

I charged upstairs to my old dormitory where a portly Brazilian chambermaid was scrubbing the floors in the bathroom, the smell of bleach infiltrating my nostrils.

"Hello," I said, "can I look in that bin please?"

She looked confused as I bounded past her and, heart-pounding, opened the lid. Accompanied by some tissues, an empty packet of paracetamol and a beer can were my shorts. My beautiful wine-stained shorts. I grabbed them, ripped open the zip pocket and pulled out my passport, clenching my fist in celebration.

"Yes!"

The cleaner was now bewildered. If I'd been five minutes later, she would have emptied the bin and my passport would have been gone forever. Did she realise the significance of this? I went for a high-five, which was turned down, but things were looking up. I had something to work with now. Hope. Next step: e-mail my mum, ask to borrow more money and get on the next flight. Simple? Almost. I was already resigned to a summer spent working in bad jobs to pay off travelling debts so another few hundred wouldn't hurt, would it? I waved my passport victoriously at the German ladies who were awaiting a taxi to take them to Christ the Redeemer before paying a grumpy teenage receptionist for fifteen minutes on the hostel's sluggish internet.

I pulled a seat up and turned the computer on, mentally preparing the e-mail I was going to send to my mum. Should I tell the full story or be selective with the truth? Introduce a mugger perhaps? I logged into Hotmail and was informed that I'd received a new e-mail. It was from Matilde, a Bolivian girl with whom I'd had a fleeting fling a few weeks previously. I clicked open. Her message was in broken English but my eyes homed in on the keyword immediately.

Pregnant.

1

I went back to my primary school recently. It has now turned into a café and community centre which is better than the student halls of residence that were mooted before angry locals fought the machine with an online petition. It's a two-storey, black-bricked Victorian building with stone stairways and high ceilings, where the narrow tarmac playground now serves as an impractical carpark. As I was ordering a coffee, I had a flashback to being in this very room as a chubby white-haired kid quarter of a century ago.

My initial meeting with Eddie was in the boy's toilets. He had shoulder-length blond hair so I assumed he was in the wrong toilet and politely pointed him in the right direction. It was our first day of school and I was meaning to be helpful, not a bully. He understood my motives and we hit it off although God knows what we talked about. What do four-year-olds have to say? As we sat down on paint-stained steps for our first registration, I shunned an affable Canadian pal from nursery and sat next to Eddie. I was a fickle shitbag back then.

As our friendship grew, we began going to one another's houses for tea. The first time I went to Eddie's, we ate beans on toast and he introduced me to his guinea pig which was called Carter. I was honoured he'd named a pet after me although it later transpired that this wasn't the truth; Eddie's dad had named the rodent after the rock band, Carter the Unstoppable Sex Machine, who had been in the news after attacking Phillip Schofield at a Smash Hits Party. Was Eddie's dad a Schofield hater? My dad, a primary school teacher, would take us out for walks along woodland trails and show us how to build masterpieces out of cereal boxes. At times, however, we had disagreements, the worst of which resulted in Eddie and I having a fistfight. While I can't recall what triggered it, I do have hazy memories of doing something I'm not proud of. I bit him.

As is the case with four-year-olds, the fallout didn't last long and we soon made up. By Year 3 we'd earned a bit of status within school, epitomised by a doubles chess tournament victory. The fact that most of our opponents didn't know the rules was not important. We were called The Crocodiles. The following year we reformed, calling ourselves The Crocodiles Return. Inspired. We'd expected the name alone to spark terror into our adversaries and were certain we would lift the much-coveted victory shield once again. The only honour greater than this was beating our bearded headmaster, Mr Sheldrick; if you claimed victory he awarded you a trophy in front of the whole school. Eddie and I swaggered into our first game, confident and cocky. We were playing a pair in Year 1.

"We can beat these two with our eyes shut," I said, smirking and plotting the four-move checkmate which had served us so well in the previous year's tournament. Unfortunately for us, one of the kids, Fred, was unusually clever. A bona fide child genius.

"Are we playing the en passant rule?" Fred asked as we were setting up the pieces.

What the hell?

"Shut up, Fred," I said. He took this as a no, we are not playing en passant.

It didn't matter. Fred skilfully poached our rook with his queen and the blood drained from my face as he proceeded to dismantle our backline, paving the way to a quick victory.

"Checkmate."

The smug little shit.

Unwilling to accept this, Eddie and I shared a glance before doing something despicable.

"No, it's not."

"I'm sorry?"

"It doesn't count. We are starting again."

"Why?"

"We just are."

Given little choice, Fred and his partner reluctantly agreed to a rematch, in which we bucked our ideas up and managed to scrape a win against our shaken six-year-old opponents. We went on to win the whole tournament again but it was sullied and I feel bad about it to this day. Fred, if you're reading this, I'm sorry. And I still don't understand the en passant rule.

***

From Year 3 onwards we went swimming on Friday mornings. I'd done fine to start with, making light work of the ten-metre certificate, which my mum had proudly sewn onto my trunks. The step up to the big pool was, however, enormous. I was comfortable in the shallows but became anxious as soon as I was aware I couldn't touch the bottom with my feet. I remedied this by remaining within touching distance of the sides of the pool at all times.

"What are you doing over there, Andy?" asked a classmate, fresh from diving to the bottom and touching it with his hand. The maniac.

"Oh, you know. I just like it over here."

After a few lessons in the big pool, we attempted the twenty-five-metre certificate. All my classmates had gone before me and succeeded, including Eddie who'd aced it and was casually sitting on a bench, chatting to the underwater kid, who had not broken a sweat. He should have been in a much higher class. Get him in pyjamas fetching rubber bricks from the bottom.

"Okay, you're up," said Winston, our Rastafarian instructor.

I set off. As anticipated, I breezed through the shallow end before hitting a mental block as the water got deeper and my heart began to pound. Focus, I told myself, it's not far. Just look ahead, don't think about what's below. As a seven-year-old, my mind training skills were amateurish and I began to panic. The water was deeper than my entire body. What would happen if my arms stopped working? Treading water frantically, I looked to the side where Winston was strolling along in flip-flops, dreadlocks sprawling down his back.

"Winston?" I gasped.

He didn't hear me. Was he looking at the female swimming instructor across the pool?

"Oi, Winston!" I called out again, thrashing my arms.

13

"Whoa, what's up little man?" he said. "Do you need the pole?"

This was the ultimate humiliation. Having Winston hold the pole out and drag you in. I'd only seen it happen twice before, both times to girls, who had been demoted to a lesser group and were surely condemned to a lifetime on dry land. I looked at the end of the pool. It looked an awfully long way away. Could I do it?

With water getting in my mouth, ears, and nose I looked back to Winston, who was raising his eyebrows, awaiting my answer.

"Pole, little man?"

I nodded.

***

A popular craze at primary school was "itchy beard." The concept was simple; if you didn't believe what one of your classmates was saying, you would scratch an imaginary beard. The bigger or less believable the lie, the bigger and itchier your beard would get. If you suspected dishonesty but weren't sure, a small, subtle itch of your chin was sufficient. As the storyteller's tale escalated into blatant lies, groups of listeners would be using both hands to viciously scratch at enormous bushy beards by its conclusion. When you fell victim to beard scratchers it was maddening. Silas, a black kid who always wore a shirt, tie, and cardigan to school was the worst; even when you were telling the truth, he would automatically start stroking his chin. It was impossible to have a conversation with the guy. I have no idea what the origins of the itchy beard craze were or whether it was common in other schools.

One of our classmates, Damian, was regarded as a tough kid; a stocky, rosy-faced rogue who wore wet-look gel in his hair. He had older brothers and sisters and thus knew things that none of us did and he was the best at Mercy, the brutal game where competitors lock hands and try to inflict maximum pain on each other by twisting their wrists until someone calls for mercy. Damian highlighted his superiority by continuing to twist his victim's wrists long after they had admitted defeat. The only way to beat him was by using your wits and asking at the start of the battle, "What's the name of this game?" My brother taught me this trick.

On one occasion, Damian was telling a story about drinking beer, which in hindsight was probably true, when Ollie, a cheeky friend began scratching his chin. Damian wasn't impressed.

"Fuck off with your itchy beard. Your mum is a prostitute. She's had more balls than Stephen Hendry."

He was nine. What on earth did this mean? It hadn't sounded pleasant so I made a mental note not to do the itchy beard thing to him. One evening a few friends were at mine for tea including Damian. You're all friends in primary school, aren't you? I was delighted as my brother had got some new football nets for his birthday which I was looking forward to showing off. There'd been a couple of chin scratches when I'd boasted of the new nets, which were not undeserved as I'd claimed they were the same nets that Leeds United use.

We were playing three-and-in and Damian was in goal, something he wasn't happy about as he was wearing jeans. I was trying to tackle Ollie in a bed of broken daffodils when, in the corner of my eye, I saw Damian swinging on the crossbar.

"Please don't do that," I asked.

"Fuck off."

Given that he was playing in my garden while my dad cooked him dinner, I thought this harsh. He continued to swing until, sure enough, the bar snapped in half and the goalposts collapsed in a heap, forever ruined. My brother, John, was raging and blamed me entirely. With most kids, if they misbehaved at someone's house their parents would be called to come and pick them up, a humiliation comparable with when your mum told you to "stop showing off," in front of your friends. To Damian, no such problem. He just left and walked home by himself, slamming the garden gate on his way. I was upset with him but he trumped this with intimidation and, fearing what he'd be like as an adversary, we soon made up.

Damian was persuasive; he'd once convinced me to swap the entire contents of my pencil case for a solitary football sticker. In fairness, it was a rare Coventry City shiny. Towards the end of the school year, he and I made another arrangement where we swapped our collection of Super Nintendo games. I gave him some classics; Super Mario World, F-Zero, International Super Star Soccer, Sunset Riders and Micromachines. In return, he gave me a collection of woeful platform games I'd never heard of. Two of them didn't work. John was unhappy with me again as I hadn't run the deal by him. A few days later he ordered me to go to Damian's house and swap back. Swapping back was highly frowned upon in those days and I was nervous. Fortunately, he was okay with my proposal, claiming to have "clocked" Sunset Riders and that Super Mario World was "shit anyway," a sentiment I vehemently disagreed with.

I arranged to meet Damian at his house after school, an even more daunting proposition. No classmates had ever been over and it was spoken about in hushed tones. His big brother was a notorious hard man and there were rumours that the family had a Pitbull Terrier. My mum walked me to the house and while she waited at the bottom of the drive, I knocked and waited. Eventually, Damian answered the door with a scowl and I stood on his porch while he sloped upstairs and bashed around for what seemed an eternity. With the sound of dogs barking in the background, we swapped back and I left the house feeling pure relief. It was all okay.

I got home and gave my brother some attitude, nonchalantly tossing the games on the sofa.

"There. Are you happy now?"

My brother looked at the cartridges.

"Where is Micromachines?"

"What are you talking about? I only gave him four games."

"No, you didn't. Twerp. Where is it?"

"I didn't give him it."

"Yes, you did. Go and get it."

I was getting worked up. Shaking. I shouted.

"I promise there were only four games!"

The severity of my lie was beyond itchy beard and my brother was livid. Even now, I don't know if I honestly thought that there were four games or if I was just too scared to go back to Damian's house. My brother, in his first year of high school and more worldly-wise than I, had no qualms about such things and after I'd given him the address he marched over and picked up the remaining game.

He was pleased with himself when he returned.

"I promise there were only four games," he mimicked, shoving the Micromachines cartridge in my face.

He'd won.

To this day, if ever my brother and I disagree on something, he will throw the line back at me.

"I promise there were only four games."

The bastard.

While I was upset about all of this, I asked myself; was it a genuine mistake or had Damian actually tried to steal from me? Soon after he moved to another school and we lost all contact. Twenty years later, I saw Damian again. A photograph of his face was on Crimewatch. Britain's most wanted for armed robbery. Perhaps that answered my question?

2

My mum grew up in Thirsk, a small market town in North Yorkshire and told us tales about a childhood spent in a redbrick home next to a slaughterhouse, crammed full of elderly aunties and uncles and mad animals. Her dad, who'd been nearly fifty when she was born, was something of a local celebrity by virtue of being an excellent cricketer and former mayor of the town. At twenty-one my mum moved to the bright lights of Leeds to study law and, one evening in the student union, was approached by a bespectacled Bob Dylan-fan, recently returned from hitchhiking across Canada.

My mum would go on to be a successful barrister and my dad would utilise his diploma from the prestigious Crewe teacher training college, landing a position at Burley St Matthias Primary school. They moved into a semi-detached at the top of a cul-de-sac near Headingley cricket ground shortly after John was born and this would be where I'd spend my first eighteen years on this planet. It was a lovely little house with French windows opening from a thin kitchen into a back garden the size of a tennis court. We held firework displays for the whole street here although I remember our neighbour, an Indonesian architect, once got overexcited and threw his sparkler into a tree, causing an uproar.

"Gus! There are children around!"

As the last to arrive on the scene I landed the box room while my brother got the biggest in the house. This would be the source of staid envy, particularly when he got a pool table. My brother and I spent most of the time in the living room watching TV, scrolling through Teletext or sitting on the floor, too close to the screen while playing on the SNES. My dad, a tall thin man with floppy greying hair spent his time pottering around the house moving and fixing things or sitting in his cherished armchair, drinking cups of tea and reading books that none of us understood.

My mum, who sported the typical early-nineties perm, blouse and thick-rimmed glasses look during my childhood spent much of her time in the backroom, stacked under piles of paperwork, occasionally venturing through to the front room where she'd turn off my dad's Kinks records to play Enya or Eurythmics. For the most part, my mum is an intelligent, logical woman but on occasion, oddities and old wives' tales from Thirsk would creep through the net, unchallenged. I once got an ear infection and was off school in agony. Rather than seeing a doctor, we went with my mum's miracle cure: heating up an onion, chopping it in half and strapping it to my ear with a piece of string. To make things worse, she had to run some errands and took me with her – out in public, where other people could see me wearing the onion.

"Are you sure this works? I feel a bit stupid."

"Stop fussing, course it works."

It didn't work.

On occasion, my parents would go away for the weekend, leaving us in the company of our grandparents. They still lived in the same house my dad had grown up in Alwoodley, a suburb of Leeds populated predominantly by elderly people. My nan was a cheerful, blushing lady who was short and round, comprised almost entirely of circles. She had the classic short, curly white/purple haircut popular among ladies of her age. When does that look kick in? Seventy? She laughed a lot, collected Capodimonte porcelain figurines and, as you'd hope for, was an exceptional cook specialising in comfort food; fry ups, Yorkshire puddings, dumplings, flapjacks, and cakes. She would feed us until we were stuffed before we'd sit, sweating in the stifling hot living room, watching Saturday night TV. My nan usually did most of the talking but now and then my granddad, a fierce, outdoorsy man who drove like a maniac, would regale a cheery anecdote from the war.

"And that was the last time I saw poor Johnny..."

Silence apart from the Gladiators theme tune on TV. Once, as I was trying to concentrate on Family Fortunes, he began telling a tale which sounded uncharacteristically perky.

"It was a beautiful beach. The sun would glimmer on the sea as seagulls flew around us. Families would be eating picnics, full of joy." He looked to the ceiling with a nostalgic smile. "There was a Lido which bobbed around in the water. It was a tough swim to get there but once we did, we'd spend hours sunbathing, diving off, laughing and joking. It was a wonderful time. I loved that Lido."

I shared a surprised glance with John. What was happening here? My granddad looked ready to continue but before he opened his mouth, something happened. There was a pause. His smile began to curl and a ferocious scowl formed as he looked out the window with a steely-eyed glare.

"And then the vandals came."

My granddad's face reddened and he raised his voice

"Those bloody vandals…"

My nan scurried through from the kitchen wearing a pair of marigold gloves.

"Not this again, Jim?"

"But they ruined everything. You don't understand…"

"Jim, that's enough!"

He spent the rest of the evening stewing silently while we watched Blind Date and felt guilty laughing at Cilla's jokes. This story had seemingly caused more pain and sorrow than any of the war tales featuring brave soldiers perishing at the hands of the German bastards.

***

Even with a "temporary" Portakabin class, my primary school was one classroom short with the solution to have classes of split year groups; R/1, 1/2, 2/3, 3/4, 4/5 and 5/6. Given that I was one of the oldest in my year – and stormed my Year 2 SATS, which I like to think played a part – I spent my final two years in 5/6, which was the best deal. It was the coolest class, offering two years of sitting on benches in assembly as the rest of the school squirmed on a cold wooden floor.

I was upset when Eddie and I moved up to 4/5 and some of our pals remained in the confines of the 3/4 Portakabin. However, I soon got over it when, after much excitement, a new kid called Jack joined my class. Barring a pair of Sri

Lankan brothers, who were exceptional cricketers but kept losing balls by hitting them over the railings, there hadn't been any new arrivals in a long time. We barely had enough space for the current crop, although with Jack this wasn't much of an issue as he was rather small. He had floppy hair, a wide grin, and bags of energy. Rumour had it that his garden was massive and his dad allowed him to have bonfires. I honed in.

"Welcome to the school, friend."

"Thanks. What's your name?"

"Enough of the pleasantries. It is true you have a treehouse?"

A couple of nights later, Eddie and I went to his despite neither of us having received a concrete invite. With delight, I discovered the speculation was true. All of it. His garden was enormous with rope swings, dens, tunnels and climbing frames. An adventure playground.

Jack's parents appeared happier to see us than he did, although there was pride in his eyes as he showed us his most recent addition, a zip line tied between two beech trees. I gazed around in wonderment, this was too much. What should we do first? Will there be time to do everything before my mum comes to pick us up?

Jack suggested the "big" rope swing, which confused me. I'd only noticed one rope swing, which didn't look too intimidating.

"That one?" Eddie asked Jack, pointing to the top of the garden.

"No, look up."

A huge oak tree towered over the dusty divot we were standing in. A frayed blue rope was dangling down, tucked behind a large nail in the tree. I followed the rope upwards with my eyes until they eventually reached the branch it was tied to. It was in the Gods. I felt nauseous.

"Watch," Jack said before scrambling up through some shrubbery to a protruding root which served as a launching platform at the foot of the tree. He hooked his foot into a loop, jumped up and soared through the air. At the pinnacle, he was fifteen feet in the air. After he'd finished swinging he clambered down and stood next to me, flicking back his hair with his hand.

"Your turn."

I was scared, my stomach fluttering. Did I want to do this? As a delay tactic, I began firing questions at him.

"How did you tie the rope swing?"

"I tied a ball to the rope and threw it."

"What kind of ball."

"A tennis ball."

"What kind of knot did you tie?"

"Are you going or what?"

With Jack and Eddie, who I sensed was also nervy, watching in anticipation, I gingerly made my way to the launch point.

"Just hook your foot in and jump," Jack shouted as I stood motionless.

"Wait a second, I'm just getting ready."

"Come on, it's easy."

"Fine," I snapped, worried that word would get around at school that I was a wimp.

Deep breath, knot in my stomach, I put my foot in the hoop.

"Will this hold my weight? I'm taller than you."

"My dad has been on it and he was fine."

Piss off.

"Right, here we go."

I grabbed the rope as tightly as I could, shut my eyes and jumped. Plummeting, I left my stomach behind me.

Wow.

Wait a second, ow.

The frayed rope was cutting deep into my hands, causing friction burn.

"Aargh!"

I whizzed past Eddie and Jack screaming before beginning my upwards trajectory. I wasn't taking in my surroundings. All I could focus on was the agony of the rope burn. This was unbearable, I couldn't take it anymore. As I was approaching the apex, I let go. I dropped through the air, thudded onto a sloped shed roof, slid down and landed in a pile of wet leaves. Lucky. Winded but lucky.

Eddie and Jack ran over.

"Are you okay?"

I groaned.

"Why did you let go?" Eddie asked.

My breath eventually came back and I clambered to my feet and showed them the grazed skin on my palms.

"Rope burn."

"Oh yeah," Jack said, "that happens sometimes."

Eddie didn't take his go.

***

In my final year of primary school, I was glad to be reunited with various pals who had been held back in previous classes. Johnno and Danny were perhaps the two I was happiest to see again. Like Eddie, Jack and to a lesser extent, Damian, the pair of them would also go on to play leading roles in my formative years.

When I'd first met Johnno, he was wearing broken Flintstones glasses repaired with Sellotape, although by the time we were in Year 6 this fashion faux pas was long forgotten as he had a wand of a left foot when we played football on the tarmac. Throughout school, Johnno and I had gone to one another's for dinner after school and would invariably end up giddy and bursting into hysterical laughter, to the annoyance of our parents.

"Not again?" my mum would say as Ribena spilt out of my mouth and nostrils as I cried with laughter because Johnno had thrown a potato at me.

Danny, who had trendy parents that worked in TV, was a good dresser, usually clad in the latest Nike trainers and football shirts. He was also the class clown and he and I worked well as a double act. Aged ten we were discovering the increased importance of earning laughs from girls. There were several pretty girls in our class and whereas previously they had been an irritation who you didn't want on your rounders team, I was becoming increasingly intrigued by their presence.

Indeed, it was in Year 6 that I had my first romantic experience. It came during a residential trip to the Lake District and was the second noteworthy event of a bittersweet evening. Following a day of canoeing and obstacle courses, my concentration was waning and while holding a plateful of hot food, I'd walked into the back of an older kid from another school in the canteen, covering his white Ben Sherman shirt in mince and gravy. He'd worn this especially for the after-dinner disco and was understandably livid. Our hip music teacher stepped in to stop things from getting ugly and a teacher from his school fetched him a faded polo shirt from lost property.

Later, I was averting his angry glare on the dance floor when a girl from his school walked over to me, chewing gum which was forbidden.

"Will you dance with me?"

I looked to Danny for guidance. He nodded.

"Sure."

I held her hands but ensured that our hands were the only body parts touching as we flailed our arms loosely in time to "Here Comes the Hotstepper." "Dreams" by Gabrielle played next and by the chorus, both of our palms were sweating and she seemed to be losing interest. Over her shoulder, the guy I'd spilt dinner on was holding a girl close to him, her head nestled on his shoulder. Imagine what he'd have been like if he still had his Ollie Sherman on? No hope for any of us. Hang on, was he touching her bum? Who were these people?

My companion noticed them and asked,

"Can we dance like that?"

I ran away. Terrified.

3

Eddie and I spent much of our time at The Turnways where both Johnno and Danny lived - a leafy circular street half a mile away from mine which was largely occupied by young families. Through Danny and Johnno, my modest social circle grew as we became acquainted with the other kids on the street. On the splintered wooden planks of a tree house offering free views of the rugby at Headingley Stadium, I met Jacob, a clever kid with a winning smile, and Johnno introduced me to Craig, a kind-hearted joker with hair crafted into a very definite centre parting. Craig's family had a huge dog, Frosty, who frightened me initially, although I warmed to her in time (pardon the pun). Frosty once went missing and was found strolling into a leisure centre a mile away.

One Saturday the group of us went to the local cinema for a matinee showing of Apollo 13. Craig was in the year above us and tall for his age so could feasibly pass for an older brother. He carried this mantle throughout our youth and would be the one to go in the shop for cigarettes and cider in years to come. For now, his mature appearance was important as the film was a PG. Sure enough, the cinema attendant said we could go in so long as there was a responsible adult to supervise us.

"No problem, he's just behind us," Danny said with assurance. "Craig?"

I turned around to see that our responsible adult had his hands on his head mimicking horns and was making a shrill squawking noise whilst head-butting Johnno.

Another time Craig got stuck up a tree. A few of us had been loitering in the park, idly kicking a flat ball around on the dog shit-strewn grass, when we came across an attractive birch tree boasting thick, sturdy branches. Johnno, Jacob, Craig and I scampered to the higher reaches before becoming unstuck by too far a reach and having to give up. We stood in the branches among the leaves admiring the park from our elevated position for a few seconds before growing restless and taking it in turns to clamber down and hop onto the grass. Craig was the last to descend but as we stood waiting, the thud never came. I looked up to see that he was sat on the lowest branch, looking down at the grass. When I say low, I mean low – from floor to Craig's dangling feet, we were talking five feet.

"What are you doing, Craig?" Jacob asked.

"Nothing, I'll be down in a minute."

A minute passed without movement.

"Are you stuck?" I asked him, confused.

"Don't be stupid."

"Well, why aren't you moving?"

"Come on, man!" Johnno said.

"Shut up."

This was absurd, was he joking? A black guy in his late-twenties was walking his dog nearby and Craig's quandary had caught his eye.

"Yo, what's going on here boys?" He started laughing. "Please tell me he's not fucking stuck?"

"I'm not stuck!" Craig said, unconvincingly.

"Well, what the fuck you doing, you pussy?!" our new companion asked, before continuing to laugh. I don't imagine he had a job working with children. We stood staring at Craig who looked close to tears. The black guy was close to tears from laughing so much.

"I'm off, boys," he said in between howls. "This is too much!"

Craig continued to sit on the low branch, not looking at us. Eventually, we talked him into lowering himself down and dropping – a basic manoeuvre – which he managed, before thudding onto the ground. Johnno looked at Craig, shaking his head in disbelief. Craig was ready to punch him.

***

With the ignominy of Winston's pole consigned to the past, we went to the local swimming baths now and then, which was fun although often resulted in injury and invariably ended with us being thrown out for either bombing or wrestling on the inflatables. During one session, I attempted to swim the length of the pool underwater. I failed but as I resurfaced I was struck by a pair of teenage girls stood a few metres away. I couldn't help but gawp at them, fascinated.

"Oi, pin dick," one snapped. "Take a photo, it will last longer."

I dived back into the water and swam away.

For my birthday, I got a mountain bike although the ungratefulness that I displayed when I first saw it was reprehensible. I'd been hankering for a Kappa tracksuit.

"What's this mum? I didn't ask for this. I don't want it."

Slammed door. What a little shit I was.

I soon saw sense and appreciated the benefits of owning wheels. Cycling down steep hills, known as the Dippers, in nearby woods became the thing to do and if I hadn't had a bike I'd have been ostracised. The Dippers were the source of many young tears with all of us suffering spectacular falls which never deterred us from returning. Eddie and Johnno were victims of humbling over-the-handlebars disasters, while I had a high speed, skidding tumble, leaving my knees, elbows and right cheek skinned and my bike in pieces. Craig slung my bike over his shoulder and helped me hobble back to my house, an act which earned him great credit from my dad. He still brings it up to this day when he's on his third pint of ale and feeling nostalgic.

"I always had a lot of time for Craig."

As well as cycling, when the weather was good we played out, something I was well versed in having spent the early parts of primary school on my own cul-de-sac with John and some other kids on the street. Most of them were older than me though and the scene had dried up somewhat. Since starting high school, they were no longer keen on playing "Octopus, can we cross the sea?" I couldn't understand this.

Playing out at The Turnways usually consisted of headers and volleys or cricket using a wheelie-bin as an oversized wicket. We were also keen on the Tig / Hide-and-Seek hybrid, Tig 123, scurrying up drives and bouncing through gardens, showing a complete disregard for people's private property. Once Jacob and I found the perfect hiding place; an empty rabbit hutch in an absent neighbour's garden. Excited, we clambered in. After the initial thrill of hearing footsteps charging past us the dark, damp cage soon became uncomfortable. Half an hour of confinement later, we clambered out and readjusted our eyes to the early evening twilight. We were expecting begrudging adulation from our seekers but the street was eerily quiet. Where was everyone? We walked past Johnno's house and saw them sat in his living room, eating crisps in front of the glow of the TV. What was this? Angered, we knocked on the door.

"Sorry," Danny said, not taking his eyes away from Dexter's Laboratory. "We gave up."

***

Jacob and Johnno played for the local football team, Kirkstall Crusaders, and over time the rest of us joined. This was with mixed success and my personal introduction to competitive action was far from smooth. On the back of Euro '96 and scoring a good goal on the street one evening, I'd already decided that I was going to be a professional footballer and would, therefore, glide effortlessly into the first team and become a prolific striker. I was unperturbed by the fact that I had an ungainly running style and was, to all intents and purposes, pretty shit.

Preparation before my debut training session was flawed as I'd been to a sleepover (the pinnacle of a ten-year-old's social life) at Eddie's house the night before. With peer pressure beginning to rear its ugly head, it was frowned upon if you didn't stay awake until sunrise and I was exhausted. On top of this, Akpo, a Nigerian friend had drawn a penis on my forehead in marker pen which I hadn't managed to fully scrub off. This was unlikely to endear me to my new teammates and coaches although I doubt first impressions of Akpo were great either; he smelt awful having had to spend time locked in a cupboard with a full bin on his head during a punishing game of truth or dare.

Akpo, at least, redeemed himself by being a good player and immediately caught Frank the manager's eye, proudly joining the first team where Johnno and Jacob plied their trade.

I, on the other hand, did not and quickly found myself with the "have-nots" – a mismatch of ages, sexes and generally not very good players, who were cast to playing at the top of a hill on some uncut grass under the guidance of someone's older brother who had an ear stud. I remained there for months. Despite my limited talents, football became the most important thing in my life. Playing, watching, talking about it, yearning for new shirts and scrolling through CEEFAX page 302 onwards. My brother was the same but, as my dad didn't give a shit about football, my mum facilitated our obsession, taking us to watch Leeds games at Elland Road and ferrying us to and from training sessions at opposite ends of the city with Blur, Oasis, Pulp, and The Verve the soundtrack to these frantic weekend runs. On our return, she'd clean our boots and cook bacon sandwiches for us while we watched Football Italia, idolising the players on show. Baggio, Batistuta, Davids, Del Piero, Inzaghi, Maldini, Recoba, Ronaldo, Rui Costa, Seedorf, Vieri, and Zidane. I loved those guys.

Frank the manager was a stout moustached man who wore a knee-length Umbro coat. He came up the hill to watch us for a few minutes each session, making notes and occasionally calling players up to the first team. I resented these players. You had to be lucky to time your moment of magic accordingly, a task made more difficult by the older brother/coach playing at full tilt and never passing the ball, often for the entirety of Frank's scouting mission. It was difficult and I always found myself feeling nervous and making bad decisions, things which I would become increasingly familiar with in later life.

Following a management reshuffle, we got a new coach in called Garry. Like Frank, he had a moustache, but he held me in higher esteem and I broke into the squad as the second choice right back, a role I would hold down with aplomb for a long time. As with any kind of football, there were plenty of ups and downs over this period. Scoring my first goal was pure unadulterated joy but within seconds Jacob and I sandwiched and clumsily bundled over their striker for a penalty and we went on to lose.

Life as a squad player could be tough with a low ebb coming when Garry chose to toss a coin to decide who should start a key game between Jacob and I. The sandwiching mistake evidently our downfall. Jacob chose tails and won, so I had to be the linesman.

As a substitute, you often had to face the indignity of running the line, a task I exclusively seemed to get given when we were playing the toughest teams in Leeds. Getting abuse hurled at you for wrong offside calls was never a fun way to spend your Sunday mornings. Even less so against teams whose alleged eleven-year-olds had beards and tattoos suggesting a lax or fraudulent ID card policy.

On one occasion, it got too much and Danny, who'd been dropped following a recent goal drought, and I came up with a bizarre ultimatum; if both of us didn't get back into the starting line-up we were going to join the Leeds Lizards, a weekend rock climbing group at Leeds Climbing Wall. Quite why we had chosen this I don't know. What would it have proven? We never did join so I presume we must have fought our way back into the first eleven. Perhaps there was a clampdown on our over-age players?

**

Concurrent with Kirkstall Crusaders, my friendship with the guys on The Turnways spanned many popular crazes; from flipping Pogs to playing Goldeneye on N64, whatever was in, we gave it a go. A fickle bunch. It must have been a pain for parents to fork out twenty quid on a flashing yo-yo only for you to soon get bored and demand new roller blades. I preferred, and was better at, the less dangerous activities. Good at swapping stickers, bad at doing a kickflip on a skateboard. To my ire, a fad which stuck around for a long time was wrestling, with countless afternoons spent "rumbling". I didn't enjoy it, was no good at it and picked up many an injury, hobbling to my bike and unsteadily cycling home. In the build-up to WrestleMania, an event I cared little about but was forced to feign interest in for popularity's sake, Craig's big brother's mate, an avid wrestling fan, picked me up and dropped me on his head. Agony.

On the occasions when wrestling wasn't on the agenda, all of us except Eddie got bang into the PC game, Championship

Manager. For some reason, Eddie couldn't see the appeal of staring at pages of data which, at best, would flash when you scored a goal.

"You don't even get to see the match?"

"That's not the point, shut up Eddie."

We would sit listening to the local radio, playing for hours on end, emerging from one another's houses with square eyes and fuzzy heads as dusk was setting. We became talented managers, taking lesser teams to great glory. However, the addiction became worrisome when I found myself waking up in the middle of the night, in a cold sweat, fretting about my decision to sell Sonny Anderson.

The finale to our primary school days included a three-night performance of Yanomamo, a rainforest musical, which our music teacher (who was eco-friendly as well as cool - the yoga type) had pushed for ahead of Oliver. Eddie was the lead narrator while Danny and Johnno were the bad guys – the loggers. I landed the role of a dancing spider.

My parents threw a leaving party at ours after the last day of school. My dad had organised some party games, which I hadn't deemed cool enough to impress my friends and I'd stropped and stormed up to my room. After all, I'd, sort of, danced with a girl now. Red-faced and sobbing into my pillow, Danny and Johnno came upstairs and gave me a pep talk.

"Come on, you're missing out!"

I wiped away my tears, walked downstairs with trepidation and found that, sure enough, the blow football and tiddlywinks tournaments were in full swing. My classmates were laughing and chatting while my mum rushed to and from the kitchen replenishing sausage rolls and party rings. It was a success. As the sun began to set, parents came to pick up their emotional pre-teens, who were now hitting the sugar rush comedown stage. With our carefree days over, I worried about what was in store after summer.

4

Secondary school saw a considerable mix-up. From my primary school, the majority went to either Ralph Thoresby, where Eddie and Jack were headed or Lawnswood, Johnno's destination. Danny and Jacob got into sought-after schools in the havens of Otley and Harrogate respectively, while Craig was embarking on Year 8 in a school I'd never heard of. I was going to none of the above.

John had got in with a bad crowd at Lawnswood and, after his mate was suspended for throwing rocks at moving vehicles, my parents decided he might be better off elsewhere and shifted him to the Grammar School. He'd got good grades and made friends who didn't terrorise bus drivers, so logic dictated I should go there too; my parents were keen for us to be given the same opportunities.

I made a couple of pals and my team won a five-a-side tournament but ultimately it didn't work out. I wasn't happy there; the teachers were too strict, I didn't like wearing blazers, didn't like rugby union and didn't like the lack of girls – just as they'd begun to fascinate me, they'd disappeared. My mum suspected all was not well – "I hate it, I'm not going back on Monday" – and shortly after Christmas, I moved schools.

I joined Eddie and Jack at Ralph Thoresby, a scattering of dilapidated, flat-roof buildings on the top of a hill surrounded by a concrete jungle of council estates. Near the school stands one of Leeds' ugliest landmarks; a BT tower built of reinforced concrete decorated with grey microwave dishes of various sizes. You can see the tower from almost every corner of the city. What were BT thinking? Surely, they have enough cash to spruce it up a bit?

In the school grounds, apart from the top field, which served as both a smoking area and fighting arena, everything was grey; gravel playgrounds and concrete pathways and ramps taking you from one grey building to another. The grounds were, at least, brightened up by tab ends, empty bottles of Fanta and packets of Nik Naks lining the floor, the afterschool litter-picking detention never keeping up with the influx of rubbish that each day produced. Circling the school was a sharp-spiked metal fence, giving the feel of a high-security prison. In Year 9 an unfortunate friend would impale his hand on the fence, the spike spearing through his palm and coming out the other side, blood gushing. He'd only wanted to sneak out and go to the butchers to buy a sausage roll, poor guy.

Three other friends had made the transition from our primary school; Tino, a kind-hearted Venezuelan, Darren, a long-haired skater and Ollie, a nutcase. After a bit of initial ribbing "posh twat," "gay boy," etc., (cheers Eddie) I soon settled into my new form and felt sure I'd made the right decision. While not the prettiest, Ralph Thoresby was a standard comprehensive in Leeds and I'm not going to overplay how tough it was – after all I'm not trying to impress a posh girl at university now (I never informed posh girls at university about my stint in a private school.) It was a bit frayed around the edges though and after an insight into blazers and cricket, it took a little while to get used to. In Year 7 smoking was not unusual, some of our classmates had got drunk and a handful had taken ecstasy. A group of guys in our year had a spell where they would meet up in the evenings and break into cars. This was all new to me, I'd thought the Dippers were the height of danger.

As well as my primary school chums I befriended Matt, Seamus, and Mads, a trio of brown-haired Championship Manager fans in my maths class, none of whom had taken ecstasy or stolen cars to my knowledge. With them in tow, I established my niche, somewhere in between the cool, hard kids and the shy, studious ones; a relatively safe purgatory. It helped that I got along well with the two hardest guys in the year, Tyler, and Shafqat, who had achieved the sought-after accolade early in their school career. Tyler had beaten someone up on the field to earn his status but Shafqat hadn't been seen in action so his title was a mystery to me. I think his brother in

Year 9 held some sway but Shafqat never showed any intention of beating me up, so I didn't question it.

My pals and I benefited from our collective height. Aside from Jack and Ollie, who made up for it with his nutcase tendencies, most of us were tall. In addition, Eddie had recently got into lifting dumbbells and Matt was the proud owner of a muscle toner, which basically gave you small electric shocks and was, in no way, scientifically proven.

That isn't to say there wasn't a bit of bother now and then. I sat next to Imran in Geography and had always thought we were pals, especially when we made wisecracks that CBD stood for Complete Bastard Dickhead. However, one lunchtime his cousin, an overweight brute with a bad haircut, casually strolled over and smacked me in the face.

"What was that for?" I asked clutching my cheek.

"Imran said you'd pissed him off."

This seemed a strange way to convey his message, not very diplomatic. Could we not have discussed it? Imran and I didn't sit next to one another in the next Geography class and I never found out what I'd said to irk him.

Matt suffered a worse fate. During a warm day, we had been pissing around on the field, doing that thing where you crouch down behind someone and your mate pushes them over. Matt, overexcited in the heat, shook up a bottle of lemonade and sprayed it on the back of a Gavin, a tall guy who was sat on the grass minding his own business. Gavin was a laidback character of the gentle giant ilk but the lemonade pushed him over the edge and he snapped, jumped up, grabbed Matt around the neck and beat the shit out of him, leaving him curled up in a ball on the floor, crying. I could kind of see his point. Water is one thing, but lemonade?

In Year 7 we had little status on the bus home. As one would expect, a group of loud-mouthed older kids occupied the back rows, listening to ringtones, smoking out of the windows and swearing. While they could be daunting and sometimes slung demoralising insults our way, it wasn't always bad. One afternoon I came out on top of a verbal battle, although admittedly my aggressor was his own worst enemy. I'd gone for a new hairdo – I imagine I was trying to impress a girl –

and had caked my fringe with gel to keep it stuck up at the front.

"Oi, look at this guy!" shouted one of the posse from the back.

For fuck's sake, what was coming next? I've just had double maths, I'm exhausted, just let me stand here, playing snake on my phone.

"Looks like he's got a full gel of tub on his head!"

Had I heard correctly?

"Gel of tub?" I asked.

His mates started chuckling.

"Don't get cheeky with me, you little shit. Look at the size of your ears. You look like the World Cup."

This was too good to be true.

"The World Cup doesn't have any handles," I Calmly responded. "Did you mean the FA Cup?"

As he looked ready to kill me, his mates were creasing it. Every dog has his day.

***

The school football team was dire. The manager, a science teacher from near Halifax, had a romantic idea of turning our ragtag bunch into champions, Mighty Ducks-esque, but the job was too big for him. An especially chastening defeat was against City of Leeds, who have produced several professional players over the years. In a failed tactical reshuffle, I started at left back and Aaron Lennon, who would go on to play for England, was on their right wing. We lost 11-1. He scored six.

Towards the end of Year 7 Darren, who'd grown shoulder length hair, landed himself a girlfriend so my pals and I started knocking around with her crowd. They wore Adidas tracksuits, crop tops and large hoop earrings and seemed much more confident and sophisticated than us. Why was this so? How had their primary school differed from ours? They were friendly enough though and I enjoyed being part of a mixed group. We listened to Venga Boys, TLC and Ricky Martin, watched videos at James' house and played truth or dare and spin the bottle in nearby parks. It was all a bit frightening but nonetheless exciting.

When I returned to school after the summer holidays I'd assumed things would continue where they'd left off with the girls but it didn't happen. By lunchtime, it had become evident that while I'd been on a family trip to France and spent many an evening at the Turnways, playing Headers and Volleys, something more significant had happened to the girls. All of them were wearing full make-up and push-up bras. They smoked, spoke differently and expressed a succinct change in attitude. It transpired that during a holiday to a campsite in Wales they'd been getting drunk, finding boyfriends and having sex. What the heck? We were yesterday's news and within days they'd begun hanging around with guys a year or two older, who smoked and wore Rockport shoes. After a glimpse into the exciting world of girls and potential girlfriends, it was gone.

It wasn't all bad though. Early in Year 8, Nelson Mandela came to visit Leeds. This was a huge deal for the city, especially given that the calibre of stars turning on the Christmas Lights had sunk as low as Mr Blobby in recent years. I didn't know a whole lot about Nelson Mandela but was aware he was a great man and didn't want to miss the opportunity to see him. At break time I managed to convince Carl, a guy in my form, to come and see him with me. It hadn't been long since he and I had been involved in a spat during a heated rounders match, so playing truant together acted as a fitting way to let bygones be bygones.

In stealth mode, we carried out our escape, opting to climb over the tricky bottom gates as opposed to strolling through the open top gates. This was questionable logic but only added to the sense of adventure. Carl gave me a foot up which I was glad about as I was incapable of the manoeuvre without assistance. He would go on to join the army and showed fitting attributes as he clambered over with style and we ran off, giddy.

After popping to Asda, we got on the bendy bus, which was in its infancy and still quite exciting. We played the then popular game of standing in the middle bit without being able to hold on, a task made trickier whilst clutching on to our provisions for the day; a pack of cookies, some Neon Nerds and two litres of 19p lemonade. The staple Year 8 diet.

We arrived at Millennium Square just in time and, despite our close proximity to a man who smelt of whisky and was shouting gibberish, managed to get a good view. Nelson Mandela arrived on stage and it was excellent to see him. There was a slip of the tongue when he thanked the "wonderful people of Liverpool" but it was a memorable occasion. I tried hard to remember some of his lines so I could show off to girls in my form. After the event, we returned to school in the midst of a sugar and adrenaline comedown. We had the ambitious intention of slipping back into the last class of the day, with our three-hour absence unnoticed. Of course, this didn't happen and we were summoned to the Head of Year's office, arguably the most terrifying place on earth.

"So, where have you two been?" he asked us, sternly.

At that age, when you're getting told off, it is very difficult not to laugh. I knew that if I made eye contact with Carl, we'd had it. I looked at the floor and mumbled out the truth. I feared a week of detention or, worse, a phone call to my mum. The ultimate punishment. After a moment of contemplation, the Head of Year replied.

"I'm impressed lads. You showed real initiative to go and see someone that you admire. Well done."

And that was it. Great day.

***

Following persuasion from Matt who fancied himself as a future celebrity, I joined the school play in Year 9. We were doing Cabaret, a risqué move for a teenage production, although our drama teacher lived on the edge. A dead ringer for Richard E. Grant, the whiff of stale smoke and alcohol which accompanied him at all times suggested a similar lifestyle to Withnail. He drank bottle after bottle of Blue Charge, the Asda version of Red Bull.

After short auditions where we read a couple of lines, Matt got the role of Cliff, a starring role while Seamus and I landed cameos as drunken sailors. This represented little progress from my dancing spider role in primary school.

Flicking through the script before our first rehearsal, it struck me how inappropriate it was for school kids to be playing the parts of prostitutes and alcoholics. This wasn't my main concern though; where were my scenes? It took a while to identify any involvement for my man but when I finally saw some action, I was stunned:

SAILOR #2 emerges.

SAILOR #2 passionately kisses FRAULEIN KOST.

What the hell? Are you kidding me? I was thirteen. I'd only kissed three, maybe four, girls before this (through the romantic mediums of Spin the Bottle and an under eighteens night at Evolution Nightclub) and in all honesty, hadn't really enjoyed it. I didn't know what the hell I was doing. I certainly wasn't ready for this. Besides, the girl playing Fraulein Kost was two years older than me. How would she feel about it? Sailor #2 was hardly a catch.

I called Matt that evening, troubled.

"Have you read the script?"

He found it difficult to offer sound advice through ruptures of laughter.

The first rehearsal was on a Saturday morning and I bottled it.

"Where are you?" Matt texted me.

"I'm not doing it."

On Monday Matt revealed that, on learning of my withdrawal, our drama teacher had seen red and thrown a pile of papers down the theatre steps in a rage. He shouted about being sick of people letting him down. Perhaps he'd had a heavy night on the sauce before? Or was he having well justified second thoughts over his choice to do Cabaret? It sounded like a wholly over-the-top reaction to my absence anyway. The show could easily go on without me.

Matt, for his own amusement and Seamus, through fear that he might have to take on my part, talked me out of quitting by springing a fierce guilt trip.

"After he'd calmed down he just seemed disappointed with Andy. And sad. Disappointed and sad."

With reluctance, I told the drama teacher I was back in, to which he seemed satisfied.

"Okay, we'll try your scene tomorrow after school."

Thirty long hours later, the rehearsal came around. I watched nervously as The Kit Kat girls practised a racy dance routine before my scene.

With nervous energy coursing through me, I stumbled onto the set, flailing my arms and pulling a stupid face.

"Cut!" the teacher shouted, taking an angry gulp of Blue Charge. "Too much, Andy. Way too much."

Why had I voluntarily re-joined this play again?

On take two, I was more understated, taking up my position in the centre of the stage and waiting for the music to stop as Fraulein Kost approached me.

My heart was pounding.

An experienced actress, she was calm and draped her arms around my neck before removing my sailor hat and putting it on.

Time stood still. All eyes were on me. This was it.

Fraulein Kost tilted her head and we kissed.

It was, surprisingly, fine. No accidental head-butts or biting and the kiss itself went considerably better than a recent teeth-banging episode in the midst of a foam pit at Evolution. I'd been worried about nothing. The lights dimmed and I was given a thumbs-up by the drama teacher. As we walked off stage, Fraulein Kost shot me a smile and complimented my acting, making it subtly clear that "acting" was all this was.

The drama teacher informed me that we would not have to do the kiss again now until the dress rehearsal which suited me fine and, leaving the theatre, I felt pure relief. Out of all the things that could have gone wrong, I'd come out unscathed. I sensed Matt was annoyed that my dignity had remained intact.

After a few rehearsals, I was beginning to see the appeal of being in a play. For large chunks, I was surplus to requirements and spent my time pissing around with Seamus and Tony (who had joined late having heard rumour of revealing costumes) backstage. Here we had the opportunity to hang around with the girls in the play who were older and cooler than us. In normal school life they would not have given us a second glance but with the ratio of boys to girls 5:1 in our favour, they happily chatted to us and, on occasion, flirted. Perhaps I'll go to drama school, I pondered as a Kit Kat girl sat on my lap one evening.

On the evening of the dress rehearsal, the atmosphere was electric. Dancing girls were doing their hair and applying extravagant makeup, guys dressed as Nazis were adjusting their outfits and Matt was pacing up and down, practising his American accent. In my full sailor costume for the first time, I felt few nerves about the kiss scene. After all, I'd done it before and it had been fine. Being honest, I was quietly looking forward to it

Our drama teacher burst in.

"Let's do this!" He shouted before flying into a passionate motivational speech. I'd never seen him so enthusiastic. My adrenaline was pumping.

"Andy, can I have a quick word?" he said as the buzz in the air settled the cast readied themselves for the start of the show.

"Sure."

I followed him into the hallway, wondering what he wanted. Was he going to offer heartfelt thanks for my decision to stay in the play? Praise my courage perhaps?

"I've decided to cut your scene with Fraulein Kost. I don't think it added to the play."

5

While the girls we'd knocked around with in Year 7 had seemingly aged six years rather than six weeks over the summer holidays, by the end of Year 8 I was also growing up inasmuch as I'd discovered the wonder of getting drunk. I'd had a few sips of John Smith's beer one evening after Craig and I had found/stolen a couple of cans from a table outside the stadium and glugged them in a ginnel, but the first time I felt the effects of booze was on New Year's Eve 1999 with my family. My mum had allowed me to have a couple of bottles of lager with the Chinese takeaway. I'd hated the taste; each sip seemed an effort, sitting at the top of my chest and bloating my stomach. I was, nevertheless, enjoying the fuzzy sensation in my head which was increasing with every mouthful. When I'd drank my bottles, I'd stolen a couple of glugs of wine and shared a can with John. By midnight I was hammered, slurring my speech and unsteady in gait. My mum took John and me for a walk around the block to clear our heads where I supposedly prattled on about my love of football in barely decipherable English.

Despite my memory of the evening being sketchy and deserving of my first sinking feeling where I was unsure of the cause, I'd enjoyed being drunk. I boasted to Eddie and the guys at The Turnways about my discovery. A couple of them had also dabbled with a can or two over Christmas and were similarly enthusiastic. We agreed that a plan needed hatching.

Craig's brother was friends with a guy with a side parting called Ronnie, who drove a car. Ronnie proved to be a more helpful friend than the one who had given me ongoing back pain. On the stipulation that he could keep the change, he was happy to buy two bottles of White Lightning cider for us from

Patel's, the local corner shop. We sat on a bench at the top of the Turnways awaiting Ronnie's return.

After a few minutes, Ronnie skidded to a halt in his Fiesta, which was entirely unnecessary but added to the occasion. He passed the carrier bag to Craig before speeding off, never to be seen again. A fleeting cameo. We hadn't formulated a plan past this point and Johnno was looking tense.

"We can't just drink on the street. If my dad sees us, he'll kill me."

His dad was a policeman.

"Fair point, let's go in here," Craig suggested.

At the edge of The Turnways is a dilapidated brick building with high voltage signs on it surrounded by a spiked fence. One of the panels in the fence was missing so we squirmed through and stood on the damp leaves and litter. Out of all the discreet spots available, this was quite possibly the worst. Craig opened the first bottle with pride – after all, it was he who had sourced the sauce – and took the first long sup.

"Ah, lovely!"

We passed it around the five of us, each taking as many swigs as possible. It was, by no means, lovely; sweet, sickly and gassy. Drinkable at least, more so than lager anyway. On the third round, Craig took an ambitious mouthful which he couldn't manage and spat it back out, cider dribbling down his chin and onto his white No Fear t-shirt. Johnno began giggling uncontrollably which set the rest of us off. We soon saw off the first bottle and the effects were kicking in; a pleasant buzz.

"Let's go somewhere," Danny suggested and we clambered back through the gap in the fence, emerging into the last vestiges of daylight. We unsteadily wandered off, briefly discussing our opinions on Ronnie's comb over (largely negative, although Craig was a fan) before moving on to the more important matters; girls and football. As we all went to different schools it was easy to embellish your status at school.

"Yeah, I've got a chance with loads, I'm just deciding who I like best."

None of us had a girlfriend.

We chatted at length about Kirkstall Crusaders, being over complimentary of one another's abilities, reminiscing about good goals and matches over the past couple of years. The familiar streets seemed different somehow. As we walked past hurried people returning from work, Craig clutching the remaining bottle under his arm, I felt as though we had one over them. We were having a better time.

With the world swirling we staggered along pavements, down back roads, through ginnels and up hills glugging, talking and laughing. Be Here Now by Oasis had just been released and, arms around each other, Johnno and I roared the choruses of the best songs. I felt on top of the world. Nothing much else mattered apart from this moment right now. The evening flew by in an electric haze and before I knew it, my curfew was up. I longed for more White Lightning.

I bid my pals a fond farewell before stuffing my face with Hubba Bubba on the way home, masking the sweet stench of cider. I snuck in just after 9pm, shouted hello to my parents before stumbling upstairs, citing history homework. Lying on my bed, the ceiling spinning, I considered how much fun we'd just had.

At football training the next morning my pals and I evaluated the evening and shared a common consensus; we should do it again. Headers and Volleys and Tig 123 consigned to the past, all we wanted to do was get drunk. Of course, with us being thirteen and Ronnie a one-off, getting hold of alcohol was difficult. We had a fighting chance; I was unusually tall, having hit a whirlwind growth spurt, while both Craig and Eddie were well-built and looked older than they were. We were, unquestionably, under eighteen but could pass perhaps for sixteen and shopkeepers were more lenient back then. "Back then" makes me sound like a wistful eighty-year-old reminiscing about the war.

Being the oldest, Craig was our first choice and he succeeded at a rate of about one in three. Waiting in anticipation around the corner, there was no greater sound than clinking glass as Craig triumphantly returned with full carrier bags. Eddie, whose bench pressing was paying off was the second choice, while I was last chance saloon and inevitably got rebuffed. My first attempt was in the Co-op. After Craig and Eddie returned empty-handed citing the "bitch" (law-abiding employee) on the checkout, I put my head down and strutted in. Heart pounding with my pockets full of coins, I perused the aisles, gathering the requested cider and bottles of WKD. There was a five-deep queue at the checkout so I placed the basket of booze on the floor, shuffling it along with my foot.

When my turn arrived, I was met by a stony-faced lady, presumably the bitch.

"Act confident, ask questions to side-track her," Eddie had advised.

"Can I buy some matches please?"

She turned her back to grab a pack. This was promising. I bent down, picked up the bottles and piled them in front of her. She looked at me with a smirk.

"You've got to be joking?"

"What do you mean?"

"Come on love, your mates have just been in. Have you got any ID?"

"Of course I do," I said in a deep voice. "Just not on me."

"Put the bottles back."

Humbling. I was greeted by shaking heads and impatient hands demanding their £3.75 back before we splintered and went home, defeated.

Shortly after this, we struck jackpot; a small convenience store run by an elderly couple where we could get served without issue, every time. The choice of drink was limited to sweet red wine or MD 20/20 but this was a problem that could be worked around. At thirteen, our tastes were hardly refined.

***

The word that alcohol was now both accessible and terrific soon spread and our drinking group expanded, with many pals from school joining us. After a few sessions of roaming the streets, we settled on a regular Friday spot; a cobbled back street speckled with puddles, known as Puddle Lane. Inspired.

Four girls who lived in the area, three from my school and one from Lawnswood, entered the fray, which would have been great only the ratio just didn't work. It was on average three to one. Carefree booze-ups soon became an unspoken battle for attention, with two or three mates at loggerheads, trying to make a girl laugh. If, on the rare occasion you got five minutes alone with one of them, you'd face scowls and jibes from alcopop-fuelled former friends.

With hormones racing, this was a trying time. Chloe, a petite blonde in my maths class, had been interested in me a few months previously but I'd not acted upon it and missed my chance. To rub it in, by the time we'd started the Puddle Lane chapter, she'd shed her braces, changed her hairstyle, wore trendy clothes and was now a bona fide stunner. Why had she stopped liking me? What had changed? How have I managed to get worse? Is it my hair? The spots on my head? It's an odd situation fighting a battle against your former self and I was deeply envious of the six-months-ago me. I resented him. The prick. While I was tormenting myself and reintroducing cast aside t-shirts, I wasn't the only one pining for Chloe's affections. Over the next year or so, she won the hearts of most of us and had short flings with some, causing widespread jealousy. She played it well, seemingly working a squad rotation system in which I didn't make the bench. Her ruse was to keep everyone thinking that they had a chance; that their time would come. She was excellent at flirting, an activity I've never mastered, and when you spoke to her, she made you feel important. It was you that made her laugh the most, you that she connected with the most. We were, all of us, unaware or perhaps in denial about what was going on, but the tacit rivalries were unbearable.

In the end, she fell in love with Danny, which was all the crueller as he was the only one in the group who wasn't interested in her as a girlfriend, the subject of his affections being an unobtainable girl who went to Lawnswood. It was all a bit complicated and, on a personal note, a bit shit.

With the romance and ratio snags, the excitement of the early Puddle Lane days waned and one Friday in October, the demise was complete. Matt, Seamus, Tony and I had skived off school as the new Championship Manager game was released on the same day that American Pie 2 came out; two huge events. Fired up after a great day, we arrived at Puddle Lane with our expectations unrealistically high to find that it was the same as ever, if not worse. Four girls to thirteen guys. As the rain began to fall and the evening descended into slurred bickering, we'd had enough. In American Pie 2, it was all house parties, rock music, and bikini-clad girls. This seemed to be the norm for teenagers in America. Why wasn't it happening to us? How could we make our lives that exciting? Something needed to change. We started a band.

6

American skate-punk music was all the rage so despite none of us being American or punks, we decided on this as our genre. In fairness, Danny and Johnno were half decent skateboarders although I, of course, was not. Despite owning a top-notch skateboard which I'd won in a Young Telegraph competition, I was dreadful and had given up after a painful and humiliating fall on a fragile homemade ramp at The Turnways.

As a grade three classical guitarist, I thought myself best-qualified to be lead guitarist but Danny and Jacob were also keen on this glamorous role. They both had new electric guitars which were better than mine so we settled on three guitarists. At least one too many. As much as I fancied being lead singer, I begrudgingly accepted that I was tone deaf so Danny and Jacob agreed to share the vocals.

Johnno got the role of drummer because his parents allowed him to have a drum kit in his room and, after much persuasion, we convinced Craig to splash his paper round savings on a bass guitar and teach himself how to play it, pronto.

We had a band meeting to discuss a name but couldn't settle on anything, so opted to use a website which generated random words and put them together. This was the days of dial up internet so it took quite a while. We went for "Falling with Superman" which I liked until years later when a man said it sounded like a Christopher Reeve hate club which had never been the intention.

Song writing sessions tended to involve sitting around in Danny's bedroom, going on MSN Messenger and eating Super Noodles. This seemed to aid the creative process and within a few weeks, we had written a handful of Blink 182-influenced / plagiarised tracks about deep topics ranging from fancying girls to being told off by your parents. Here are some lyrics to one of our songs. The title hints at our American influence and is also contradicted somewhat by the opening line.

Spring Break (Lyrics: Andy, Jacob and Danny circa.2001)

Verse
Summer spent by the pool, showing off and acting cool,
Was our main priority at the time (at the time),
Another predicted mistake led my feelings to break,
I ask myself why, oh why?

Pre-chorus
Ignorance to reality (ignorance to reality),
Can't believe that I didn't see,
That we were crashing down,

Chorus
Can't believe that I didn't see, can't believe that I didn't
see, (oh-oh-oh-oh-oh-oh-oh)
Can't believe that I didn't see that we were crashing down.

In the initial creative outpouring, we'd penned three other tracks: "Best Friend's Room," "Growing Older" and "Nowhere Left to Turn." Factoring in a couple of Blink 182 covers, we soon had our set list and felt ready to hit the Leeds circuit.

We got our first break when my mum arranged a gig for us at her work. It was good of her to sort this out, although performing to a seated middle-aged audience in a seminar room at Leeds Magistrates Court was not how I'd envisaged the beginnings of punk rock stardom. I tried to win over the crowd with a well-rehearsed air jump to which they looked on completely baffled.

We recorded our first four-track CD at a place called Sponge Studios, where we were greeted unenthusiastically by the bearded men who worked there. They didn't seem to rate our chances of world domination highly after Craig sought assistance for a technical fault and it turned out that he had neglected to switch on his amplifier. I designed the album cover on Microsoft Paint and we burnt an ambitious number of CDs which we tried, largely in vain, to sell.

Soon after the release of our CD the band had a shakeup. We hired a new lead singer called Dylan - a short Leeds United fanatic with a bad hip, who was scouted after a heartfelt version of Sitting on the Dock of the Bay at the Lawnswood talent show. I had met Dylan many years previously, at Beavers. After reminiscing about a trip to the Bradford Photography museum when Yannick, a mischievous Beaver had wreaked havoc, Dylan and I seamlessly resumed our friendship and he was a strong addition to the band.

We also hired a band manager, a balding middle-aged guy called Paul, to take our practices on Friday nights. He was a nice guy but far too keen to add searing violin solos to our songs which were almost always inappropriate. Some girls came to watch our band practice once so I decided to play a basic solo in "Spring Break" with the guitar behind my head. Unfortunately, I hadn't practised my party piece nearly enough and got the solo horribly wrong, ruining the performance for everyone.

We played a couple of semi-successful gigs – by the definition that over ten people turned up and we didn't get booed off – at the New Roscoe and Joseph's Well. During one of them, I suddenly noticed that I couldn't hear the bass guitar. I looked over to see that Craig, who'd always been easily distracted, had stopped and was stooped down, kissing his girlfriend mid-chorus. This was fourteen years ago, and today he is still with her and they have four kids.

Unfortunately Falling with Superman did not last quite as long and after our definitive gig at the esteemed Headingley Community Centre, the band broke up citing creative differences.

I still think we could have made it and haven't given up hope of reforming one day.

*****

Year 10 was a magical time; a thrilling glimpse into the adult world of which we were on the cusp. Everything was new and exciting; new experiences and emotions, new friends and new music, the joys of boozing and an increased interest in late night films on Channel 5. Concurrent with Falling with

Superman, our social fabric was evolving and when Friday nights moved from Puddle Lane to pastures new – a field near a Co-op where a larger group, predominantly from Lawnswood hung around – life improved dramatically. While the collection of characters was diverse, everyone was convivial. There was no resentment that we went to rival schools and within weeks, our circles had amalgamated forming a huge contingent for weekend drinking sessions.

I'd heard murmurings that one of the guys, David, was a hard man not to be taken lightly, but on meeting him this couldn't have seemed further from the truth. Clad in a red No Fear hoody and baggy jeans, he was laid back and pleasant, giving me a pound when I didn't have enough for my wine. David's subgroup consisted of Patrick, a basketball player from Meanwood who wore Nike jogging bottoms, Jared, a cheeky-faced chap who wore a beanie hat, Kirk, who was surprisingly strong despite a wiry frame and Dom, who caked his jet-black hair in gel, hairspray and mousse.

I was already familiar with some of the guys through football; Noel and Morgan, a pair of towering ex-Kirkstall Crusaders teammates and Sam and Charlie, who I'd played against on Friday afternoons in the past. Both Sam and Charlie wore permanent smiles and were excellent players, although it soon became apparent that while Sam didn't drink, Charlie was partial to weekend self-destruction, drinking and smoking himself into a stupor before getting up to win man of the match the next morning. This is only doable when you are a teenager or Tony Adams.

It appeared that Liam, who had an eyebrow piercing, tattoos, and a full-time building job, and Billy, who was well over six feet, wore shiny loafers and did something to do with property development, were already fully-fledged adults and I tried to act mature around them.

"Yeah, tell me about it. It's been a tough week of graft for me too," I'd say, referring to my paper round.

Alfie and Stuart, a pair of sporty, energetic guys, were easy to get along with while Jed, Sunil and Leroy, a trendy trio from Hyde Park, boosted our street cred levels. I became acquainted with Clarence and Chris, a pair of handsome musicians who played in successful local bands – considerably more successful than Falling with Superman anyway – and Dylan introduced me to Alexander, Martin and a guy called Rodney, who I recognised.

"Have we met before?" I asked him and recalled that we had.

Two years previously I'd been walking to the park. I was bouncing a deflated basketball and minding my own business when I was interrupted by a kid I had never seen before. He was tall and lithe with blond hair and freckles.

"So, you like basketball then?"

"Um, yes."

He fell into my stride uninvited and told me that he too liked basketball, but didn't play as much as he'd like to. Who the hell was this confident kid? He seemed about my age and was friendly enough but it didn't seem normal to me to just start talking to someone you don't know on the street. It still doesn't. Is it?

We chatted idly for a few minutes before he told me his name was Rodney, turned up his drive, and said goodbye. I carried on walking to the park bouncing my deflated basketball. Shortly after this, I was on the bus home from school when I saw Rodney again, a couple of stops from my house. He beckoned me to get off which I did. He looked pleased with himself. Like he had a plan.

I walked down the road with him and we chatted. Rodney told me that he had a couple of friends at my school, which I didn't doubt if he approached everyone who was walking down the road and befriended them. At the top of his street, he darted off and rummaged around in a bush, unearthing a bottle of Lambrini, the cheap wine synonymous with teenagers and chronic alcoholics. He'd stashed it there the previous Friday, he told me. The circumstances surrounding this were unclear. Was he involved in a social life beyond Puddle Lane?

"Let's down it," he said, his excitement contagious.

We headed to a park a few minutes away and took it in turns to neck the drink until the bottle was empty. As soon as we had finished it I was hit with a deep sinking feeling. I'd said I would go straight home from school as my grandparents were over for an early dinner. Shit. I'd only been with him for fifteen minutes.

Giggling, we said goodbye and I stumbled back to my house, feeling increasingly intoxicated as the sugary wine worked its dubious magic. On arriving home, I was dizzy and felt sick. I sat at the dinner table with my grandparents, picking at my fish fingers and chips, barely saying a word. If I did it would be apparent that I was drunk. At 4 pm on a Monday. Aged thirteen. My grandparents would be appalled.

***

Making all these new friends was great but mixing with other schools provided us with something even more significant; the opportunity to meet new girls. Among the girls at my school I was regarded as okay, but a bit of a prat. My most recent relationship had lasted two days, never recovering after I chucked a giant ball of Blu-tack at Duncan in a Science class, he ducked out of the way and it hit my new girlfriend plum in the back of her head. I'd had a couple of previous blink-and-you'll-miss-it relationships where we did little more than hold hands at break time not knowing what to talk about, but things were getting more serious now that everyone had hit puberty and I was realistic about my chances of future classroom romance. They were slim.

My old primary school friends, Abbie, Jemima, Sophie and Joanna had all gone to Lawnswood and, perhaps still dining out on my Year-Six-class-clown glory days, they held me in reasonable enough regard to introducing me to their friends. This led to me securing my first proper, tangible girlfriend. Her name was and still is I suppose, Carly; a sweet girl with pale skin and dark hair. One Friday night when autumn leaves were lining the pavements and there was a cold bite in the air, Danny and I were showing off, talking about our plans for the band and making wisecracks. This seemed to impress her and, assisted by a mutual appreciation of Blink 182, our romance blossomed.

In the infancy of our relationship, Carly and I would meet up a couple of times a week to walk around streets and through parks, holding hands and occasionally kissing. Before these dates, I would cover my entire torso in Sure roll-on deodorant and chomp on half a packet of Airwaves. I lent her my hoody once when it was raining and felt far too cold but pretended I was fine, which suggested to me that this was more serious than my preceding flings.

I was embarrassed to call her on the phone at my house – I have a deep voice which carries through walls – so whenever I wanted to speak to her I would steal money from the change pot and walk to the telephone box at the bottom of the street. Eventually, after much embarrassment, I admitted to my parents that I'd got a girlfriend. My dad half-heartedly tried to do "the chat" one evening when I was walking down the drive. Sensing where the conversation was going, I said I was in a rush and sprinted down the street.

We shared a special winter together. Our parents allowed us to go to each other's houses where we would listen to Dido while burning Pound Shop joss-sticks or, if conversation lulled, watch EastEnders. My midweek curfew was 9.45pm if I'd done my homework beforehand. On Fridays, it was 10.30pm with a licence to stretch to 11pm without reprimand. At weekends, we'd stand together on the field drinking sessions, or attend the house parties which were starting to happen - the highlight being a raucous event hosted by a ponytailed Colombian called Fernando in a back-to-back terrace in Beeston. Sadly, the honeymoon phase wasn't to last and after four months we had a bust-up at Billy's party and the relationship was over. Finished. The reason? She'd been sick on me. I'd deemed this unforgivable although looking back, I was a dickhead about it. It hadn't been deliberate and I'd egged her on to share another bottle of El Velero. Relationships were transient in those days and she soon started going out with Johnno. No hard feelings.

7

Jack was friends with Emilia, a girl on his street who went to Leeds Girls' High School and she sometimes hung around with us in his attic bedroom, where we would play pool and listen to Motown music, thinking we were cool. She talked about sex with an intimidating openness, although made it subtly clear that she had no interest in sleeping with any of us. Her preference was older guys who did things like drive cars and smoke weed. Emilia was a bit annoying but tolerable and I owe her a great deal of gratitude after she sowed the seeds for one of the best evenings of my teens.

Leeds Girls' High School were doing a fundraising ball at a nearby hotel and she provided Jack with five invitations. I can't remember what they were fundraising for – perhaps an upgrade to first class flights on their Year 11 ski trip? Jack asked Eddie, Tino, Jacob, an eccentric curly-haired guy called George and me to join him. We readied ourselves at mine, putting on our suits, sharing dabs of the fake Armani aftershave that John had bought me for Christmas, and swiftly working our way through the eight-pack of Carling that my mum had provided for the occasion.

My dad gave us a lift to the hotel as we chatted animatedly to dispel our nerves. How was this going to go? Would we be treated as cool outsiders – a bit of rough – and gain the attention of some well-to-do young ladies, or would we be condemned to sitting in the corner while the private school boys wowed them with fine wine and caviar?

The five of us flashed our invites at reception and swaggered through to a large function room which was had been elaborately decorated with balloons and bunting. I rubbed my eyes. The room was full of girls with fancy hair-dos wearing beautiful frocks. Full of girls, but no other boys. None.

What was going on? I shared a glance with my pals who also had raised eyebrows and wide eyes. Was this for real?

Emilia, our one contact in the room marched over to us, wearing a blue ball gown and a fascinator. She had a face like thunder.

"The Grammar School Boys were banned from coming because of their poor grades. What kind of a shit night is this going to be?"

"Are you joking?" I asked.

"No. You losers are the only boys here."

"And that's going to be the case all night?"

"Unfortunately, yes. I'm going for a cigarette."

What news! We were outnumbered by twenty to one. Was karma finally balancing itself out after those testing times on Puddle Lane? For the rest of the evening – and for the only time in my life – I felt like a rapper at a yacht party. Well, if you swap the Cristal for a flask of Glen's vodka and Armani suit for Asda George. With us being literally the only male option, groups of girls approached us. We didn't have to make the first move. On the dance floor, there was no need to subtly dance into a girl's vicinity before trying to make eye contact agreeable enough to permit you to put your hands on their hips. Girls were asking us to dance with them! This was unheard of. And terrific. All five of us secured slow dances, kisses, phone numbers and MSN addresses in the whirlwind four hours that followed.

"So, how was your night?" My dad asked on the drive back home.

"Nothing short of excellent."

***

While I shared a few text messages with one of the girls from the ball and got into another lengthy MSN conversation with another, nothing ultimately came of it and I didn't secure a new girlfriend. I would rue this missed opportunity, especially since, in a lifestyle change which didn't encourage romance, I started smoking weed.

When I was eleven I'd smoked a cigarette with Craig's brother in a ginnel and such was the burning guilt, when I returned home I told my mum and started crying. At fifteen, in the same ginnel, I was introduced to cannabis, taking my first drag of a joint with Craig and Phil, a short ginger-haired lad who had recently moved to the Turnways. I was tougher by now and while I felt uneasy about my debut dalliance with drugs, it didn't incite tears. In fact, I quite liked it. Cannabis tasted much sweeter than cigarettes and after inhaling the smoke and withstanding a small coughing fit, I enjoyed the fuzzy light-headedness that followed. I shared a glance with my new acquaintance and Craig, who had both already smoked a substantial amount by now, and we began chuckling.

After the laughter waned we became anxious that Johnno's dad, the policeman, may catch us.

"He sometimes walks down the ginnel on his way to Patel's," Craig said, concerned.

We passed around the rest of the joint frantically until only the stub remained.

"Andy, because this is the first time you've got stoned, you need to swallow the end of the joint," Phil said.

"Why would I want to do that?"

"Come on, man. You've never heard that rule?"

"No. Craig?"

"Yeah, you should swallow the joint, Andy," Craig agreed.

Feeling a little paranoid I put the stub in my mouth and washed it down with flat Irn Bru. Craig and Phil burst out laughing.

"You idiot, I just made that up," Phil said, wiping his eyes. "Bet that tasted nice!"

This little prank would be representative of my spell as a cannabis smoker. While I liked some aspects of being stoned, I never fully felt comfortable with the stoner scene. This was a snag really because, from fifteen onwards, weed becomes a prevalent part of the social setup.

A new lingo had developed among my mostly middle-class, mostly white peers. When we were smoking, people – including me – spoke in a stronger-than-before Leeds accent, with a hint of Jamaican and said things like:

"Easy, mate. Give us a burn on that spliff, yeah?"

"Yo, this guy is Redeye Jedi, man!"

"Browny's a safe guy man, he always sorts us with a sick Henry." (It took me weeks to realise that a Henry was an eighth.)

I didn't know Browny or any of the other nicknamed drug dealers that roamed North Leeds and wasn't entrusted making the calls or getting in the car to carry out the transactions. Despite being a nifty table tennis player, my hand to eye co-ordination has always been poor and I never mastered the art of rolling a joint. I downloaded a "How to skin up," video on Kazaa but it was no good – I was more interested in previewing snippets of a Jenna Jameson video which was taking days to download. Rolling a well-crafted joint became a status symbol and those who could do it expertly were held in reverence. My stock, however, began to fall. Being able to down a can of Fosters in one no longer held much significance.

For all my gawkiness with cannabis, I did enjoy the feeling of being stoned. Mildly stoned at least. When a few of us shared a joint or two, we'd laugh, get into deep nonsensical conversations and when I arrived home I'd become engrossed in whatever straight-to-DVD film was showing after midnight on BBC2. Unfortunately, being mildly stoned didn't cut it for long and a range of new activities were implemented to make us all get as stoned as possible, as quickly as possible.

We would give one another blowbacks, an intimate process where you'd hold the lit end in your mouth and blow smoke out of the other end so your mate would inhale a big hit. There was a variation of the blowback called a crucifix, where you would receive a blowback and a third pal would stand behind you and squeeze your chest. Craig's brother told us that this got you "completely fucked" and who were we to doubt him?

When his mum was absent, Charlie, the hedonistic footballer invited us around for smoke outs; we would hot-box his greenhouse outside or sit in his bedroom, shutting all the windows and doors before lighting the joint and leaving exhaled smoke swirling around the room, unable to escape. During one such session, Craig got up and left the room. After sitting in hazy silence for half an hour, Danny turned to me.

"Where's Craig?"

"Good question."

We explored the downstairs rooms and the garden but there was no sign. Becoming concerned, we walked into a tiny office room on the second floor. It was pitch black and Craig was sat on a swivel chair, forehead on fist, chin protruding à la Bruce Forsyth.

"Are you okay, Craig?"

We picked him up and took him into the light of the hallway. His face was green, his eyes red slits and he was shaking. He managed to make it to the toilet before being violently sick. Danny and I burst out laughing and I added the word "whitey" to my fledgling cannabis vocabulary.

The parents of a lad at my school won over £2 million on the lottery and moved into a huge converted farmhouse where he held extravagant parties. I spent the entirety of one of these in his bathroom with four other guys, taking it in turns to lie in an empty bathtub and smoke a joint while our peers sealed us in with cellophane, creating an airtight box filled entirely with smoke. We'd get out with bloodshot eyes, bad heads and nausea and stand in silence while the next unfortunate clambered into the tub. What the heck were we playing at? Why were we choosing to spend our Friday nights doing this? There were pretty girls drinking and dancing in the giant kitchen downstairs. My success at the Leeds Girls' High School fundraising ball seemed a lifetime away.

8

My musical pals, Chris and Clarence were both cool and witty and I made a concerted effort to try and show that I too possessed these character traits. Comparable to playing tennis against a superior opponent, you must raise your game when socialising with guys wittier than you and I could, just about, hold my own. If I managed to get a chuckle from them, I'd feel great, my mood boosted by two notches. However, sometimes – akin to shanking an ambitious backhand crosscourt winner out of the court – I'd try too hard and get a lukewarm response before going quiet as the conversation drifted on to unfamiliar topics.

Clarence's dad lived a five-minute walk from mine and his house became the go-to for watching football and films while drinking stubby bottles of Bier De France. Around this time a questionable habit began whereby we would rent low-budget erotic thrillers and listen out for good lines. We would then incorporate them into conversations at parties leaving our peers baffled.

"Never has one man been so blessed."

"I'm sorry?"

"With a body, so beautiful."

"Why are you being weird?"

One evening, we picked a couple of videos up from Blockbuster and I put them on our family membership card which my mum let me use. We watched the first half an hour of one but had to turn it off as it was both bizarre and awful. On leaving Clarence's I forgot to take the DVD back to the shop. You can probably see where this is going but before things came to a head, a pertinent episode took place.

The following week my dad was moving some stuff around in the house. This is something that dads do from time to time whether necessary or not. I got back from school and walked upstairs into my room at the very moment he'd picked up my bedside cabinet. Why a bedside cabinet needed moving away from the bedside was not clear. A career change? You wouldn't have thought this posed much of a problem but under the cabinet lay a collection of top-shelf magazines, amassed over the past two years. I stood there in stunned silence. My dad said nothing, moved the cabinet to the other side of the room as if nothing unusual had happened and quietly left the room. Never mentioned again. At least not to me anyway, I imagine he had a laugh with my mum about it over their Saturday evening bottle of wine.

A couple of weeks later, a letter from Blockbuster arrived in the post.

"Andrew," my mum said, clutching it in her hand.

LATE RETURN FINE. Film: Chained Sinners and Medieval Fleshpots.

"A word."

You can't talk your way out of that, can you? My parents must have thought me a sex-crazed lunatic.

***

Buoyed by my newly expanded social group, so long as I wasn't too stoned, I assumed that socialising was easy now – I'd cracked it. Sadly, I was brought crashing down to earth one unfortunate evening. The disaster was, in no small part, down to a jumper I was wearing. I have benefited from my brother's hand-me-downs many times over the years but on this occasion, I fell afoul of our age gap and generational fashion fads. When John was sixteen, Take That were famous the first time around and curtain haircuts were cool. Turtleneck jumpers were also in, so as he cut his teeth on the nightclubs of Leeds, I imagine dance floors were filled with sweaty men whose odour was masked by Lemon Hooch and Lynx Africa. When he grew out of his prized turtleneck – a gleaming white number – there was pride in his eyes as he handed it over.

"This jumper has served me well. Treat it with respect."

I'd admitted that John looked trendy in it but there was a nagging doubt in my mind that apart from Andi Peters on

CBBC, I hadn't seen anyone else wearing one for a while. Did any of my friends own one? Pushing these fears to the back of my mind, I chose to debut it at a house party Matt and I were going to. It was hosted by a guy I didn't know very well who was a bit weird. When pulling the jumper on at home my head got stuck. Wrestling through the cotton I was hit by the early throngs of a panic attack before emerging through the neck hole, red-faced and breathless. I was pleased with the look but it was too hot so I took my t-shirt off and put the jumper back onto my bare skin. Itchy but cooler.

The party was in full swing when Matt and I arrived.

"Uh, hi," the host answered, hesitantly letting us in before leaning over the bannister to kiss a bespectacled girl. We walked in with trepidation and I realised I didn't recognise anyone. Arriving at a party as an outsider is tricky and can go either way. There's a chance you'll be new and exciting and talk to some girls but the likelihood is that you'll find yourself stood alone in the hallway, peeling the label off your beer and feeling anxious. Matt, who'd brought a flask of Glen's vodka, ploughed straight into the action heading into the living room. He was wearing a new Bench t-shirt and was going through a purple patch where several girls fancied him. I glanced through but the room was busy. Too busy. Intimidating. I'll have a drink to settle my nerves, I told myself. Upstairs sounded quieter but would have meant interrupting the host's on-stair romancing so I made a beeline for the kitchen. Once there I could put my beers in the fridge. It would give me a reason for being in the room. A task.

On the way through, I overheard two lads in baseball caps.

"Looks like Ian Botham's walked in," one of them said. They laughed.

This seemed a dated reference. Could it have been deliberate? A clever double-edged insult, suggesting that my jumper belonged to a bygone era. I pretended I hadn't heard and put my head down.

"Oi, Botham."

I continued walking, thinking that I might go straight out the back door – Call it a bad night and get home for Match of the Day. A vague acquaintance stopped me in my tracks. He was wearing a solitary golf glove.

"Easy, Andy. Fancy doing a bucket?"

I didn't know what this meant so wasn't sure whether I fancied it or not. He hadn't mocked my turtleneck though and I appreciated this.

"Sure."

I followed him into the backroom conservatory where drum and bass music was playing and the stench of cannabis stung my nostrils. We sat down with a group who were cross-legged on the floor huddled around a half-full bucket with a cloudy Pepsi bottle bobbing around on the surface. They grunted a few hellos that were neither friendly nor hostile.

"Your turn, dude," a small chap said.

I didn't know what to do.

"It's alright, you go first," I replied. "Dude."

"Nah man, I'm baked."

Shit.

An energetic mixed-race guy stepped in. He was older than everyone else and wearing coloured contact lenses making his irises appear purple. Coloured contact lenses were fashionable for about two months in 2003. God knows why. He looked frightening.

"If you pussies want to have a little chat, I'll go again."

Okay, an opening. Just watch what he does carefully. He put the bottle to his lips and plunged it into the water. A girl in a Nirvana t-shirt lit the half joint which was stuck in the side of the bottle like a straw in Kerplunk. The bottle filled with smoke and Purple Eyes sucked in, smoke flooding into his mouth and out through his nostrils. He'd done this before.

"Fine, I'll try," I said.

The apparatus was repositioned by the girl in the Nirvana t-shirt who was evidently a bucketing expert. I copied my purple-eyed predecessor, sucking in as the bottle filled up. It was strong. And it kept coming. I tried to take it back but was hampered by my lack of smoking experience and burst into a coughing fit, causing my chest to hurt and my eyes to stream. I felt my stomach churn and metallic saliva forming at the back of my mouth. Oh god, was I going to be sick? The cross-legged crowd were laughing as I did everything in my power to hold back vomit. After a succession of small swallows and deep breathing, nausea ceased. I was, however, very stoned.

"This guy nearly pulled a whitey!" someone said. It sounded like they were speaking from the other end of a tunnel. "That's even funnier because he's wearing cricket whites!" the small guy said. He looked like a wooden puppet. I sat, out of my mind, as the crowd – including my fickle acquaintance, the bastard – mocked my turtleneck, and inability to do buckets.

"Yeah, but cricketers don't even wear turtlenecks, so what are you on about?" I managed to muster but it fell on deaf ears. After I'd said it I wasn't sure if I'd spoken at all. Had I just thought it? Following another round of buckets, which I politely declined, the piss taking and all conversation petered out into silence. The drum and bass music stopped so the girl in the Nirvana t-shirt stood up and pressed play. She came and sat next to me.

"Hey, don't let them tease you about the jumper."

Was she stroking my back?

"Thanks."

"I've got a nipple piercing."

I mustn't have heard her correctly. I chose to ignore it.

"So, do you like the jumper?" I asked.

"No, it's awful. And you're sweating. Why don't you take it off?"

I couldn't tell her that I had nothing on underneath.

"It's okay. I think I'll just keep it on."

"Suit yourself."

She shuffled around the circle until she was sat next to the man who looked like a puppet. Was she stroking his back now? What the hell is going on?

This was too much. I stood up. I was feeling dizzy.

"Yo, cricket man," Purple Eyes said. "I'm off to the shop to get some munch. Wanna come?"

This was the second last thing I wanted to do. The last thing I wanted to do was sit in this circle of strangers who'd been taking the piss out of me.

"Sure."

We left the conservatory and walked up the drive where the host was now kissing either a different girl or the previous one had removed her glasses. Outside, the cool air felt good on my sweltering skin.

"Guess how many days I've been awake for cricket man," Purple Eyes asked on the way to the shop.

"Um, I don't know. Two?"

"Try again."

"Three?"

"Four, mate. I'm on speed. I'm buzzing."

Excellent. We discussed what he'd been up to over these four days. It turned out he'd done quite a lot, he'd kept busy. Mostly doing drugs and dancing. One thing he hadn't done, he informed me, was eat. He fancied a cheese string and some Pringles. He dance-walked as I stumbled alongside him, dehydrated. I was feeling too cold now. After walking for fifteen minutes there was still no sign of the shop. My companion continued to chat away, regardless of whether I responded or not. I felt very odd, like I was outside myself, watching the two of us walking along. Why did he have cat's eyes?

We got to a corner shop where the bright lights and buzzing of fridges were unnerving. Was the man behind the counter starting at me? He knew I was stoned. Shit. He's going to call the police. I needed to go. Purple Eyes was rummaging through the shelves, grabbing numerous items, including a can of minestrone soup. He should have picked up a basket.

I decided I didn't want to be hanging around with a weird guy on Class A drugs anymore. As a stoned, paranoid and insecure teenager, I would have felt much more comfortable sat in my bedroom alone. I turned and darted out the shop and broke into an unsteady jog, heading the opposite way from the party, towards a park.

Purple Eyes shouted after me.

"Oi, cricket man."

Shit.

I continued running.

"Go on then, fuck off!" he yelled as I ran into the night. "I don't give a fuck anyway."

"Okay, see you around," I shouted back. "Nice to meet you."

"Fuck you and your shit jumper!"

I never wore the jumper again and I never saw him again. I wonder if he's been to sleep yet?

9

My real friends – the ones who didn't judge me on my jumpers – and I drifted away from the fields by the Co-op to bigger and better things. A hill half a mile away. It had been christened Tellytubby Hill by our predecessors, a name which I never liked. It seemed infantile. And at fifteen, having now had a proper girlfriend, I was a man. Now and then, brave friends with relaxed or absent parents held house parties but Tellytubby Hill became the Friday night constant, whatever the weather. The one plus about doing this in the winter months was the increased chances of holding hands with a girl.

One spring evening I sensed a change in the atmosphere. A handful of guys from Lawnswood were wearing smart shirts and shoes and seemed distracted. Liam was wearing a silver bracelet which I hadn't seen before.

"What's with the shirts?" I asked.

"We're going to town."

"I'm sorry, what?"

"Our fake IDs have arrived. We're going to Dust."

Afterwards, stories were rife about this inaugural night at Dust, the name of a ska, punk rock and alternative night at a club Called Bassment (not a spelling mistake, a clever play on words). They'd got in without issue, drank, danced, kissed some girls and got home at 3 am. It sounded wonderful. I was cripplingly jealous. I didn't have a fake ID and besides, there was zero chance my parents would allow me to go to a nightclub.

Every subsequent Friday the same thing would happen. Whether we were at Tellytubby Hill or someone's house, a divide was forming. Some of the guys were clock watching. Not because they had to be home at 10.30pm like me, but because that was when the club opened. Each week, the group going to Dust grew; one or two more got hold of a fake ID or a brother's provisional driving licence and were getting on the night bus as I was skulking home to watch a Shannon Tweed film in my room with the volume turned down. (I'd thrown my top shelf magazines away in a fit of guilt and embarrassment following the bedside cabinet incident.) After a while it became unbearable. I needed to do something.

I scraped a tenner together and bought an "international student" ID. It was passable and said I was eighteen, unlike some of my friends who were claiming to be in their late twenties despite not having hit their growth spurt.

The next step was to get an alibi. I lay on my bed one night listening to the Red Hot Chili Peppers and mulling over my options. Midway through "Scar Tissue" it came to me. Johnno was one of my oldest pals and my mum knew his parents. My new pal, Charlie, the decadent footballer's surname was Johnson and he was often referred to as Johnno. Charlie's mum was of the, "I'd prefer to know what they're doing than have them keep secrets," ilk and not only allowed him to go out on Friday nights, but also let him have mates to come back and stay at his afterwards. Perfect.

"Mum," I said breezily as she was doing the ironing one evening. "I'm staying at Johnno's house next Friday."

"Okay." I wasn't lying. Clear conscience.

Since hatching my plan, I'd been giddy. In GCSE art class on the Friday morning, I felt more excited than I'd ever been about anything. My heart was racing and while attempting a Monet-inspired piece, I snapped two pastels through lack of concentration. The night finally came around. Following strict instructions from Patrick and Rodney, I put on a smart shirt and shoes, which didn't go with my baggy jeans, and applied a generous amount of hair gel, going for a larger quiff than normal. I was wearing my special-occasion Kangol boxer shorts which I'd bought from TK-Maxx – my mum still bought me Y-fronts and I was too embarrassed to tell her that I didn't like them so hid my Kangol boxers and hand-washed them for weekends. I procured a four pack of Fosters from my kitchen and walked to Charlie's house where I was met by a flurry of energy and excitement. A rock and metal Kazaa playlist was blaring from his computer speakers and friends were drinking cans, laughing, popping in and out to smoke, comparing IDs and applying too much aftershave. The anticipation was tangible.

At 10pm we went to the bus stop and bustled on to the number 1. I was buoyant until a short man shouted from the back.

"What the fuck is this? The fucking Play Bus?"

"Fuck off, man," Patrick countered, but my confidence was shattered. Play Bus? Was it that obvious? I wasn't going to get in, was I? By the time we'd arrived in town I was a bag of nerves and fell silent as we walked through the Merrion shopping centre. Groups of actual men and grown-up women were stumbling around, drinking and gallivanting. I felt like a child.

"Right, quick one at a pub to get warmed up?" Liam suggested. He'd as-good-as left school now and had been drinking in pubs for a while. I had not.

"It's fine, we go here every week," Charlie reassured me.

It was no problem. The fake ID worked like a charm and I bought my first ever pint in a pub. A seminal moment. The atmosphere was cordial and I was surprised by how welcome a group of definitely-underage idiots were. Rodney and Charlie were listening to the musings of a middle-aged man with a comb-over and I found myself talking to a black man on crutches by the bar. He asked me if I thought he looked like Thierry Henry.

"Um, yes. I suppose so."

When I was twenty-eight the same man approached me, in the same pub. He'd aged well.

"Hi Thierry," I said and we picked up the conversation as if time had stood still for thirteen years. Bizarre.

Just after 11pm, we were ready to go to Bassment and my anxieties resurfaced. Even the guys who'd been ten times or more (how many times you'd been to Bassment was a sign of status at the time) seemed a touch on edge as a Friday morning plan was put in place; two by twos and one three. As a debutant, I was placed in the three, flanked by Liam the builder and Billy the teenage property magnate.

So as not to draw attention to ourselves, our entrances were staggered. Once the preceding pair had got in, they'd text to confirm it and the next pair would wait a few minutes before heading in. My trio went last. As we stood around the corner from Bassment my companions were calm; smoking and speculating as to whether a purportedly promiscuous girl was likely to be present tonight. We got the text, waited three minutes and it was time. Feeling lightheaded and with a sweaty back, I feigned assurance, walking with an unrehearsed swagger. I could see the silhouettes of two bouncers leaning on the wall beside the door entrance to the club. Were they watching me? The short walk felt like a mile. When we finally arrived, the bouncers moved in front of the door, blocking the promised land for now. One was a giant, with coarse skin on his face. The other was shorter but muscular. They were both drinking bottled water.

Through the few gaps between the two men, I could see steps leading down to the club, where sounds of merriment and whiffs of smoke and beer were drifting up to street level. "The Middle" by Jimmy Eat World was playing. How I longed to be down there.

"Alright Terry," Liam said to the shorter bouncer and they shook hands. What the hell? He knew their names? Were they mates?

"Alright lads. How are we doing?" Terry said, then shook Billy's hand too. My friends greeted Terry's huge partner, Doc, strolled through the door and stood at the top of the steps. I looked at the floor and shuffled forwards. I was expecting either Doc or Terry to block me with a robust arm, but to my astonishment, Terry gave me a stern nod, and that was it. I was in. My fake ID surplus to requirements. Phenomenal. With my arms around my friends' shoulders, the final chorus of the song getting louder as we walked down each step, I felt as though this was it. Life started now.

There was a small, quick moving queue to the foyer where you paid, giving me enough time to reach into the deep pockets of my baggy jeans and scrabble together the £3.50 entrance fee. This would leave me with £6.50 for drinks. I didn't need bus fare, I'd walk home. Hell, I'd run home, such was the adrenaline pumping through my veins.

We got to the front and were met by a man with a dyed pink goatee and long, strawberry blond hair. He was friendly, taking my money, stamping the back of my hand with the word Dust and wishing me well. He seemed okay but I later found out that he wore sandals at all times and referred to himself without jest as Jesus, which made me reassess my opinion. Hands stamped, my pals and I turned the corner and entered the club. "The Taste of Ink" by the Used had just started. The club was tiny but the atmosphere electric. It smelt of smoke, sweat, and perfume. Overwhelmed I took in my new surroundings.

On my immediate left was a small booth where a stern DJ in his thirties was nodding along to music and drinking a can of Red Stripe. In front of him, the dance floor, not much larger than my living room, was rammed with a mix of girls with dyed hair wearing netting and bracelets on their forearms and intimidating looking men wearing band t-shirts: Rancid, System of a Down and NOFX. I recognised Clarence's big brother in the middle of the action – he was wearing a flat cap and smoking a cigarette. There was a giant black man, about six feet seven, wearing a Chelsea football shirt. How had he got in with that? There was a pair of white guys wearing basketball vests with thick chains around their necks and bandanas. I don't think they were joking. They were dancing near, but not with, the tall black man. Nobody else was wearing a smart shirt and shoes.

Resisting the temptation to dance we bustled through the lively crowds, Liam hugging a girl with garish pink highlights on the way, and made it to the brightly lit bar at the back of the club.

"Andy!"

I turned around to see Rodney and the rest of our group huddled in a dark corner. Seeing that all of them were also dressed far too formally, I felt reassured. Perhaps this smart dress code was our look? Our niche? My pals ran over and, shouting and laughing, we hugged one another, jubilant.

"What can I get you?" a bubbly bargirl with dreadlocks asked me when the furore had died down.

Shit, what do you drink in clubs? I scoured the fridges and shelves behind her, then worried I was taking too long, panicked.

"Um, a Newcastle Brown Ale please?"

David, who had customised his formal attire by sewing a Greenday patch on to the smart jeans he was wearing, shouted into my ear.

"Get an absinthe."

Ever impressionable, I followed his advice. A Newcastle Brown Ale and absinthe. That classic combination.

"£5.50 please," said the girl with the dreadlocks. She was singing along to the music and I fancied her. I had one pound left.

"That will keep you going all night!" David said after we had necked our absinthe. He claimed it was 70% proof and illegal. I doubted the validity of both claims. I was sitting with pals in the dark corner, sipping my Newcastle Brown, when "Superman" by Goldfinger came on. Charlie and Rodney's eyes lit up and the three of us headed for the dance floor which was packed with people skanking and shouting along. I'm a terrible dancer, especially skanking – all arms and legs like an elk – but I recognised the song from hours spent playing Tony Hawk's Skateboarding on the PlayStation and sang along with accuracy, justifying my position in the centre of the dance floor. Such was my passion, I landed a handshake from the tall black man in the Chelsea shirt. I felt ten feet tall.

This was the start of a ska section with songs following by Catch 22, Mad Caddies, Less Than Chris and Reel Big Fish following. Despite my band's lack of a horn section or any proper musicians, we were going through a ska phase at the time so I knew the songs. I was in dreamland. Is that girl looking at me?

The genre subtly shifted to hip hop, with "Walk this Way" by Run DMC acting as a buffer before Beastie Boys, Missy Elliot, and Roots Manuva tracks. When "Gravel Pit" by Wu-Tang Clan came on, the white guys wearing bandanas were in their element, their right arms raised above their heads bouncing along to the beat. I thought they looked a bit daft but they'd attracted the attention of a group of girls, including the one who might have been looking at me, so I tried to copy them. I didn't feel comfortable doing this and no longer knew any of the words to mask my dancing deficiencies. I signalled my thoughts to Rodney, who was doing an odd dance where he flashed his right hand towards the floor and back up repeatedly, and we headed back to the dark corner to regroup. I was sweating.

"Fancy a drink?" Rodney asked, red-faced with hair gel dripping down his forehead.

"Can I get anything for £1?"

"No."

"I don't suppose..."

"Yes."

Rodney fought his way to the bar and returned with two bottles of Heineken. He was flush. A budding entrepreneur, he'd set up a mini paper round empire whereby the newsagent gave him hundreds of papers and he employed paperboys to the groundwork. He took a share of the profits without having to deliver a paper. He also got £30-a-week Education Maintenance Allowance, all of which he planned to spend in Bassment. There were flaws in the EMA system; the guy whose family had won the lottery claimed it.

"Are you having a good night?" Rodney shouted in my ear over the M.O.P. track that was playing.

"Yes."

Sitting down with my pal, sipping room-temperature Heineken, I glanced around the club. I saw a guy in the year above stood at the bar wearing a North Face coat. He must be hot? He also had headphones in his ears, which struck me as both odd and arrogant. What was he listening to? A couple of attractive blonde girls from Lawnswood had arrived fashionably late and sashayed through the crowds getting admiring/leering glances from men in black t-shirts. I fancied one of the girls quite a lot, even more so right now. In the strobe lights, her blonde hair looked almost white, her eyes wider, her breasts bigger and she was wearing a short, denim skirt. She caught the same bus as me in the morning and sometimes laughed at my jokes at Tellytubby Hill, which was excellent. Alas, she had a boyfriend and I begrudgingly accepted that she was, for now, out of reach.

This did not stop me from changing my behaviour as soon as I'd caught her eye. She had been going to nightclubs for months already so I wanted to show that I too felt comfortable in this unfamiliar social setting; not giddy and intimidated.

Despite my heart rate having increased rapidly, I hoped to appear cool and relaxed, so slumped down in my chair, nodding along to the music and tapping my foot. The girls gave Rodney and I a little wave then headed to the bar where they were accosted by the men in bandanas who were keen to buy them drinks.

From where they were stood I was in the eye-line of the girl I fancied so, for the next few minutes, every one of my actions was based on the chance that she might be paying attention to me. I wanted her to know that I was having fun – a good time guy – so laughed exaggeratedly at something Rodney said. I tried my hardest to make Rodney laugh too. I wished she'd seen me shaking hands with the tall black guy earlier.

The girls declined the advances of the men in bandanas and their boyfriends came over and whisked them off to sit in a corner at the other side of the club. This was probably no bad thing since it meant I could stop putting on this stupid performance. The boyfriends looked affable, like they were okay guys but, of course, I hated them.

"Look at those dickheads," I said to Rodney who agreed. I think he fancied one or both of the girls too and had also altered his behaviour since they had walked in. The punch-in-the-gut feeling didn't last long. After finishing my beer, I was over it. This is my new life now, I'm a clubber. Look at all the girls – a quick headcount suggested there were between twenty and thirty here. I was in the process of undoing the top button of my shirt for a more casual look when the opening chords of "Chop Suey" by System of a Down began. Rodney and I shared a glance before springing up and heading back to the dance floor where the ratio was now 90% men and a mosh pit had formed. Men were beating the shit out of each other. Was this fun? I stood on the periphery deciding whether to get involved. If I didn't, would I have failed? Was this an unspoken initiation?

"Yes, Andy! You having a good night?" Charlie yelled before grinning maniacally and ramming his body into a man with a ponytail. Liam had his arms above his head, fists clenched and eyes closed screaming, "Angels deserve to die!"

I hadn't expected this kind of music to be his bag.

I couldn't stand on the edge of the dance floor for the whole song. I grimaced, looked to the floor and stepped into the mixer, half-heartedly barging into a chubby black-haired man wearing a Motorhead t-shirt. My rib hurt. Was a mosh pit like going in for a 50/50 tackle in football? Were you more likely to get hurt if you weren't fully committed? I bounced off him and into the back of a sweat-dripping guy who I recognised as a sixth former from my school. He didn't look happy to see me. There was a moment where our eyes met before he scowled then shoved me hard, nearly flooring me. He was screaming along to the song.

"Why have you forsaken me?"

It was all very dramatic.

I managed to get through the song without sustaining any further injuries beyond the almost-definitely bruised rib which would cause discomfort for six weeks. Despite the violence, there was a cordial atmosphere. When people fell over, they were picked up and there was back-slapping and hugging, beads of sweat swirling through the smoke-filled air.

The next song was "Know Your Enemy." My brother was going through a Rage Against the Machine phase so I was familiar with the song. The man with the ponytail was a fan, shouting along furiously. Rodney was doing his unique flashing right-hand dance again; ostensibly suitable for all genres. The tall black man had re-joined the dance floor which seemed to calm the mosh pit down. Nobody wanted to bang into him. I sang along to the bits I knew and mouthed the words I didn't, trying to lip read the man with the ponytail. At the end of the song, where Zak de la Rocha shouts "All of which are American dreams," over and over again, the chubby man in the Motorhead t-shirt and I locked eyes. He pointed at me and roared in my face.

"All of which are American dreams."

Feeling uncomfortable I pointed back at him.

"All of which are American dreams."

I looked around to see everyone else was shouting along. This was an odd sight – tens of teenagers in Leeds, impassioned about early-nineties American politics. The man in the Motorhead t-shirt was becoming louder and more aggressive with each recital. He had wild eyes.

"All of which are American dreams."

I was exhausted when it finished and, as "Epic" by Faith No More started, I was ready for a break and left the dance floor alone. I needed to gather my thoughts so headed for the upstairs toilet despite not needing to go. At the top, someone tapped me on my shoulder. I assumed it would be one of my friends and was surprised to see a small tanned girl with black hair. She looked like the Portuguese footballer Rui Costa.

"I haven't seen you in here before?" she said. Thick Leeds accent.

"No, it's my first..."

"Want to pull?"

"I'm sorry?"

She put her finger in her mouth, pulled out some chewing gum, flicked it on the floor then leant in to kiss me. Shocked, I clumsily reciprocated and we stood kissing outside the toilets for the entirety of the song. Her breath was a mixture of peppermint and Lambert and Butler cigarettes. She took my hand and we walked downstairs together.

"Let's sit down."

Unfortunately, there were no available seats. "Down with the Sickness" by Disturbed had cleared the dance floor and was proving an appropriate time for folk to take a breather. The girl was unconcerned and sat on the floor under the stairs. She grabbed my arm and yanked me down to join her, her strength belittling her small frame. We resumed kissing for a few more seconds then sat in silence. This was new territory for me. What's the protocol? What are you supposed to talk about? Should I ask for her number? My mind was racing. Why was I sat on the floor kissing a girl who looks an awful lot like an AC Milan midfield maestro? How has this happened?

We continued the process of kissing sporadically and sitting in silence holding hands for a good fifteen minutes. I wasn't sure whether this was fun or not. "Private Eye" by Alkaline Trio had started and I liked the band. In the corner of my eye, I could see Rodney and two other friends were heading back to the dance floor. I wanted to join them. Can I leave the girl? Is that acceptable? Am I in a relationship now? I looked at her. I didn't think I fancied her at all and we'd hardly hit it off conversation-wise. What was I playing at? On the dance floor,

I noticed that Rodney had taken his t-shirt off and was doing a silly dance, pretending to be a hen. That made the decision for me. I stood up. The girl remained seated. She was nonplussed.

"Bye," I said.

"Bye."

As I turned my back she was lighting a cigarette.

While it was a fleeting, ultimately unsuccessful romance, it had boosted my mood further. I was in a club and I'd kissed a girl. Magnificent. I reunited with my pals and we laughed and danced our way through the punk rock section of the night, with music from my idols at the time; Blink 182, Greenday, NOFX, Rancid, and Pennywise. Oh, what fun I was having. By 2 am the crowd had thinned and the music became more relaxed. Those remaining on the dance floor stood in a circle with their arms around one another singing along to "Drive" by Incubus, "Santeria" by Sublime and "Concrete Schoolyard" by Jurassic Five. As I looked at my friends' drunken, happy faces, I felt a wave of euphoria coursing through me.

The last song of the night was "Jammin'" by Bob Marley. Midway through the lights came on, the flick of a switch snapping me out of my halcyon dream and crashing back to reality. I looked around at the remaining clubbers – fellow late-night stalwarts. Everyone looked tired. Men had bags under their eyes and matted strands of wet hair stuck to their foreheads. The guy in the Motorhead t-shirt had a nasty looking cut below his eye. Liam was stood in the corner with his hand up the top of the girl with pink highlights. Girls' mascara was running and their hair all over the place. One was crying and being consoled by the tall black man. What was she so sad about? Rui Costa was kissing the man with the ponytail under the steps where I had sat with her. Shards of broken glass, crushed cans of Red Stripe and tab ends were littering the floor. The smell in the air was disgusting. The place was disgusting. But I'd just had the best night of my life.

10

The only snag with my new lifestyle was the cost. To feel comfortable, it was necessary to have £12 for Dust, which was well beyond my paper round wages where I'd hit a glass ceiling at £6 per week. We'd done work experience placements towards the end of Year 10, which I had hoped may open doors to paid employment. While organised classmates were networking and finding exciting gigs at radio stations and newspapers, I did nothing and had to use a list that school provided for people who hadn't sourced anything themselves. From the list, I secured two weeks' work at Fleetwood Hall, a hotel and conference centre near my house.

My first shift began at 6 am on a Monday. I was greeted in the restaurant by a small, camp man in his late thirties who introduced himself as Norman. Given the time of day and large pile of dirty plates in front of him, he was surprisingly perky.

"Morning! You must be the work experience?"

Given the time of day and large piles of dirty plates that would soon be in front of me, I was unsurprisingly un-perky.

"Yes."

"Great. Put these on." He chucked me a yellow shirt and apron. "Don't worry I won't look."

He made a point of covering his eyes with his hands while I put the shirt on.

"Pick up a cloth then and let's get you started on the plates. No time like the present!"

"Okay," I said glumly.

"I'll be sorting the coffee machine."

With that, he bounced off singing along to the Victoria Beckham and Dane Bowers song, "Out of Your Mind" which was playing softly through the speakers.

An hour later I'd finished the pile of plates. It was hard work. I leant against the table, exhausted.

"Hey, hey. Hope you're not slacking off!" Norman said, emerging through a fire escape door, smelling of cigarettes.

"No," I protested, "look, I've finished."

"You think you've finished? Good one!" He laughed. I didn't. "Come and join me in the kitchen, my friend."

In the industrial kitchen, a red-haired, scowling chef was slowly stirring a giant vat of baked beans. Norman pointed to piles of plates on an adjacent table. They weren't dirty.

"But haven't they been cleaned already?"

"They have. By me. Now they need polishing. You'll need a fresh cloth and a jug of hot water. I can see you've got a lot to learn, my friend!"

"Hmm."

"I'm going to go and finish up on the coffee machine."

He bounced off, whistling "Out of Your Mind" again. Surely there were better things for me to do than clean already-clean plates? The chef was busy and made it quite clear he wasn't keen on chatting. As I polished, with the humming of the kitchen equipment overpowering the radio and the stark lighting shining on the metal tables, I felt a pang of loneliness. Was it going to be just me, Norman and the solemn chef all day? Is this what working life was? I glanced at my watch to see it was only 7.15 am and consoled myself that I would have still been in bed otherwise. At least I was being productive. It would have been nice to get a pay check at the end of it but you can't have it all.

Norman returned half an hour later, once again smelling of cigarettes. He asked me to pick up as many plates as I could and follow him back to the restaurant. He defied his thin frame by expertly carrying two large piles as my arms shook under the weight of one. As we arrived at the restaurant I was relieved to see that another colleague had arrived.

"Good morning, Mariana!" Norman said. "What time do you call this?"

"So sorry," she said in a Spanish accent. She looked hurt. "I thought I start 8 am?"

"You do Mariana. I'm only joking!"

"Not so funny."

"This is the work experience," Norman said pointing to me. Did he know my name? I introduced myself and as Norman departed for another cigarette, Mariana and I set the tables for breakfast. Her English was iffy but I can listen to a Spanish accent all day. She was attractive – petit, olive skinned and dark brown eyes. I learned she was from Almeria and spending a year at Leeds University. Some basic arithmetic told me this meant she was at least four years my senior and therefore I had no chance. Comfortable with this, I felt no nerves and we settled into pleasant conversation. I gathered she didn't like Norman.

The grumpy chef and Norman began setting up the breakfast buffet and Mariana and I were asked to stand at the door and greet guests. By 8.45 am no guests had arrived. I was getting restless. A man in his sixties eventually ambled in and I showed him to an available seat, of which there were many. Norman raised his eyebrows and nodded his head aggressively at Mariana who picked up a pot of coffee. The man went to the buffet, returned with a precariously full plate and sat down again. Over the next two hours, three more guests arrived, Mariana poured them coffee, I cleaned up their plates and they left. That was the extent of the action. The rest of the time was spent standing around, doing nothing.

"Okay, good breakfast. Well done team!" Norman said, closing the restaurant doors at 10 am. "Now let's prepare for lunch. Mariana, you and I are going to strip the tables. Work experience, can you get back into the kitchen and polish the plates? Sorry, I'll stop calling you that. What's your name again?"

I stood near the sullen chef and polished plates for two long hours before two more colleagues arrived, looking annoyed, at midday. Gianluca was a twenty-something Italian student with a goatee beard and Dwayne was from another school and also doing work experience. They were both incredibly lazy and I liked them. Gianluca spent his time rolling cigarettes and trying, fruitlessly, to flirt with Mariana, while Dwayne believed he had cracked the system.

"If you tell Norman you are sorting out the store cupboards, he'll leave you alone and doesn't come to check. I just sit there. It's great."

I liked the sound of his ploy but didn't want to push it on my first shift. Norman and Gianluca's smoking and Dwayne's skiving meant that for most the afternoon it was just Mariana and I polishing, setting tables, serving coffee and cleaning up plates. As much as I was fond of Mariana, I wasn't having fun and was mightily relieved when 2pm finally came around.

"Work experience," Norman said after I'd taken off my apron, "someone's called in sick. I don't suppose you can help with the conference this afternoon?"

I was desperate to go home. Instead, Gianluca and I served tea, coffee, and biscuits to thirty or so suited salesmen who were locked in animated discussion – "It's a numbers game, we are on the frontline!" Gianluca just couldn't have given less of a fuck about the job and got annoyed with a salesman who asked for a refill.

"Can't you see I'm busy?" he snapped, before leaning back against the wall and rolling a cigarette.

While I enjoyed talking to Gianluca about Italian football and admired his cool demeanour, the division of labour was wildly disparate. My legs were aching and I was ready to sleep for ten hours. After the last salesmen departed leaving a room of mugs, plates, and crumbs, Gianluca said, "I need to speak to Dwayne about something urgently," and sauntered off, humming.

Dejected, I started loading the crockery onto a trolley. Norman walked in.

"Where's Gianluca?" he asked.

"I don't know."

"Right, well looks like it's you and me to finish up, my friend!"

He was whistling the Dane Bowers and Victoria Beckham song again.

As I walked home I was physically and emotionally ruined. Is this what working life is? This is what I've got in store? The shift had seemed far too long. It had lasted forever. Is this what people do, day after day, forever? Fucking hell.

The rest of the week was much the same and oh, how I hated it. Chatting to Mariana was the only glimmer of sunlight. On the final Friday, I legitimately had to fetch a trestle table from the storeroom where I found Dwayne sat on a cardboard box, eating a Danish pastry.

"Come and join me mate. Do you want a cake? A bag of crisps? You name it."

Was he stealing the hotel food? The alternative was preparing a coffee station with the elusive Gianluca so I sat down, relieved to take the weight off. Dwayne handed me a can of stolen cherry cola and as I was pulling back the ring pull, Norman walked in.

"Well, well, well, my friends. What have we got here?"

While I wasn't officially sacked – after all I'd been working for free – I was advised that a future career at Fleetwood Hall was unlikely.

***

Not to be dismayed by my work experience failings, shortly afterwards I got a Saturday job at a John Filan's frozen food shop. John had been working there for a couple of years but had moved on to a better-paid gig at Bryan's fish and chip shop and recommended me to his manager Sheldon for the vacancy. It's not what you know, eh?

As I was deemed too young to man the till, the majority of my shifts were spent wandering around facing up. This is a demoralising task, turning the products on the shelves so that the labels are facing the customer and my grafting could be instantly undone by one heavy-handed customer. Sheldon was a plumper and less camp version of Norman and shared his penchant for pop music, insisting that a 6-track CD was played on a loop all day, the compilation including hits such as "Superstar" by Jamelia and "I'm Outta Love" by Anastacia, both of which I still know all the words to.

The facing up was, in truth, just killing time. The real reason I was employed was to help with the weekly delivery which took an hour or so. It wouldn't have made financial sense to solely come in for that when my wage was £2.55 an hour though.

The delivery was strenuous labour. A large bald man threw boxes of varying size and weight at me from his truck whilst saying things like "Man up, soft lad." I, in turn, chucked the boxes down a ramp to a colleague, Dean, who had to put the boxes in some kind of order. Dean was unapologetically striving for the management role and wore a shirt and tie to work. This was unnecessary. He was older than me though so landed a marginally better deal in the process by virtue of being indoors and not being demeaned by the bald man.

While I was at work, most of my friends had a much sweeter Saturday arrangement where they would play 5-a-side football. Annoyingly, a few of them would often come into the shop on the way to say hello/take the piss out of me. On one occasion Patrick and Sam came into the shop and swept a load of Panda Pop bottles onto the floor and ran out, laughing.

"Pick them up," Sheldon said gravely. "And tell your friends that they aren't welcome in my shop."

That was it. The following weekend I couldn't face it anymore and called in sick. When you work four hours a week this isn't acceptable, is it? I put on a weak voice and splutter, assured Sheldon that I would be back in the following week and put on my football kit.

On meeting Dylan and Rodney outside Safeway's to get a taxi to football, something terrible happened. In a case of drastically bad luck, Sheldon was walking straight towards me. What was he doing? I'd never seen him leave the shop before.

He was scowling. I considered running away but it was too late.

"Morning, Andy."

I froze.

"Morning," I replied, making a tactical decision not to be the first to bring up my earlier phone call. "Where are you going?"

"I'm going to get some change for the till. More to the point, where are you going?"

"Um, I'm just getting some air. I'm really not feeling good."

This wasn't going to cut it. I was with two friends. All of us were wearing shorts and shin pads.

Incredibly I didn't get sacked and the incident was never mentioned again. How had I got away with it? Had Sheldon forgotten?

A few months later I was called into his office for a yearly review. I was surprised and happy to hear that he was giving me a pay rise. He congratulated me and handed me an envelope with my wage and new terms. My increase was one penny an hour. Four pence a week. He hadn't forgotten.

***

Meanwhile, back in school, I was gearing up for my GCSEs, exams that our teachers put a disproportionate amount of pressure on. It was implied that a failure to get five Cs meant your life was effectively over. You'd be on the streets battling heroin addiction within weeks.

I wasn't too worried about my subjects apart from French and Science. French just seemed unnecessarily complicated. Why is a candle masculine but a sponge feminine? Who'd made these decisions? Fortunately, my mum was quite handy at French and spent many a fraught hour going through my work with me, creating vocabulary tests and rewarding me with a can of Fosters if I passed. This blackmail worked and I managed to scrape the desired C.

I found Science even less comprehensible. I couldn't get my head around photosynthesis, the periodic table or the formula for speed and struggled badly. My progress had further been hampered by being in a class with Eddie, Jack, Matt, Seamus and Mads so large parts of the lessons that I didn't understand were spent pissing around. Science facilitates pissing around like no other subject. If you're allowing teenagers to wear silly coats and goggles and giving them fire, magnesium and pig's livers to play with, what do you expect? We hid a pig's liver in Jack's bag during one lesson and it took him until after lunchtime to realise why he smelt of piss. I also played a cruel prank on Eddie where I passed him a Bunsen burner stand which I was holding with tongs and asked him to put it away, not mentioning that it was still boiling hot. He took it off me and, of course, burnt his hand. I still feel bad about that but got my just desserts when I accidentally set alight to my hair with a Bunsen burner, my wet-look gel proving highly flammable as my quiff went up in flames. Head under a cold tap did the job and there were no injuries but my charcoaled hair needed a restyle.

By Year 11 I'd been demoted a set and was on track to flunk science completely – something I was told would be a huge problem in terms of my, as yet unrecognised, career aspirations. The benefits of being middle-class were that once my parents identified my scientific shortcomings, they got me a science tutor. I forget his name but he was a large-headed man of around seventy, with curly white hair. He smelt of baked potatoes but was a talented scientist with a kind demeanour and, as he patiently talked me through my AQA textbooks, things began to make sense and I started to improve. Still, I resented the weekly lessons and was always in a foul mood beforehand. From 6pm – 7pm, I wanted to be eating crisps while watching the Simpsons and Hollyoaks.

One week, it was 6.15pm and he still hadn't arrived, which was uncharacteristic. My dad was annoyed about this as he'd have to rearrange tea plans, and he went into the hallway to call my tutor before returning to the back room, looking shaken.

"You won't be having your lesson tonight, Andrew."

I felt a surge of relief and contemplated how I might spend this new 45 minutes that circumstances had presented. Perhaps I'd have two bags of crisps.

"Why not?"

"Well, I'm not quite sure how to say this. Your tutor died this morning."

This was unexpected news. He'd seemed fine, the poor man. I felt awful but vowed to get my head down and continue to spend Tuesday evenings working through my science books. It's what he would have wanted. I over-performed in the end and dedicate my B in Science GCSE to his memory. With a bit of tweaking, I think there's a script for a film in there, isn't there? James Van der Beek starring as me and Sir Ian McKellen as the tutor, perhaps?

11

Lurking below the surface of my formative years was something unpleasant. Between twelve and seventeen I was mugged more times than is reasonably on. I'd estimate nine times. Nine muggings. Getting mugged is rubbish. The first time it happened was at the bus stop at the bottom of my street on a Monday morning. Johnno and I were stood waiting for the number one as usual, which stopped at Lawnswood and Ralph Thoresby. Lawnswood was a cheaper fare so if we got on together I could say "20p please" when I should have been paying 32p. With that kind of dishonesty, I suppose getting mugged was my just comeuppance.

Our tormentor was an oddly cheery chap a few years older than us.

"Can you give me your bus fare?" he asked with a smile.

There were a few other people stood at the bus stop and nothing about him was particularly frightening so I, kind of, stood up for myself.

"Um, I'm sorry I can't do that. I need it for the bus. Do you mind if I don't?"

It was a polite exchange so far. We just disagreed on the issue re. my money. Surely we could come to an amicable arrangement?

He turned to Johnno.

"How about you? Can you give me your bus fare?"

Johnno shook his head.

Things took a turn.

The cheery criminal pulled a knife out which, I must admit, alters the mood. It was only a craft knife and while I thought it unlikely he would murder us, it gave him the upper hand in negotiations. Johnno and I handed him our bus fare and dinner money before walking back to my house to tell my mum. We got to spend the morning off school and had the excitement of a trip to the police station. I'd only lost £3 and, knife aside, it hadn't been that scary. A light introduction to getting mugged. The mugger got caught later that day and we were informed that he'd carried out a spate of similar bus stop offences over the previous week.

The nice-but-dim mugger was not, sadly, representative of all muggers. During the coming years, an influx of gangs began patrolling the streets of my leafy, middle-class neighbourhood. The area was becoming popular with students who the gangs had identified as easy targets, likely to be in possession of cash and mobile phones. Be it with pals or alone, my heart sank whenever I saw a group of hooded lads strutting in my direction. There were no niceties with their opening gambit, usually along the lines of:

"Yo. Let me make a call from your phone, blud."

"Lend us a quid, mush."

I never saw the point of this charade. We all know that you aren't going to make a call then return my phone, don't we? The money isn't a lend, is it? I lost a couple of phones and a few pounds in these scenarios but my pride wasn't damaged too much as there wasn't much you could do about it. I've never been anything close to resembling a fighter so when outnumbered by hoodlums, I offered little resistance.

I preferred getting mugged when I was on my own. With pals, there was always that horrible moment where you glanced at one another hoping that someone had an answer and was going to save the day. On one occasion, we were outnumbered by eight to five. Of course, we were going to lose. In the middle of the ordeal I saw a glint in Craig's eyes and thought; he's going to do something here. He's got a plan! He did have a plan, only it was a self-serving one. He turned, sprinted over the road and ran into Safeway, where he hid. It worked. While we were turning our pockets out again, he was safe. In Safeway.

Out of the all these shitty incidents, there was one time when we came out on top. Eddie, Tino, Ollie and I were at the bonfire fair in town. I was working out the best way to spend the £4 that my mum had allocated, leaning towards sugary food instead of the Hard Rock ride which would certainly incite nausea. Are fairground rides fun? I still don't know the answer. A couple of yobs approached us. One of them reached into the pocket of his Adidas poppers and revealed a shiny blade. Brilliant. Goodbye candyfloss, hello miserable walk home.

Ollie wasn't in the mood; the walking embodiment of small-man syndrome, he'd had enough. We'd once had to drag him away from five angry skateboarders while he shouted that he would fight them all, at the same time, on his own. You couldn't deny his self-confidence. As soon as he saw the knife, rather than handing over his belongings, Ollie punched the mugger in the face. Rock beat scissors.

"Run."

This was, as I said, a one-off and my biggest humiliation was yet to come. I'd just got together with Carly and along with some mates, we were sauntering aimlessly around the streets hoping that an irresponsible pedestrian might go in the shop for us to buy some cider. As the sun was setting, we were strolling up a quiet street when a gang collared us. They were becoming well-known and the leader was notorious for being a violent maniac. He had short, curly hair stuffed under a Nike TN cap and tilted his head downwards when he spoke to you, his pale irises sitting just below sharp eyebrows.

There was the usual ritual of, "Yo. Lend us a quid, blud," before things took a more sinister turn. Looking at me, the leader said.

"Yo, you've got a long face."

I couldn't argue with his observation.

He turned to Craig.

"Yo, look at this guy's hair. Spike."

Where was this going? Feeling humiliated, I looked at Carly, then at the floor. She can't have been impressed. Did she like my long face? It got worse.

"Long Face, kiss Spike."

What the heck?

"You heard me, Long Face. Kiss Spike or I'll fucking rough you up, mush."

I looked at Craig, who was as stunned and crestfallen as me. For the record, his hair wasn't even that spiky. Even the ringleader's posse seemed a bit uncomfortable with his idea but grunted a few laughs. I didn't know what to do. Safeway was too far away and even if it wasn't, it's probably frowned upon to leave your new girlfriend in the midst of a mugging while you save yourself.

"Why do you want us to do this?" I asked feebly. "I don't understand?"

The ringleader grabbed my head and his sidekick grabbed Spike's head and they tried to shove us together. As our faces were nearly touching one another and I could see Craig wincing, the thugs had mercy. They gave us a shove, called us "fucking faggots," and swaggered off down the street, leaving us sad and humiliated, not knowing what to do or say next.

I tried to brush it off to save face in front of my girlfriend.

"We didn't actually kiss each other though, did we?"

Although we didn't split up there and then, it wasn't long before our relationship ended and she started going out with Johnno. Long Face was not deemed as future husband material.

The bastards. That event was, I believe, the last time we were done over by that gang, although I did come across the two leading members in different milieus later in adolescence. A year or so later I was walking to the park when their second-in-command, a tall dark-skinned chap approached me alone. Not again, come on?

"Yo. You hungry, blud?"

Oh god, what does this mean? What horrific ritual is coming? Is he going make me eat a slug?

"I suppose so."

"Do you want a free pizza?"

I looked at his t-shirt and noticed he was in Domino's attire. This could be legitimate?

"Wait here."

He ran over the road into Domino's and came out with a fresh twelve-inch pizza in a box.

"Nobody came to pick it up so you can have it."

"Um, thanks."

Guilty conscience?

After my time at John Filan's came to an end I got a weekend job at Subway sandwich shop. When I arrived for my trial shift, the guy showing me the ropes was, you've guessed it, the gang kingpin, his curly hair stuffed inside a comically small Subway cap. Had he turned his life around? Was a violent past a prerequisite for working in the fast food industry? Where are the transferrable skills? Teamwork? Timekeeping?

"Easy, mush, I'll show you how to use the till..."

During our time working together, which spanned over a year, neither of us mentioned his psychopathic past. How do you bring it up?

"I don't suppose you've still got my phone? Also, while you're at it, could I have my dignity back too?"

I wouldn't say that we ever became mates but there was a small moment of redemption. In the middle of one shift, I caught him with is hand in the till. Maybe he wasn't quite on the straight and narrow yet? I didn't say anything and, at the end of the shift, he came over and stuffed a tenner in my pocket. The romantic in me likes to think that, similar to the Domino's man, this was a belated apology for tormenting my friends and I, however, it was probably hush money.

As I got older and began to look more like an adult, the muggings became less frequent. There was a minor incident where I was swarmed by a bunch of kids and they nicked my crate of Bier De France. After they'd taken my crate one of them politely asked me if I had a bottle opener. Another, not so politely, chucked a bottle at my back as I walked off.

By eighteen the muggings stopped. It was over. I'd come out the other end in one piece. I'd like to say it was a character building chapter of my life but really, it was just shit. If any youngsters are reading this and thinking of mugging someone, don't do it. It's a nasty thing to do. Miss out the mugging phase and go straight for a job in fast food. Much more honourable and Subway are always crying out for staff.

12

The summer after completing GCSEs was one of the best of my life. Beginning in style, my Sunday League football team, Lawnswood YMCA, won the league on the last day of the season sparking wild celebrations. While my contribution to our success comprised predominantly of ineffectual substitute appearances, I won a pint-downing contest after we'd lifted the trophy which gave me as much veneration as our player of the season, for a few minutes at least. Being an under 16s team, it should probably be questioned why such a contest was allowed to take place.

The following week, seven of us went to Newquay for my first official lads' holiday. I had been away with friends unsupervised before on short cycling and hiking trips in the North of England. These were great fun apart from when long-haired Darren inexplicably decided to bring a huge, heavy suitcase for a weekend's walk from Whitby to Scarborough. We each had shifts lugging it along the rocky coastal tracks on triangle-shaped wheels but some people (including me) didn't pull their weight and squabbles disrupted camaraderie. What was Darren thinking? Why didn't his mum advise him that the suitcase was madly impractical?

Anyway, Newquay was a different animal. It was the place to go for celebrating the end of your school days. There was promise of surfing, beach parties, easy entry nightclubs and promiscuity and it sounded tremendous. Our ensemble comprised of Johnno, Jacob, and Eddie as well as Stuart and Alfie. Beguilingly, Alexander had found his way onto the list, despite the fact that none of us knew him very well.

We arrived at Leeds bus station early in the morning and chatted about our plans for the week and how best to live on our modest budgets. We were averaging £12 a day, so plotted ingenious cost-cutting techniques such as living off a giant vat of pasta and drinking cheap cider before heading to the nightclubs.

"We'll just have to be careful and make sure we don't waste any money," I said. "Only buy stuff we need."

Alexander had slipped away into a newsagent unnoticed and returned with a grin on his face and a glistening magazine in his hand.

"What have you got there, Alexander?" I asked.

"It's the official Championship Manager magazine. Bumper edition."

"How much was that?"

"£8.50."

Who was this guy?

Morale was sky high, to begin with, but that's nothing an 11-hour National Express ride can't quash and by Birmingham, the buzz had died down as people moaned of headaches and aching legs or fell asleep. Alexander remained upbeat throughout, happily flicking through his magazine, smiling from ear-to-ear.

We arrived at our accommodation, The Surf Lodge, late in the evening, and were welcomed by a long-haired man in his late twenties who showed little interest in us. Exhausted, we resisted temptation to hit the town, instead of crawling into our dormitory and getting straight to bed. I was keen to get a good night's sleep but was disturbed by the sound of flipping pages in the bunk above me. I looked up to see Alexander using a head torch to read his magazine.

"Andy, did you know that the Collyer brothers who invented Championship Manager fell out because Paul didn't go to Oliver's wedding?"

"No, Alexander, I did not."

I finally drifted into a deep sleep and woke up to the sunshine seeping through the curtains. It was a warm, hazy morning and we headed to the beach, accompanied by the sound of seagulls squawking. We breathed in the fresh salty air, splashed about in the cold water and kicked a ball around before setting up a camp (one towel) and sitting on the sand. This was before the days of smartphones and Spotify so our music for the day, and indeed the week, was an old-school hip-hop compilation CD on Alfie's ghetto blaster. As we sang along to "Ignition" by R. Kelly, I felt deliriously happy. You can't beat the opening hours of a holiday, can you?

The beach was quiet but nearby a pair of older girls were sunbathing. I wanted to capitalise on my mood and did something uncharacteristic.

"I'm going to talk to them."

"Really?"

"Watch and learn..." I began, before the enormity of the task ahead kicked in. "Will someone come with me?"

Eddie begrudgingly agreed and we ambled over, trying to look laidback as though this was normal behaviour for us. We were sweaty and covered in sand.

"So," I opened with, as we stood a few feet away from them, "what are your names?"

They were surrounded by piles of magazines debating how much weight a Sugababe had lost and a scandal involving Federico from Big Brother.

"What do you want?" asked one of the pair, without looking up.

Shit. Eddie stepped in.

"He just...um...we just wondered if you girls are on holiday or local?"

"We're local." She still didn't look up. "Why?"

My time to shine.

"You should be able to help us then. We are looking for a good party tonight, are there any clubs you recommend?"

A good time guy with a hint of sophistication.

She looked up at me, shook her head and picked up a magazine.

"Well, I guess we might see you later then?"

We walked off and returned to our pals who were laughing.

"Shut up, I'd like to see you try." I snapped, my good mood kicked into the long grass. I'd perked up by the time we were getting ready for our first night out, although the old school hip-hop compilation was wearing a little thin already. I'd heard "Rappers Delight" at least ten times. We shirt-and-shoesed it and strutted the half mile from The Surf Lodge into Newquay town centre, drinking cans of Carling and passing around a bottle of Vladivar vodka for vomit-inducing gulps.

The first bar we came across was a Walkabout on the cliff edge. The clientele seemed to be actual adults but, equipped with the fake IDs that had been proving successful at Bassment, we went for it. Eddie and I were the tallest members of the group so paired up on the frontline. A bouncer as wide as the two of us together rebuffed us.

"Why not?" Eddie asked, politely.

"Look at you. No chance."

"Come on, we're on holiday?" I said.

"Don't get cheeky."

"How is that cheeky?" Eddie said. "Go on, just let us in."

"Right, that's it, you little shit."

He grabbed Eddie in a policeman's hold and held him over a railing above a vertical drop down to where the waves were crashing on the sharp rocks below. This had escalated quickly. Eddie expressed apologies in between yelps of pain and gladly the bouncer didn't hurl him over the edge, instead releasing his grip and shoving him in the other direction. For the second time today, flustered and scared, Eddie and I returned to our waiting pals.

"Good start."

Unperturbed we continued into town and were encouraged to find that several groups of sixteen-year-olds were also milling around in high spirits, the glow of inebriation obvious through loud voices and unsteady gait. After a couple of less dramatic refusals, we finally found success in The Rock Club, a dark, sticky-floored venue where a DJ in his fifties was playing "Back in Black" uncomfortably loud as people ranging from sixteen to forty, mostly in black hoodies, danced, drank and smoked roll-ups. Due to its similarities with Bassment, I felt at home in the dingy room and had a good night, drinking lager out of plastic cups and singing along to Greenday with my arms draped around my pals. This was not really Stuart and Alfie's cup of tea – they were more into old school hip-hop – but it was the first night and they persevered for a while before departing circa 1 am, shortly followed by Eddie, Jacob, and Johnno.

This left me with Alexander. After leaving the club we staggered onto the street and got talking to a bunch of lads from London, which was quite exciting given that I didn't know anyone from down South. They were passing around a flask of Glen's vodka and Alexander gleefully accepted the bottle. He was being unusually vocal and dominating conversation with quips and Championship Manager tips that nobody had asked for.

Our new friends invited us back to their hostel to continue drinking. They'd been fishing earlier in the day and wanted to show us their biggest catch, a coy carp which they were keeping in a bathtub. Alexander was keen to join them, alas it was 3 am and I was growing tired so we politely declined, signifying the end of a brief friendship. Alexander paid for a taxi back to The Surf Lodge and we snuck into our dorms where the rest of our pals were sleeping soundly.

***

"Ugh…"

I opened my eyes open and blinked repeatedly to adjust to the morning light and stared at the sagging beams on the bed above me. What was that noise?

"Ugh…"

There is was again, what was going on? The room smelt of sweat, smoke, and petrol.

"Argh…"

The noise was coming from above. It was Alexander. In a Domino effect, his grunting began to awake the rest of my pals who, one by one, sat up rubbing their eyes.

"Are you okay, Alexander?" Alfie asked.

"No."

"What's wrong?"

Before Alexander could answer I heard his stomach churn and his large head appeared over the side of the top bunk. Without any further warning, he was violently sick, the grey vomit dripping onto the floor forming a lumpy puddle inches away from my face.

"For fuck's sake," Eddie said. "Go to the bathroom, Alexander."

"Ugh…"

Alfie and Jacob began laughing before the room fell quiet for a few seconds.

Alexander was sick again. This time throwing up on the bunk bed ladder, with strings of vomit dangling from the rungs.

"Oh no," Eddie said.

"What's up, Eddie?" Jacob asked.

Eddie leant over the side of his bed and was also sick, vomit splattering on the floor.

"Now look what's happened, Alexander," he said angrily. "Another one of us has been sick."

"Sorry, Eddie," Alexander said. "Ugh, I don't feel good at all…"

The scene was vile, the room like something from a horror film. This didn't deter Alexander from wanting to stay in it and after locating a bucket, he unsteadily clambered back into the top bunk and lay down again, closing his eyes.

We left him and headed out for some food and a walk around the town, discussing the previous night out and planning the impending one. When we returned, late in the afternoon, Alexander was in bed but the vomit had disappeared and the room no longer stank. He was reading his magazine.

"How's it going, Alexander?" I asked.

"Awful. I've paid for new sheets and for the room to be cleaned. That's all my money gone. I won't be coming out again."

"Really?"

"To be honest, I never want to go out again anyway so it's not a problem."

He stuck to this, spending the rest of the week barely leaving his bed except for trips to the lounge to watch films in the evening. His first lads' holiday was effectively over after one night.

The remaining six of us were more active, playing tennis or going for walks during the days and heading into town by night. We discovered Beach Club, a busy nightclub that accepted fake IDs and seemed to be the hotspot for GCSE finishers. Here we drank £1 bottles of blue WKD and with Sean Paul, Usher and Mario Winans providing the soundtrack, tried to dance with girls. It was a fun, lively atmosphere but my memories of the venue are tarnished by the resident DJ, a man in his thirties, saying quite possibly the worst thing I have ever heard anyone say. He stopped the Craig David song that was playing and shouted to the crowds.

"This place is absolutely dripping with minge!"

Now, I know that DJs are not always the most refined types and, secured from the bustling dance floor by their little booths, they can get away with a fair bit, but come on? That's unforgivable.

Another venue which gladly accepted our modest custom was Tall Trees, allegedly Newquay's oldest nightclub. Tall Trees had a winning marketing gimmick; it shone strobe lights bearing its name onto the sky which could be seen for miles around. Quite how they were funding this was a mystery as, when we got in, the vast, decrepit club was almost empty save for a smattering of folk stood around the periphery of a dance floor which lazily lit up in a rhythm unrelated to the music. It appeared Beach Club was the market leader even though their DJ was a likely candidate for the sex offenders register.

Nonetheless, late in the night, I enjoyed a small slice of romance on the sparse dance floor, sharing a kiss with a curly-haired, bisexual break-dancer. It was one of those typical teen romances where you barely speak for the duration and she left without us having exchanged names. Still, I strutted back to my friends with my mood and confidence elevated, the failed chat-up attempt on the beach a distant memory. Indeed, blinded by this brief encounter, I held Tall Trees in exaggerated high esteem, believing it to be the best nightclub in the world and persuaded my pals to go again the following night.

"Can't we try somewhere else?"

"Somewhere else that shines lights onto the sky? Yeah, good luck with that, Stuart."

And so, we returned. This time it was a techno and hard house night and much busier than before; the dance floor was packed, which confused me as the music was dreadful. Take me back to dancing to Run DMC with my bisexual break-dancer. Eddie and Alfie jostled to the bar, getting a round of drinks before bringing them back to the alcove we had located.

With the repetitive thud of the music, it at one another speak and none of us were enjoying ourselves. I felt a touch guilty. Perhaps we should have listened to Stuart and gone to see Tim Westwood at Koala Club after all? A girl in a luminous crop-top danced over to us and sat next to Jacob. She was pulling some strange expressions, curling her mouth into unusual shapes, eyes wide. She addressed the group:

"Anyone got any gurners?"

"Jellsters? What do you mean? A jellyfish?" Jacob asked her, confused.

"Jellyfish? What are you talking about?"

This was a bizarre conversation. After she spelt it out to us, we eventually deduced that she meant ecstasy so sadly for her, the answer was no, we do not have any gurners. After this exchange, it became clearer as to why people were enjoying dancing to this terrible music; looking a little clearer, almost everyone was on gurners. Apart from us. We left shortly afterwards and headed back into town, having a pint in The Sailor's Arms, a busy late-night pub before splitting into splinter groups and roaming around town, trying to get into bars. I remember little from the night apart from walking home with Johnno. Midway through the journey, we shared a glance with one another before bursting into laughter. About nothing. We laughed and laughed until we were howling and crying. Nothing funny had happened, it was inexplicable. It was like time had turned back to our primary school days and were having dinner in my backroom, testing my parent's patience.

The next day I looked through the front section of my JanSport rucksack which had been acting as an unsafe safe. I was upset but not surprised to find that I had less than one pound to last me for the remaining two days. Was Newquay over for me, like Alexander? I didn't want to spend my remaining days lying in the dormitory which still smelt of vomit. I called home and frantically explained my plight to my dad.

"Andrew, how's the holiday? Have you visited the Lappa Valley Steam Railway?"

"No, not yet. Um, please can you wire me some money?"

"You don't have a bank account, Andrew."

"Oh, what does wire mean? They always say it in films."

"What's the address of The Surf Lodge? I'll post it to you."

"Thanks."

I borrowed a tenner from Stuart to get me through and, on the final morning, was delighted when the long-haired Surf

Lodge owner informed me that I had post. The envelope had been sent first class and written on the front of it, in marker pen was:

URGENT! EMERGENCY! FOR THE ATTENTION OF ANDREW CARTER.

I opened it to find a crisp twenty-pound note. Thank you for that, Dad. I'll pay you back one day.

For our final hurrah, we drank beer and listened to the old school hip-hop album one last time at the Surf Lodge before walking the now-familiar route along the cliffs into town. It's lovely on holiday when you feel acquainted and comfortable in your settings and know the lay of the land, although the final night had a touch of melancholy about it. I was going to miss Newquay.

We enjoyed a fitting finale, well, aside from Eddie that is. He'd received a text message from Sarah, a young lady he'd met earlier in the holiday and headed off to meet her and her sister in the Sailor's Arms. The rest of us returned to Beach Club but shortly after arriving, Jacob heard rumours of a literal beach party which sounded promising. It was a clement, starlit evening as we strolled the short distance down to the coast to see hundreds of teenagers gathered around glowing campfires with ghetto blasters blaring and guys in flip-flops playing the guitar while the waves gently lapped on the shoreline. This was what I imagined life would be like in California or Thailand, I didn't know such things happened in our country. I was spellbound.

Jacob and I bought an overpriced four-pack from an astute teenage businessman who'd loaded up from Asda before it shut and sat on the sand, reminiscing about the holiday and speculating about what our futures held.

"Malia next year?"

We got chatting to some girls from Hampshire, who had just arrived in Newquay and gladly assisted when they asked us which clubs we'd recommended. (Take note, hostile girls on the beach on day one.) Indeed, one of the girls and I got along well and to my delight, she said she was moving to Leeds in September. What were the chances? With her pretty face flickering in the glow of the campfire, she wrote her phone number on my arm in mascara and we made loose plans to meet up later in the year. I seem to recall saying I'd show her around the clubs, which was a touch misleading as there was only one club that let me in in Leeds. Walking home with my pals, I was as happy as can be – a wonderful end to a wonderful holiday.

This wasn't the case for all of us. Back at the hostel, Eddie had returned early, alone and was lying in bed, stewing.

"What happened?" I asked after we'd bustled into our room in the early hours.

"I went to the Sailor's Arms but Sarah wasn't there. I had a pint on my own then went to the Beach Club but they didn't let me in so I came back."

"Oh, sorry to hear that. It's only one night though, you've enjoyed the rest of the holiday, right?"

"Yes, I suppose so."

"More than Alexander, anyway?"

Alexander suddenly sat up, awake.

"What are you talking about? I've had a brilliant holiday. I've had a great night out, I've watched Training Day three times and I've nearly finished my magazine. What more could you ask for?"

13

Within minutes of arriving at the college open day, I was sold. Ralph Thoresby was due to be demolished the following year, a telling sign as to the state of the building and, after five years in the same place, I was ready for a change. Besides, I'd spotted an inordinate number of attractive girls in the Sociology taster class.

While some of my mates from school had been grouped together, I didn't know anyone in my form, which was both daunting and exciting. A clean slate. Aware of the importance of first impressions, I was a bag of nerves on my first day. I seldom impress from the offset; I often get undeserved dirty looks from men on the street, numerous friends have since admitted they didn't like me when we first met, and I've always found it nigh-on impossible to chat up previously unknown girls.

Wristbands were in fashion at the time. Should I wear mine? What about a cap? After much deliberation, I played it safe – jeans and t-shirt, no accessories. My only insecurity was my eyebrows; without a hint of irony, I'd shaved tramlines into them over the summer, which had almost grown back but not quite. At least I'd fared better than Eddie, who – at a sleepover at Matt's – had been talked into shaving his eyebrows off entirely. He'd looked like a serial killer.

As twenty or so folks stood outside our form room, old acquaintances were chatting while shy strangers stood in silence. I noticed that two guys had gone for both wristbands and a cap while another was wearing a full, smart suit, his attire suitable for a job interview with Alan Sugar. What was his game? A tall, boisterous Sikh bounded down the corridor and introduced himself to everyone, shaking hands and making gags. I admired and, indeed, envied his confidence.

After a few minutes, our form teacher arrived; a tall, purple-haired lady, wearing an elaborate floral gown. She unlocked the door and advised us to take seats, the shrewder folk aware that where you sat now could be your seat for the whole year. I waited accordingly and engineered my move so that I was sat in between the boisterous Sikh and a frizzy-haired guy wearing baggy chequered trousers.

The teacher was staring straight at me, smiling.

"Andrew Carter?"

"Um, yes."

All eyes were on me.

"I know your parents. I knew you when you were this high," she said, gesturing with her hand to indicate a miniature person. I was certain I'd never seen this lady before, although my memories of being three foot tall are admittedly hazy.

"They bought a house from me in the eighties."

"Oh, okay."

"Sorry, I'm embarrassing you, aren't I?"

"No," I said, burning up, "not at all."

The brief conversation ended and people shuffled their bags around. The teacher leafed through some paperwork for a few seconds before the buzz was replaced by a long silence.

"Tell Neil and Janet, Cindy says hello."

Cindy was not a name I was expecting. This was not a strip club. We played a standard get-to-know-you activity, where you say your name and something interesting about yourself, discovering that some people liked rugby, others were keen on dancing and one girl had a belly button piercing.

It was the turn of the guy in the suit.

"Hi, I'm Will," he said. He was well spoken and cocky. "My real name is Andrew but I hate that name."

Hate that name? I hated him. At least he'd given me ammo for my interesting fact. I was going to say I supported Leeds United but two other guys had already used this one.

"My name's Andrew and I happen to like my name," I said, generating a couple of muted sniggers but not as much of a laugh as I'd hoped for.

At break time I was dismayed to see Will and the boisterous Sikh getting on well and retreated to the safety net of meeting my school buddies and Martin, a friend from football, in the common room. A lean guy wearing a leather jacket and ripped jeans strode through the doors and strutted towards us. He was causing quite the commotion, earning admiring glances from a group of heavily made-up girls.

"Easy, Andy. What's up?"

He offered me a high handshake to which I connected well. I knew him. We'd been in Beavers and Cubs together and, more recently, bumped into one another at a park and shared a weak joint. He oozed charisma which I hoped might rub off on me.

"Hi Cameron, I didn't know you were coming to this college?"

The six of us began chatting animatedly, the prevalent topic of conversation, of course, being girls. We had each identified several potential wives and it was only 10.30 am. Cameron's arrival had boosted our kudos but no sooner had girls been looking our way than their attention was diverted. Ten or fifteen older looking guys swaggered into the common room; muscular, chiselled athletes, some of whom had beards. They were wearing blue tracksuits informing us that they were in the football academy. How could we compete?

Following little consideration, I'd picked Law, Sociology, English Language and Psychology, but within two weeks I'd dropped Law because it was incomprehensible and swapped English Language to English Literature on a tip-off from Jacob and Cameron about the calibre of girls in their class.

As well as Jacob and Cameron, my nemesis, Will was in the English Literature class. Following some jesting about Othello, he and Cameron had hit it off and to my irritation, Cameron invited him to join us for a pint after the class. He wasn't wearing a suit this time and, after discussing Leeds United's demise and sharing a cigarette, I begrudgingly accepted that he wasn't too bad. Will introduced us to a pair of guys who also had one-syllable names, Lee and Jim. They liked The Strokes and The Libertines, shared a proclivity for dressing well and looked cool when smoking. Strong additions. This was good. Now, where are the girls?

Over the course of the first term, many of my pals found romance in the shape of either short flings or actual girlfriends. Following a rendition of "Mysterious Girl" at a karaoke night,

Matt won the heart of Lucy who would go on to become his wife and, after wooing her with his Ford Fiesta and sharp dress sense, Will got together with Tilly who he would marry some eleven years later.

I, however, was suffering from a crisis of confidence. While I was adept at getting the odd classroom giggle, I was finding it increasingly difficult to initiate meaningful conversations with girls. Throughout Year 10 and 11 this wasn't an issue so why was I regressing? Small fish, big pond? Didier Drogba in his first season at Chelsea? Would my form improve like his? While I had a good set of friends, we weren't even big fish in our-section-of-the-upstairs-bit-of-the-common room, this honour held by the boisterous Sikh and his mates.

Friday nights were still spent at Dust although it had become a little samey/identical every week of late. I'd recently tried to rekindle the flame with Rui Costa and she'd said, "Who the fuck are you?"

After elaborate planning we went to Creation, an enormous four-story club full of dance floors, bars and ambient rooms frequented by pointy side-burned men with women sat on their laps. The different areas were linked by a labyrinth of confusing corridors meaning large portions of my night were spent on my phone, lost.

"Where are you, Eddie?"

"I'm at the bar," he shouted, his voice barely audible over a Sean Paul track.

"Which bar?"

"What?"

"Which one?"

"I can't hear you. Where are you?"

"I don't know."

It was nonetheless an entertaining night and one that opened my eyes to a nightlife beyond a dank and dingy cellar. Cameron was wearing a leather jacket which was impractical on a sweaty dance floor but went down a storm. At one point, he was spotted slow dancing with a 51-year-old called Sue.

I was starting to discover that for all his charm, Cameron was hedonistic and slightly mad. During a Tuesday-afternoon English lesson, while the teacher was reading out an emotive scene between Othello and Desdemona, I noticed he had a paper bag on his lap. Every few seconds he was dipping in and nibbling its contents.

"What are you eating?" I asked, expecting him to say, perhaps, Liquorice Allsorts.

"Magic mushrooms, do you want some?"

"Oh, I'm okay for now thanks, mate."

On the walk home, they kicked in and he went loopy; talking gibberish while plucking leaves from trees and studying them with wonder. It was a long walk. I was relieved to turn off at my street.

"Right, this is me then, mate. Get home safely."

He was staring at the sky, transfixed.

"Look, Andy, the clouds are dancing."

"Bye, Cameron."

***

Will passed his driving test which broadened our horizons in that we drove to more scenic spots to smoke; five guys crammed into a tiny Fiesta was uncomfortable but it beat sitting at home and struggling to access MSN Messenger on our gallingly slow dial-up internet. In local parks and luminous BP garages, we shared good times, chatting about subjects ranging from Shakespeare and George Bush to football and our chequered ambitions for the future.

Over Easter, Will, Cameron and I performed in the Passion Play at Leeds Cathedral. Will had advised me it would be a good way to raise our stock and get noticed in college. We'd stayed at mine the night before, got drunk, and slept through our alarms. My mum had to come in and scrape Jesus, Barabbas and Pontius Pilate from a dearth of empty cans on my living room floor and bundle us into her car where ashen-faced and fragile, we ran through our lines a final time. During the play, I noticed one of the girls in the choir, a petite blond with big eyes and a sweet smile and in between my bumbled lines I couldn't stop staring at her.

With the Passion Play providing a common interest I started chatting to her at college and was pleased to find that we got on well. Her name was Cara. During one free period, I found myself strolling into town with Cara and one of her mates – also a girl, also attractive. Happy to have found myself in their esteemed company, I was trying to show off with a range of poor to average jokes when a suited man approached us.

"My apologies for being so forward, but have you two ever thought about being models or actresses?"

You two? I caught his eye and he looked a bit awkward.

"Sorry, you three. You too, sir."

I think he had flatteringly but mistakenly assumed that one of the girls was my girlfriend and didn't want me to think he was a sleazebag although his slicked-back hair and sickly-sweet aftershave did little to suggest he wasn't. Perhaps he just didn't want to hurt my feelings? After a long pause, he unconvincingly added.

"We are always on the lookout for male talent too."

The man proceeded to give us some well-rehearsed spiel about how his agency had once scouted a Hollyoaks star. As an avid Hollyoaks watcher at the time, I asked him who this star was. He hastily diverted the conversation.

"So, here's my card guys, give me a call and we will get you booked in for a meeting at the office."

It had been an odd encounter. Afterwards, the girls laughed it off and didn't appear to think much of it. Does this sort of thing happen a lot to girls? Despite a bad feeling in my gut, I kept hold of his card and on the bus home began planning my life as a celebrity.

The following day I was in town when I bumped into Matt. I asked him what he was up to. He looked excited.

"You'll never believe what's happened, Andy. I've been scouted by a talent agency! I'm going to an appointment at the office now to discuss my portfolio."

This was a coincidence, wasn't it? I told Matt that I too had been scouted but hadn't booked in my appointment yet. He suggested that I tag along with him for some moral support. Maybe they could fit me in too? This seemed like a good idea and the two of us followed the vague directions on the back of the business card until we found ourselves in some rented office space above a William Hill.

A receptionist advised us to take a seat in the waiting area where a few other soon-to-be-famous stars were sat nervously. A stony-faced woman with a clipboard swept into the room.

"Who are you two?" she asked.

Matt gave her his name to which she nodded approvingly and said that someone would be with him soon.

I explained my situation and she looked me up and down.

"So, you haven't actually booked an appointment?"

"No."

I took out the man's crumpled business card from my pocket as proof that I had been scouted. She looked at the card, and me, dismissively.

"I don't think you are what we are looking for. You can go."

I was crestfallen. My celebrity dream was over already. Matt looked at me apologetically as I sadly walked out of the office and went home.

Later, Matt called me and enthusiastically told me that they wanted to start on his portfolio as soon as possible. Not wanting to appear bitter, I congratulated him. I wanted him to remember me when he was famous. If I stayed on his side maybe he would bring me along to some glittering award ceremonies?

Over the coming days, he had some photos taken and proudly showed me when his portfolio was finished. Most of the pictures involved him wearing an unbuttoned tuxedo jacket and bow-tie, which would have been fine, only he wasn't wearing a shirt.

"They are great, aren't they? The agency is in touch with some shops and TV representatives so it's just a waiting game until I get some offers," he told me. "They only cost a couple of hundred quid but that's nothing, is it?"

"You had to pay?"

Some twelve years later, after one unsuccessful audition for a Costcutter advert, his big break still hasn't come. The waiting game continues. I can't knock him too much though, after all, my chances of becoming a star were deemed so unlikely that the agency didn't even try to rip me off.

14

The encounter with the sham talent agency did, at least, provide a topic of conversation with Cara. Shortly after the encounter, I managed to get her phone number.

"Can I take your number so we can keep each other updated on how it goes with the agency?"

"Sure."

Transparent but effective. We settled into texting one another now and then and within a couple of weeks, I'd fallen for her. Did I have a chance? I couldn't tell. Comparable to timing your moment of magic when Frank walked up the hill in the early Kirkstall Crusaders days, I tried to engineer my best moments to correlate with Cara's presence. When she sauntered into the common room I hoped I'd be in the process of making my friends laugh or perhaps standing with the cool black guy who was in my Sociology class.

When we chatted as a pair I felt like we got along well and I made her chuckle. However, I wasn't sure what to read into this as I'd detected that she was generous with her laughs. I once saw her in hysterics while chatting to a dry guy from the football team who I didn't like and concluded that I was nothing special. She was probably texting loads of guys; a diminutive heartbreaker. Nevertheless, when she left for the day I missed her and when I got home I replayed the conversations we'd had during the day. How had I come across? Was I overdoing it when, unasked, I boasted about how much I'd drank in Creation?

One Wednesday evening I'd got home from the late shift at Subway when I received a text from Cameron, who had also just finished work. He was a barman.

"We're going to Heaven and Hell. I'm on my way to yours."

Feeling a surge of excitement, I splashed some water under my armpits to cover the smell of bread and cheese and he arrived within minutes. Heaven and Hell did a £10-all-you-can-drink offer, which was both reasonable and irresponsible. While we were optimistic about the night ahead and pleased with our spontaneity, we were facing a conundrum; between us, we had just £25. The surplus £5 was necessary to catch the night bus home but how were we going to get there? After discussing this over a can of Carling and the just-finished-work endorphins still pumping, we elected to jog. It was an unseasonably balmy night and, wearing jeans and smart shoes, by the time we'd ran the two miles, I was sweating buckets and had blisters on my feet. Not a great look, although Heaven and Hell was not the most refined of venues. It unfailingly smelled of vomit.

It was after midnight when we arrived so we had just two hours in which to have fun. On our way in I saw Aaron Lennon getting rebuffed at the door. He'd recently broken into the Leeds United first team so his age was common knowledge. As I strode past him I felt a sense of closure after the 11-1 loss a few years previously. You might go on to play for England and earn fifty grand a week but who's winning now, Aaron? The club had three sections: Hell, which played aggressive techno music and was usually frequented by wide-eyed men on pills, Purgatory, which was for RnB and hip hop and a bit intimidating (I'd once seen a couple having wild sex on a table) and Heaven, which played cheesy pop music and had the lowest probability of violence. Hell, despite being, well, hell, always had the quietest bar so a sound tactic was to get your drinks in there before heading to the top floor. Cameron and I got four alcopops each, downed one, felt a bit sick and headed upstairs clutching the remaining three.

"Love Shack" by the B52s was playing when we arrived in the jam-packed room.

"I'm just going to the toilet," Cameron said, "I'll find you in a second."

I was bustling through crowds and scanning the room for a familiar face when I felt a tap on my shoulder. It was Cara. Wearing a stylish yellow dress and with newly curled hair framing her pretty face, I felt a wave of delight. I'd never seen her outside of college hours. Could this be the night? I hoped she wouldn't notice that I was drenched in sweat and smelt of sandwiches.

"Hi Andy, you're friends with Pontius Pilate, aren't you? Are you out with him tonight?"

"He's just gone to the toilet."

"Will you tell him I'm just sitting over there?"

"Um, sure."

Cameron returned and, through gritted teeth, I passed on the information.

"Thanks, do you think I've got a chance?"

Fuck you, Pontius. You charismatic, handsome twat.

"I'd say so, yes."

A weird guy from college approached me. He was very drunk, encroaching on my personal space and explaining his theories behind 9/11 in one of those conversations where only one person talks. In the corner of my eye, I looked to see that Cameron and Cara were holding hands. This wasn't right? I'd been putting in groundwork for weeks, agonising over what to say in text messages and making sure I looked my best on Thursdays when we shared a free period together. Cameron had done nothing. They'd barely spoken to each other. Torturing myself, I continued to glance over until, sure enough, they began to kiss. It was done.

"Sorry mate," I said to the weird guy who was now talking about the flaws in a Freudian theory he'd been reading about in Psychology. "I don't mean to be rude but I just don't give a shit."

I trudged off and considered going home but couldn't as Cameron had our remaining fiver. I went down to Hell and sat at the bar ordering drink after drink, staring into space and hopelessly hoping that a girl might approach me. Of course, it didn't happen. Instead, I watched as a skeletal man wearing a t-shirt saying: "So many women, so little time" stumbled up to a stunning brunette in a black dress, grabbed her hips and whispered something in her ear. I expected her to turn around disgusted and maybe slap him. She did not. She smiled at his t-shirt and leant in to kiss him. Life just didn't seem fair. I tried my best to be a decent guy but that didn't seem to get me anywhere. I needed to be more proactive. I couldn't just sit around waiting for a girl to come over, I wasn't good-looking enough for that. A frequent criticism when playing football was that I waited for the ball to come to me rather than trying to get it. My dormant love life was comparable. I continued to sit, stewing.

At the end of the night, Cameron found me and we caught the bus home together. He was, of course, chirpy. I hadn't discussed my feelings for Cara with him so he had done nothing wrong and there was no reason to fall out with him. I didn't want to entertain a conversation about potential date venues though.

With furry teeth, bloodshot eyes and a splitting headache, I took the bus to college the next morning. After toiling in a Psychology class, which dealt with the Freudian theory that the weird guy had been critiquing eight hours previously, I was concerned that I was sweating out alcopop. It was a long hour and I left feeling lightheaded and weak. Needing to eat something, I staggered to a nearby row of shops and bought a tuna sub from Highway, a sandwich shop perchance influenced by my own employer. Walking back, I was wolfing it down with barbeque sauce on my chin and crumbs on my t-shirt when I was stopped in my tracks by Cara. She was fine. Fresh faced.

"Morning Andy, did you have a good night?"

She'd caught me off guard. I'd been eating far too quickly and could feel the sandwich curdling in my WKD-lined stomach. This was bad news.

"Sorry, I'm not feeling too…"

I ran off, dashed up a ginnel and was sick, the luminous vomit splashing over my Vans trainers. I would never have been good enough for her, who had I been kidding?

***

Heartache aside, college life was good. Under the stewardship of Alec, a flame-haired guitarist who wore baggy jeans, we formed a band. Will had caught wind of this and told us he was a great singer on the basis that he'd been in a choir at primary school. During our first practice, at his mum's house, it transpired that he was, by no means, a great singer. I couldn't understand why he'd lied? He was always going to get found out as soon as he opened his mouth. It's wasn't a lie that had legs.

We politely booted him out and replaced him with Cameron, who could sing a bit and also rap. Yes, rap. The band had just one gig, at the clubhouse of my former football team. It went well, although we overdid our encore playing at least two too many additional choruses of "Get Away" by Lenny Kravitz as people began to spill out of the function room and back to the bar, where they didn't have to shout over my heavily distorted power chords.

One Friday evening Will had a free house and invited a few of us round. As was so often the case, the plan for the evening didn't stretch beyond buying some cans and after an hour we were restless.

"What shall we do?" I asked.

"Well," Cameron said. "I have got some 'shrooms on me?"

Did he always have magic mushrooms on him? What was his problem? We discussed the idea and, with trepidation, I agreed to try some. Why not? We were in a safe, familiar environment after all. What could go wrong? Aside from Jacob, who declined, we each nibbled a handful then continued to sit around doing nothing, now with the addition of fear and a foul, earthy aftertaste lingering in our mouths.

"Nothing's happening," I declared after half an hour, "can I have some more?"

Cameron passed the bag around again and we continued sitting, waiting. They were dud. This was rubbish, I wanted to go home. I could still catch the last bus, Call this one a write-off and get back for Jonathan Ross. As I was planning to make my move Jacob's phone vibrated, which was the most exciting thing that had happened since we arrived. I glanced over at him and saw his eyes light up and his mouth curl into a smile as he read the screen.

"Does anyone fancy coming to town?"

"Absolutely not," Eddie replied. "Why are you suddenly keen?"

"Oh, it's nothing. I just fancy it. Should be a good night."

I didn't want to go either. I was not in town mood. Once you've pictured yourself at home, on the sofa, eating Quavers, it's difficult to vanquish the image. Besides, I was wearing an ill-fitting t-shirt with a cartoon alien on the front. I had no recollection of the purchase. What had I been thinking? Jacob looked disappointed at the collective response.

"Okay, I'll level with you," he said. "That text was from a girl. She said she's going out and wants to see me. Sorry, I mean, some girls are going out and they want to see us."

"Being on mushrooms is terrifying in busy places," Will said. "Rule me out."

"Surely one of you will come out?"

What followed was comparable to when you are playing football and the keeper shouts,

"Who's next in?" and everyone looks at the floor.

"Fine, I'll come," I said. "Can you lend me a tenner?"

"Sure. You won't regret it, this will be a great night."

Tired and filled with reluctance, I readied myself to go. As we were leaving I turned to Will.

"Is it really terrifying?"

"Yes, but these are duds. You'll be fine."

"Well, okay. See you later then."

"Bye."

Jacob and I got the last bus to town which, to rub salt into the wound, went straight past my house.

"This is going to be a great night, mate."

If you keep repeating something, it doesn't make it true.

"Yep, can't wait."

My mouth was feeling a bit dry but other than that, nothing. We stopped talking, which Jacob, furiously texting on his phone, was unconcerned about. I dug a two-pound coin out of my pocket and began twirling it through my fingers. When I was in primary school, Akpo's uncle liked two-pound coins so much that he used to buy them for two pounds twenty. As I was contemplating his questionable business nous, I felt a wave of something odd. A headrush.

I blinked and stared wide-eyed out of the window on to rain splattered streets. Everything was shimmering. Shop fronts, lamp posts, pedestrians. Shit, this was a bit weird.

"Are you okay?" Jacob asked.

"Well, everything is shimmering."

In the city centre the bus pulled up at its stop and I felt as though all eyes were on me as Jacob and I walked down the aisle. I stood at the front of the bus and looked back at the passengers. Did everyone else know that everything was shimmering? Should I tell them?

"Are you getting off or what?" the driver snapped. "You can't just stand there."

I stumbled off the bus, feeling very peculiar now. Was I having fun? I don't think I was. It was after 11pm and the streets were full of revellers. Jacob was walking with intent.

"Come on, Andy. Hurry up."

I gazed with a confusion at glittering street lamps and swirling buildings. I stared at the slanted faces of Picasso pedestrians.

"Just act normal, Andy," Jacob warned as we approached the entrance to the club. "You're being weird."

This was a big ask. How could I act normal when the bouncer was a giant lizard? We were ushered in without issue and I unsteadily followed Jacob to the upstairs room where a Libertines track was playing to a lively skin tight-jeaned crowd.

The source of Jacob's texts found us before we'd got to the bar.

"Hi," she said, with what I think was a flirtatious grin, although her eyes looked like a snake's.

"Is he alright?" the girl motioned towards me.

"Yep, he's fine," Jacob said. "Drink?"

The girl took Jacob's hand, they walked off and that was the last I saw of them. I didn't fancy a drink and found a seat in a dark corner adjacent to the busy dance floor. I stared at the crowds, who all seemed to be grinning maniacally with animated faces. This was frightening. I blinked several times but couldn't get out of this cartoon-world. The strobe lighting didn't help. This was frightening. While I knew it was down to the drugs, it was difficult to convince myself that I wasn't going insane. After sitting through a Smiths song and blinking repeatedly, I'd had enough. I didn't want this anymore. I've tried it and I don't like it. Make it stop.

A guy from my college had spotted me and was walking over, looking like an elongated version of himself. He was a cool customer; cap, Fenchurch t-shirt and Nike Air trainers. He smoked roll-ups and knew DJs. Our paths crossed at college but I was far too wary of how I acted around him to become proper friends. I was desperate to impress and show that I too was a cool guy. My issue with being cool is that you aren't allowed to laugh much; it's all nodding, sipping bottled beer and speaking in streetwise accents not concurrent with being white and middle class. I've never been much good at it. Alone, wearing a t-shirt with an alien on it and hallucinating wildly perhaps demonstrates why not.

"Easy, Andy," he grunted.

"Uh, hello."

"Who you out with, dude?"

The peak of his cap was growing. It's not real, I told myself. The peak of the cap isn't really growing. Or is it?

"Andy? Why are you staring at my head, man? Are you okay?"

"I'm feeling a bit off-colour if the truth's known."

The letters on his t-shirt were spinning.

"Are you high, Andy?"

"Nice t-shirt, man."

"Uh, sure."

He walked off. I was keen to get home but there was a lot of difficult admin necessary to achieve this. I'd need to leave this club, walk through town, find a bus stop, produce bus fare, get off at the right stop, find the hidden key by the wheelie bins and sneak in without waking my parents. God, this was overwhelming. I tried to gather my thoughts by staring at the ceiling, where streams of colourful water were pouring onto the dance floor. Surely that's dangerous? Why aren't people reacting?

In the corner of my eye, I was surprised to see the cool guy bouncing back towards me. He was holding a pint of orange juice.

"Drink this," he said, handing it to me.

"What? Why?"

"You're tripping, aren't you? The vitamin D will help."

I took the glass from him and guzzled it down. It tasted divine.

"You'll be fine now," he reassured me before disappearing back into cartoon darkness.

I felt revitalised, I'd had the magic potion and I was cured. I was Prince of Persia. Prince of Persia can make it home. Easy. I stood up and fell back down again, slumping into my chair. Maybe not just yet? The multi-coloured water was now flooding the dance floor. I didn't want to get wet, it was a cold night. I needed more potion. Where was my saviour? I had to find him. I got up, managed to stay on my feet this time and roamed into the darkness. Had he gone downstairs? This place was a labyrinth.

An arm grabbed my neck. A bad guy.

"Come on mate, you're out of it."

"I need orange juice"

The bouncer led me downstairs and pointed me in the direction of a taxi. I have very little recollection of how I got home but somehow managed it as I found myself in my bed, staring at the ceiling. Being at home did not provide the anticipated solace and I lay, writhing, staring at my ceiling. The lines were bending to create a tapestry of religious imagery; seeing the Virgin Mary's face was unnerving. Where had that come from? The Passion Play?

Despite my delirium, as sunlight seeped through my curtains and the familiar sound of wood pigeons signified a new day, I was very aware of the situation. I had taken mushrooms and hadn't slept a wink. I continued to lay on the bed until eventually, mercifully, the hallucinating ceased and I began to settle into more ordinary thought processes.

I received a couple of texts from Will. They'd had a great time. I told him my night had not been so great. Terrifying and endless. At 10am my mum shouted from downstairs.

"When are you getting up? Do you want some breakfast?"

"Do we have any orange juice?"

15

Perhaps unsurprisingly given my lifestyle, I flunked my exams, getting two Ds and an E in Psychology. I'd fancied myself to do well in Psychology but the entire year underperformed after it emerged that we had been learning the wrong syllabus for a whole term. I was disappointed but soon perked up as that summer, twenty of us were going to Malia. Although we were only going away for two weeks, my mum seemed to be holding back tears as she said goodbye, muttering something about "growing up too fast" and that she was proud of me. It seemed a strange time to say this. Why was she proud of me going on a booze-fuelled 18-30 holiday that she was primarily bankrolling?

We were staying at Ilissos apartments, ramshackle accommodation just off the main road, five miles away from the main strip. The apartments were run by an angry Greek lady called Maria who had wiry black hair, couldn't speak English and disliked our assemblage from the offset. Her potbellied husband, Costas, was of a calmer temperament and sat by the bar, supping Mythos beer while Maria worked herself to the ground.

On entering the strip for the first time I was overwhelmed; flashing lights, scantily clad girls, quad bikes flying past and loud club music booming out of the hordes of bars with names like Newcastle Bar, Bar UK and Club Sex. There was also a worrying amount of steroid-bound men in vests who were older and likely much tougher than us creating an underlying scent of pending violence in the sticky air. I'd imagine that anyone over the age of thirty, or with an ounce of class, would find the place revolting, but for a group of sixteen and seventeen-year-old idiots, this was paradise. Kind of.

We drank fishbowls through novelty straws, hugged and danced with one another and befriended a forty-year-old man from Liverpool on a punching machine. He was on holiday alone but compensated for this by being tremendously strong. The marathon nights out on the strip tended to last until sunrise. Every night we would split up into splinter groups and recount our various adventures while dicking around in the pool the next day. People's night out recollections were full of incident and/or lies, typically featuring romance, heartbreak, tears, scuffles and at least one crashed quadbike.

At 6 am one morning, my friend Dom had still not returned to the apartments. Concerned, we went to look for him and left the apartments to trudge along the dual carriageway. We hadn't got far when a figure emerged on the horizon. And something else. It was Dom, rolling an enormous tyre down the road.

"Why have you got a tyre, Dom?"

"I've pushed it back. All the way from the strip!" He said, proudly.

"But why?"

"The taxi wouldn't let me in with it."

"Go to bed, Dom."

In Malia, I did something stupid. Stupider than Dom's tyre and arguably the stupidest thing I've ever done. One morning, Dylan and I were feeling surprisingly fresh and went for a hike up a mountain outside the town. We were looking forward to taking the moral high ground when we returned to the hotel to find hungover friends still in bed.

"So, what have you been up to today, Liam? We've had a great day, let me tell you."

"Fuck off."

It was a searing hot day and once we'd arrived at the top, we were dripping with sweat and out of our modest water rations. The dusty path became indistinct on the way down as we staggered through undergrowth hoping we were heading in the right direction.

"I don't recognise any of this," I said to Dylan who reassured me that we would "snake back around" and end up somewhere familiar. We had no drink left and while not in panic mode, this was becoming unpleasant. After slipping into silence as we plodded along, we eventually came out at steep road winding down the mountain side. We followed it for a few minutes before seeing a large warehouse, surrounded by wire fencing.

"Do you reckon we can get any water in there?" I asked. The gate to get into the premises was ajar and nobody was around. We ambled onto the forecourt, found a six-pack of bottled water propped outside the warehouse and guzzled it down. The shutters of the warehouse were up and it was wide open so we decided to explore.

"Fucking hell, what have we found here?" Dylan said.

Inside, box upon box, crate upon crate of beer, wine and spirits were stacked to the rafters. We wandered around and helped ourselves to a couple of bottles of coke and headed out. Energised, we followed the road down the mountain and ended up a mile or so away from our apartments. It had worked out to be a tidy circular walk in the end.

Later that afternoon I was sat with Dylan having a Mythos beer by the pool. We began to discuss the events of earlier in the day.

"Do you think it's always unmanned?" I said. "They had all sorts there. We could easily take a few crates if we go on the quad bikes?"

"Shall we go now?"

"Yes."

I have never been a thief and even as a seventeen-year-old idiot, this was hugely out of character. I don't know what had got into me; caught up in the whirlwind of holiday excitement, seeking danger and adventure? Feeling as though the world owed me one after the Psychology AS-Level injustice? Maybe it was simply that I was running out of money and needed booze for the rest of the holiday. I honestly don't know.

I sat on the back of Dylan' quad as we drove back up to the warehouse. We casually strolled through the gates and helped ourselves to two crates of beer and a crate of alcopops before walking out. We stuck one crate under the seat and I precariously held on to the other two as we sped back to the apartments. On our return, we dished the contraband out to eager pals. Some were impressed at our tale but others raised eyebrows and gave - what I appreciate now - was deserved criticism.

"You've been breaking into warehouses and stealing booze? What the fuck are you playing at, Andy?"

"I take it you won't be drinking that Smirnoff Ice then, Billy?"

"I didn't say that, did I?"

That evening we were doing football shirt night. This is – exactly as it sounds – a night where all of us wore football shirts. An inspirational idea, mooted after we'd found a stall selling a wide range of fake shirts for a pittance. I'm usually a bit of a misery about themed nights – I don't see the point – but I was keen on the opportunity to sport my new Greece shirt with Charisteas on the back.

The mood was buoyant as our colourful party flooded into a quiet bar at the top of the main strip. We'd been coming here every night and had built up a rapport with the manager, a Greek guy in his fifties who gave good deals on beer and free shots of a fruity spirit which I suspected was Robinson's squash. I was stood chatting with Will and Rodney when something kicked off behind us. I wasn't sure what had happened but a watermelon was smashed to pieces on the floor and Eddie and Patrick looked guilty.

"That watermelon was very special to me!" the manager screamed before picking up a knife and chasing us out of the bar, waving it. Things had escalated quickly.

Later, once things had calmed down and we were in a bar where the owners didn't chase you with knives, I was sat next to Dylan.

"Shall we go back to the warehouse?" he suggested.

"Now?"

"Why not?"

"Well, it's dark. I could do with getting some more booze though. It was easy last time, wasn't it?"

"Yes, it's easy. It will be fine," Dylan reassured me.

It's not really fine at all, is it?

"We could do with one more coming though. To keep lookout and help us stock up." I said.

"Yeah, good shout. Who do you think will be up for it? We need someone a bit reckless and morally questionable."

I walked outside where Cameron was stood, chatting to a shot girl and smoking a cigarette.

"Fancy an adventure?"

"Do I?"

We took a taxi back to the hotel. I hopped on the back of Dylan' quadbike, Cameron got on his own, and we drove into the Greek mountains to steal from the warehouse for a third time that day. At 1 am, wearing football shirts, drunk. As Dylan wound his way up the steep sloping roads, my nerves began to shred. In the darkness, this seemed much more sinister and I began to fear that we were pushing our luck. What if someone catches us?

"Right, here we are," Dylan said as we parked up the quad bikes by a streetlight outside the fence. The shutters were still up inside the warehouse but the entrance gate had been padlocked. You'd have thought this would put us off.

"Will you give us a foot up, Andy?"

I helped Dylan up before Cameron and I unsteadily clambered over. Some dim lights were shining in the forecourt but inside the warehouse, it was almost pitch black.

"Let's go, this is stupid," Dylan said.

"We're here now," I said, "we can't leave empty handed."

"I can't see anything mate. I don't know what's what."

"Stop talking," Cameron snapped in hushed tones. "Just grab one each and let's get out of here."

We fumbled around, each picked up an indeterminable crate and scurried towards the fence.

"I'll climb over first then pass them to me," Cameron suggested.

We heaved them over and were ready to flee when Cameron said.

"Fucking hell, we've hit jackpot! These are boxes of Champagne!"

On this news, Dylan and I returned to the darkness of the warehouse and each grabbed another box. We scrabbled them over, loaded the quad bikes and set off.

Cameron was driving behind us as Dylan led the way down the now-familiar mountain road.

A few minutes into the drive, I saw a light further down the mountain heading towards us.

"What was that?" I asked Dylan.

"I didn't see anything."

Cameron had dropped off and was twenty metres behind us.

We turned a corner. Now it was unmistakeable. Two cars were driving towards us. Fast.

"Fuck, fuck, fuck," I said, clutching on to the champagne crates.

"What shall I do?" Dylan asked.

It was too late to think. They'd seen us. Sirens began to screech. We were, to use the technical term, fucked. Dylan pulled over by the side of the road and I put the champagne crates on the floor, awaiting our fate. Cameron stopped behind us as the police cars skidded to a halt in front of us. The doors on each car sprung open and four policemen flew out and ran over to where we were stood. The other two ran past us, towards Cameron.

"Why?!" shouted a tall, well-built officer in his forties, raging. "Why?!"

"I'm sorry," I said. "I'm really sorry."

I started to cry. Dylan did too. This didn't stop the officers whacking us both around the legs and arms with a metal truncheon. It hurt. They bent my hands behind my back and handcuffed me. It was way too tight, the cold metal digging into my wrists.

"Where he go?" roared one of the policemen from behind us. "Where your friend go?!"

I turned to where Cameron had pulled over. His quad bike was there but he was nowhere to be seen. The policemen snapped at one another in Greek for a few seconds before two of them headed into the mountains, shining bright torches on the ground, shouting.

"Where are you? We fucking kill you! Where are you?"

Dylan and I were whacked again and bundled into the police car, leaving our quad bikes and the boxes of champagne abandoned by the side of the road. The policeman drove like a madman down the mountain as his colleague shouted into his walkie-talkie, presumably to Cameron's chasers. We sped along the main road for ten minutes until we pulled up at a small police station. The policemen shoved us into an empty waiting room and one sat next to us while the other stormed around, talking on his walkie-talkie, looking ready to kill someone.

I glanced at Dylan whose cheeks were tearstained. He shook his head. We'd fucked it. Well and truly. While our own fate was uncertain, and would likely not be enjoyable, I feared even worse for Cameron. He hadn't had much of a head start, what would they do when they found him? We'd been compliant and they'd still roughed us up.

The angry policeman returned to the waiting room and stood over us.

"Why?!" he shouted again, before slapping Dylan on his head. I clenched my teeth awaiting a whack and was surprised when it didn't come. A third policeman, who spoke better English, entered the fray – an elderly chap who was holding a notepad.

"Where is your friend?" he asked. "What's his name?"

"I don't know."

"What happened?"

In the stark lighting of the police station, it was dawning on me that we had committed a reasonably serious crime so, to dig my way out, I lied. I made up a complete cock and bull story that we'd been out on the quad bikes for an innocent ride when a bunch of older lads from London had pulled us over and demanded that we carry their boxes of booze down the mountain or they would beat us up. Gladly, Silas, the chin scratcher from primary school was not here. This was a tall tale but with adrenaline pumping and genuine tears streaming down my face, it somehow sounded convincing. The policemen nodded and, thankfully, didn't whack me again. The two who had arrested us headed into a back room leaving the elderly policeman to keep an eye on us.

No instructions were given and we sat waiting in anxious silence. For hours. By 5 am, I was so tired that my fear was diminishing. The elderly policeman, who also looked exhausted, flicked on a small TV in the top corner of the waiting room. Highlights of an Olympiakos football match were on and he began watching with interest.

"Is this your team?" I asked.

He looked at me and smiled.

"Yes, very good team."

"Rivaldo is a great signing," I said.

His eyes lit up.

"Yes, fantastic player!"

In a bizarre scene Dylan and I settled into a comfortable football conversation with the old policeman. He complimented my Charisteas shirt and we talked in depth about Greece's unlikely success at the Euros. We were getting on so well I almost forgot what was going on. At 6 am, the furious policeman who'd arrested us came out of his office and asked to have a word with our new mate. They walked into his office leaving Dylan and me unsupervised for the first time. After a brief respite, the magnitude of our situation hit home once again. We shared a nervous glance. We could hear muffled conversation from behind the doors. Were they discussing our fate? Did this waiting room represent my last taste of freedom before a lifetime behind bars in a Greek prison? The three policemen eventually emerged. The old guy told us to stand up. The furious guy looked less furious.

"Go," he said.

"Excuse me?" I asked in disbelief.

"You can leave now," the old guy clarified.

"Really?" I said. Did I want him to change his mind?

Dylan scowled at me to say, "shut up," before making a tilting motion with his head. The old guy gave us a grin, the furious guy, a frown and with the morning sunlight shining through gaps in the nearby mountains, we were released into the outside world. Freedom! We walked fifty metres or so away from the police station before hugging each other in pure relief.

We animatedly dissected the events of the past few hours and were certain that if it weren't for building a rapport with the old policeman, we would not have been released. Rivaldo had saved us. We talked about how stupid we'd been and I vaguely remember making a pact that we would never drink again. Dylan' face suddenly dropped.

"Where's Cameron?"

With all this exhaustion and emotion, we'd forgotten about the small issue of our on-the-run friend. Relief turned to fear as we began to speculate about his whereabouts. Had he been caught? Beaten up? Worse? Even if he'd got away, a dark night in the harsh mountains with no provisions, wearing flip flops and a fake Real Madrid goalkeeper's shirt would not have been ideal. It took half an hour to get back to Illisos, where we ran to Cameron's room and frantically hammered on the door. His roommate, Martin answered, unimpressed to have been awoken at this hour.

"Have you seen Cameron?"

"No, he's not back yet," Martin said, rubbing his eyes. "Did you guys have a late one?"

Shit. Where was he? We charged into my room where Eddie was sleeping soundly, snoring. I shook him awake.

"Where's Cameron?"

"I don't know, fuck off."

We proceeded to rattle on Patrick's room, Rodney's, Dom's, Liam's and Stuart's, awaking angry friends who each said the same thing. They hadn't seen him. The last room was Alfie's. A deep sleeper, it took a few minutes to stir him until he groggily answered the door. We were frantic with worry.

"Where's Cameron?"

Alfie rubbed his eyes and pointed to the floor.

"He's in here mate. He got in about half an hour ago, why?"

We woke him up and Dylan and I hugged him. His face, arms, and legs were covered in dirt and scratches.

"What the hell happened?"

The fuss died down and Cameron, Dylan and I sat on deckchairs by the pool as the hum of the morning traffic began. Cameron told us the story of his night. He'd sprinted as fast as he could into the mountains and hidden behind a large rock where he'd heard the policemen shouting after him, their voices gradually getting louder until they were stood six feet away from him. They shone their torches on the rock, didn't think to look behind it and after a few seconds turned and headed in the other direction. Such was Cameron's terror, he'd remained crouched behind the rock for five hours until the sun rose, at which point he hobbled back to the road and walked back to our accommodation. We never did find out what happened to the quad bikes and champagne. Perhaps the policemen had a party? The whole thing was ridiculous. Lesson learned. I have not considered breaking into a warehouse in a foreign country since. Not once.

16

Turning eighteen was a mixed milestone. Shortly before my birthday, I got beaten up outside a working men's club. A girl from my school had hired it out for a party and there was a good blend of my pals from Lawnswood, Ralph Thoresby and Notre Dame in attendance. It was a decent evening comprising of cold sandwiches, soft crisps and a casual policy on underage drinking.

After the party had finished – with an arms-round-shoulders circle to Hero by Enrique Inglesias – six or seven of us were loitering on a grass verge outside. We were considering whether to go into town when we were swarmed by a gang of ten-or-so hooded hoodlums. I saw David get smacked in the face and, being the pacifist that I am, went to grab him and pull him out of the melee. In doing this, I left myself exposed as a fat guy wearing a Nike TN cap ruthlessly landed a right hook. I felt my cheek immediately pop and clutched it in agony. Holding back tears, the brawl continued around me and, while some of my pals gave it a good go, we were ultimately outnumbered and less robust than our angry counterparts. It later transpired that the reason behind the attack stemmed from the romantic success of some of my friends with "their girls." I'd barely spoken to a girl all night so, out of all the times I've deserved a punch, this was not one of them.

As sirens wailed, our enemies scattered and ran into the night, leaving us bloodied, bruised and broken. We would be going to town tonight, only in the back of an ambulance. David, who'd broken his nose and I, with a shattered cheekbone, had sustained the worst injuries despite Patrick claiming his bust lip was life-threatening.

A&E on a Saturday night is horrifying. Drunks, druggies and fighters – and that was just my pals – sat under the stark lights wounded and impatient. David, whose night had gone drastically downhill since a dance floor smooch at the working men's club, was started on by a man who had cut off his thumb.

"What the fuck are you looking at? I've lost my thumb but I can still smack you."

Rodney was sat next to man who had broken his knuckles. Punching a dog. A nurse gave us some strong painkillers which worked well so rather than waiting to see a specialist, I went home in the early hours with my apple-sized cheek forcing my eye shut. When I awoke the next morning, my apple-cheek was bigger still, the painkillers had worn off and I was in a living hell. My worried parents took me back to the hospital where I would spend the next five days having – and recovering from – surgery to reconstruct my face. I wasn't left disfigured but even now, fifteen years later, in the words of The Weeknd, I can't feel (a section of) my face.

I spent my eighteenth birthday itself working the late shift at Subway, alone. My manager, a troll-sized jobsworth who, according to my colleague / former mugger, blew his wages in brothels, refused to let me have my birthday off even though I'd told him weeks in advance that I'd appreciate it.

"Rotas are rotas, Andy."

Making meatball sandwiches for drunk students while still sporting a swollen face was a grim introduction to adulthood. There was, at least, an acquaintance's party going on that evening which promised to go on late. I was hopeful I could steal some of her birthday attention and muster a night out of sorts. I shut up shop early, did a superficial clean of the surfaces, and hopped in a taxi with drops of barbeque sauce smudged into my trousers.

I arrived at the working men's club she'd hired at 11.30pm to discover that rumours of a late licence were false. The lights were on, the bar had a metal shutter pulled down and empty glasses and leftover food on paper plates were lining the room. Apart from a few people of parental age who were tidying up, everyone had left.

"Do you know where they went?" I asked a man in a Leeds Rhinos top who was simultaneously eating a sausage roll and dragging a tower of chairs across the dance floor.

"You've just missed them. They got taxis into town."

"Whereabouts in town?"

"I don't know."

No problem, I thought, I'll just ring Eddie. I got my phone out of my pocket to see that the screen was smeared in Southwest sauce and the battery had died. Why was I always having a bad time in and around working men's clubs? I walked home and went to bed.

The following morning, I told my mum about my non-event of an eighteenth and she took pity on me.

"Do you want to have a few friends over here next Friday? Your dad and I are going to see a Rod Stewart tribute act so you'll have the house to yourself until midnight."

I couldn't believe my ears. This was perfect. I spread the word far and wide, informing almost everyone I knew with the exception of my manager at Subway. When it's known you are having a party, your popularity skyrockets for the days preceding it.

"What are you up to this weekend, Andy?"

"I'm sorry, have we met before?"

A couple of hours before the party began, my mum drove me to the Co-op and bought some crates of lager and snacks before I showered and put on a trendy New York Yankees top I'd recently bought from TK-Maxx. I opened a can of Fosters, put on a Cypress Hill CD and waited for the masses to descend. Only they didn't. At 7.30pm, just three guests had arrived; Matt, Lucy and Seamus. My parents came into my room, seemed satisfied that it wasn't going to get too wild and left to go to the Village Hotel.

"So, Kettle Chip anyone?"

By 8pm, I was becoming concerned that a washout beckoned. Upper sixth form had only just begun – hosting a successful party would work wonders for my ailing street cred. How would I live it down if it bombed? There was a knock at the door, I sprung up and ran downstairs to welcome Will, Eddie, Cameron, Lee and Jim in. They were carrying bags full of lager and in high spirits. A group of girls from college were walking up my drive behind them, smoking cigarettes and giggling. I looked down the street to see droves of teenagers, some familiar, many not, flooding towards my house. Hurray.

Within an hour, the house was full to bursting with eclectic music ranging from Dr Dre to Falling with Superman playing in each of the different rooms. The back garden was misty with clouds of smoke and the smell of cannabis swirled through the autumn air. People were overflowing down the drive and onto the street. It's a funny thing having a house party – the relief that people have shown up is almost instantly replaced with a fear of how these people are going to treat your house. In my living room, a bottle of red wine lay open on its side and a kind soul had stubbed a cigarette out on the carpet. I walked into the kitchen to find that Patrick had taken a bite out of every apple in the fruit bowl.

I gulped down a bottle of El Velero wine and staggered around, talking to my pals and trying, in vain, to relax. In my bedroom, an extremely pissed man was thrashing chords on my classical guitar using a 2p as his plectrum and a sinister-looking group wearing jogging bottoms were doing cocaine on my bedside table.

"Hi, guys, glad to see you're having fun but do you mind, perhaps, not doing that in here?"

"Who are you? Fuck off."

"Right you are then."

The girls from Lawnswood had arrived, including my ex-girlfriend, Carly. Following the end of a relationship with a tree surgeon, she was newly single and we shared a nostalgic hour-or-so and another bottle of wine together. It crossed my mind to try to rekindle the old flame but I was distracted by the sound of a commotion outside. I walked out and was informed that the guy who'd broken my cheek had shown up. Now it's one thing assaulting me but turning up to my party too? That's pushing it, pal. Eddie took it upon himself to pass on the message that he wasn't welcome and shoved him down my drive and off the premises.

"That'll teach him," I thought. "He may have beat me up but who's winning now?" I stumbled upstairs to find that a bedroom window had been smashed by an amiable guy from college. He was deeply apologetic but the window remained smashed. Everything was spinning by now and in unclear circumstances, I too managed to smash a window. This was greeted with a cheer.

From there on in, things are hazy ("Hazy" incidentally, was the name of my favourite song by Falling with Superman. Unfortunately, we never performed it live.) My parents returned from the Village Hotel much sooner than I'd anticipated – it felt like they'd just left. I tried to sober up, expecting a serious rollicking but, to my surprise, they each grabbed a can of lager, chatted animatedly to the guests and took photos, including one of my mum with her arm around a guy who is now in prison. The police arrived shortly after midnight and shut the party down. This was a cool way to finish and, as I made a half-hearted attempt at cleaning up the detritus that my house had become, I felt proud that the night had been a success. I can't imagine the cost to fix the mess was cheap but, to my parents' credit, they never mentioned it. It was, however, made clear that a party would not be happening again.

17

Yes, got it. Number 2! I scanned the other boxes to confirm that I was right. Not many to go now, I'm going to complete it. Brilliant. I hadn't turned the volume off the Sudoku game on my phone and was enjoying the repetitive electronic beeping to the extent that I was tapping my foot in time and nodding my head as I sat on the toilet.

Loud house music flooded into the room as a door opened and I heard voices outside the cubicle. Who are the people outside? What do they want? I looked back down at my phone screen but the numbers no longer meant anything. They were blurring into one another. I felt dizzy. My mouth was tingling. How does Sudoku even work? Shit, what time is it? I need to get out of here. Where is Will? What are those guys talking about outside? They sound like good guys.

I pulled my jeans up, put my phone in my pocket, stood up and opened the cubicle door. There were two men stood by the sinks, talking loudly. One of them looked like Jermain Defoe. Was it Jermain Defoe? What was he doing here? Does he know how to play Sudoku? I walked past them to a free sink and splashed cold water on my face and through my hair. It felt good. I put my hands on the sink and looked in the mirror. I looked excellent, the best I've looked in ages. A bit pale maybe, but otherwise excellent. My eyes looked a bit weird too. Why does the corner of my mouth keep twitching?

"You having a good night, mate?" Jermain Defoe asked me cheerily.

"Yes, thanks. You?" I asked, then found myself walking over to him and putting my arm around his broad shoulders. He reciprocated and we walked out the toilets together, having a great conversation about the music in the club, which we agreed was fantastic.

"Have a good night, mate!" I said to Jermain as we left the toilets. "I need to find my friend."

"You too, pal!" Jermain said, then danced off down a mirrored corridor.

I found myself in the main room which was much busier than I remembered. All I need to do now is find my friends and I'll be able to complete the Sudoku game. There were lots of thin green lights flashing around. I liked them. Perhaps I'll stay in this room for a bit? My friends will find me, won't they? Is that man drinking a Red Stripe? I like Red Stripe.

"Where did you get that, mate?" I asked the man.

"At the bar over there, buddy."

"Where? I can't see a bar?"

All I could see was mist, lights and faces.

"No problem. You can have mine, mate," the man said, smiling. He handed me his near-full can and walked off into the crowds. What a nice man. I hope he succeeds in his quest to find the bar. I'll buy him a drink next time we meet.

I took a sip of the drink and it tasted heavenly. Where are my friends? I wonder if they will help me find the bar so I can buy the man a drink. A girl danced up to me and told me that my t-shirt was cool and a man with a bald head agreed. Terrific.

I found myself in the middle of the dance floor looking up at the thin green lights. They were intriguing. The music was good as well. There were no words but that didn't matter, I liked the beat.

"Oi, Andy!" Will shouted from somewhere. I couldn't see him because I didn't want to take my eyes away from the thin green lights. Something bad might happen if I do. I felt a friendly arm around my neck.

"We've been looking for you for ages!" Eddie said. "Look at me mate."

I looked at him. His face was damp with sweat but he looked cool tonight. I liked his t-shirt.

"Wow," Eddie said after looking at my eyes for an unusually long time. "Mate, you need to come outside for a bit. I'll get you a glass of water."

"Come on, I'll give you a cigarette," my friend, Will said. How kind of him. Although everyone is kind in this place.

Everyone is so nice. I followed Will outside to the smoking area and took a few deep breaths in the cold night air.

"Are you having a good night?" he asked me, laughing.

"The best. I met Jermain Defoe and he's going to teach me the secrets of Sudoku."

"Great. Sit down for a minute mate. I think you've just come up. You need to chill out a bit."

"I want to dance with the nice girl in there. Nothing funny though, I'm not going to try it on. We are just friends."

Eddie returned with three pints of water and the three of us sat down on a wet wooden bench. It was quite cold out here. Not too cold though. I liked it.

"Don't disappear like that again mate. We were worried about you," Eddie said. His pupils looked large but it suited him. He looked great.

"I won't, I love this place," I said. "What time is it?"

"1am," Will said, fumbling to open a fresh pack of Marlboro Lights.

How did we get to this club? I tried to remember. We'd been at The Shoes then Eddie had booked a taxi. Who was the man with the Berghaus jacket in the pub? Was that tonight? I hope the man in the Berghaus jacket is alright. He seemed like a good guy. The outdoor smoking area was packed with all kinds of folk. Whilst sipping my cold water, I caught segments of conversations:

"I've been coming here since day dot, this is my Zen," a muscular middle-aged man said, solemnly, to a young woman in a crop top. He was holding a can of Red Bull that looked too small for his gorilla hand. She was looking at him intently, her elaborately made-up eyelashes fluttering over saucer eyes.

"Oh, wow, that's amazing!"

I couldn't help but agree with her. It was great news that he was in his Zen. Good for him.

"You know what, mate?" said a bespectacled man to his pal, also bespectacled. "I fucking love you."

"I love you too mate. Do you have a cig?"

A man, who was almost certainly gay, was locked in conversation with a woman in her forties who had a pixie haircut and looked like she worked in HR.

"You look so gorgeous," he gushed, "I love that top!"

"Aw, that means so much to me, hun. You look gorgeous too!"

She couldn't compliment his top as he wasn't wearing one but they hugged. I smiled at them and they smiled back. I continued to observe the diverse crowds, chatting, mingling, dancing and smoking with the thud of a repetitive bassline seeping out from the nightclub and I felt a sense of profound joy. Both nothing and everything made sense at once.

"Let's go for a dance," Will suggested. I thought he hated dancing? My surroundings were moving quickly. Everyone in here has so much energy. I stood up. My jaw was hurting a little – why was that? We headed back into the sweltering hot club where the thin strips of light were no longer green but electric blue. On the way, the crowds were whooping and cheering, pointing their fingers towards a beanie-hat-wearing DJ, I identified that a new track had begun. It sounded very similar to the previous one, but I liked it. The DJ was incredibly talented.

Will, Eddie and I bustled our way to the middle of the crammed dance floor and pogoed up and down, with our arms around one another.

"I fucking love you guys!"

This was amazing. I didn't want it to end.

***

I didn't feel too bad the day after. A little hollow and twitchy, sure, but I happily sat on the sofa drinking sugary tea all day and managed to force down a Safeway pepperoni pizza while watching Pop Idol in the evening. Michelle McManus' stirring rendition of "Your Song" did almost bring me to tears but I didn't see this as unusual behaviour. Surely I speak for the nation in saying that it tugged at the heartstrings?

Before this, I'd taken a pill once before, at a party hosted by the guy whose family had won the lottery. I'd been exploring the many nooks of his converted farmhouse when I fell into a spare bedroom to find a schoolmate called Jamal. He was watching a porn video and dancing to the background music.

"Sorry, Jamal. Am I interrupting?"

"Do you want a pill?"

"Um, okay."

The night was a bit of a blur after that. I spent much of it sat in the front of our lucky host's dad's Ferrari, pretending to drive it with Rodney and Gavin, the laidback guy who had once beaten up Matt. I don't think Jamal's pills were very good and, as I was throwing up the following morning, I had no great desire to try them again.

Until the opportunity presented itself again, at least. Comparable to getting drunk for the first time, once you have taken a good pill for the first time, you are very keen to do it again. And again. In my defence, they were far too easily accessible. Every time we were in the Shoes, the man in the Berghaus jacket was stood by the bar. He had a deep cut below his left eye and looked permanently angry but you couldn't deny he'd landed himself a prime business location. To get his attention, you simply had to give a little nod. He'd then meet you in the toilets and the transaction could be carried out. Three for a tenner. He bought pills in batches which each had different symbols on them; PlayStations, smiley faces, Mitsubishi triangles, Pokémon and, at the top of the pile, purple hearts. They blew your mind.

The following weeks and months were a whirlwind of repetitive music that I would never listen to during the day, long and wide-ranging conversations with strangers, chain-smoking and walking home at sunrise. I'd look at the bill posters for nightclubs plastered in Headingley and would easily be able to identify which the pill nights were. If the posters included neon writing, a silhouette of a sexy woman and/or mentioned a sound system, they were suitable. The venues we frequented included Wire, Mission, Space, Kerbkrawler (yes, double K), Mint and Stinky's Peephouse, which was my favourite because it had a heated beer garden. After one endless night at Stinky's, Cameron and I got a taxi back to mine as the birds were chirping. In my room, unable to sleep, I put a compilation of Gabriel Batistuta's greatest goals on the computer and Cameron danced more passionately to the Euro disco backing music than Hussain had danced to the porn soundtrack. After watching the video for a tenth time, I told Cameron I was going to bed. He looked me in the eye, shook my hand and said.

"Have a safe trip mate, I'm staying in the club. This DJ is wicked."

On occasion, we ventured to Subdub, a dub reggae and drum and bass night at the West Indian Centre. This was always an unusual event. You could stumble into a backroom to find a group of elderly Rastafarians playing Dominoes, wonder into another to find drag queens dancing around handbags and eventually wind up in an enormous, euphoric nightclub, where the bassline made your ears bleed and topless men danced on top of speakers. We once saw a mass brawl kick off outside. A man had been released from prison that day for a crime he claimed to have played no part in. He found the man who had set him up for this injustice in the outdoor smoking area of Subdub and chose this as the perfect location to settle the score. That was my comprehension of events anyway – it could have been something very different. I just sat on a wall, smoking.

There were snags with this new lifestyle. It was illegal, unhealthy, bad for your brain and stomach, and beginning to cause rifts among my friends. It was a minority of us who were taking pills and while some were unperturbed, others were understandably against the idea and fell out with us. They looked down their noses at us and assumed that we were looking down our noses at them now that we were serious clubbers. This was not, of course, the case. I was aware that taking drugs and dancing all night did not make me cool. The opposite in fact; wide vacant eyes, grinding teeth, sweat patches, bad mechanical dancing and being overly complimentary to everyone is not very cool at all. I just enjoyed doing it. Every night was an adventure.

If the non-drug takers caught wind that we were on, considering being on, or coming down from ecstasy, they wouldn't speak to us. One weekend I was watching Soccer Saturday with Dylan. He had stayed in the night before – I had walked home from a club with a frizzy-haired medical student at 10am. Leeds came back from 3-0 down to beat Southampton 4-3 and Dylan was going mental – fist clenching, jumping and shouting. This should have been tremendous – a magnificent comeback and football at its best but I just didn't have the serotonin to muster any enthusiasm. I sat, slumped on the sofa with dead eyes. Dylan was appalled.

As any film or book about drugs will tell you, the glory days don't last forever. Within a few months, the highs were getting lower, the lows higher. I struggled to hit the euphoric heights of the first few times and the pills would often make me feel wired and anxious, not euphoric. Where's my euphoria? Give it back. The pills were wearing off quicker and I'd find myself feeling sad, scared and confused when surrounded by the oddballs of society that gather at these events. When the music stopped and the lights came on at the end of a night in Subdub, it was truly horrific. So horrific, in fact, that I'd rather not talk about it.

I was less inclined to chat with strangers and becoming aware of the artificiality of it all. None of this was real. I hadn't found a lifelong friend in Jason from Bridlington in the toilets of Stinky's where we discussed the pros and cons of him starting building college. Ryan, the hard-man from Hunslet was not actually my mate, was he? While we'd hugged a lot, and exchanged phone numbers, we weren't going to text each other and meet up for lunch like we'd planned, were we? I didn't really have anything in common with Sharon, the forty-four-year-old mother of three, who I spoke to for two hours about childcare while smoking an entire pack of Lambert and Butler's, did I?

When I got home I'd lie staring at the ceiling, my addled mind whizzing with fragmented beginnings of thoughts. It was unpleasant. The ensuing days I'd try to feel better about myself by doing innocent, day-to-day activities; play football (I was getting worse at this), go swimming, walk through the park, buy a newspaper – but it didn't work. The comedowns were not just deeper, but much longer. I'd still be feeling emotionally unstable on a Wednesday. It was time to pack it in. Or, at least, cut down.

I nipped the habit in the bud at a good time. Taking ecstasy was not going to expand my mind in a way conducive to boosting my A-Level grades and from February I stopped being a moron altogether and, to use a cliché, got my head down. A-Levels - even Sociology ones - are tough. The jump from GCSEs is massive and I would later discover that A-

Levels were, in fact, more difficult than my degree. I worked harder than ever before - harder even than at John Filan's - and managed to claw back my poor AS-Levels results to secure a B, C, D and an E in General Studies. General Studies doesn't count though. One of the essay questions was: "Describe human skin."

My results were unspectacular but not terrible. Will and I opened our envelopes together to discover we'd got identical results. While I clenched my fists, and planned for a life in academia, which would not have to be facilitated by clearing, Will stormed off, close to tears, vowing to re-sit his A-Levels.

18 (to 30)

Kavos is a seaside village on the island of Corfu in Greece, in the municipal district and the municipality of Lefkimmi. (Source: Wikipedia, 2017)

To celebrate the end of sixth form, I went to Kavos with 35 friends.

Having survived Malia, I felt better equipped for this kind of holiday. I was eighteen now and promised myself that there would be no nights in the slammer this time around. I was a new man, a reformed character.

We arrived at Kavos airport at sunrise and were met by our club rep, a man in his early twenties called Steve. He had spiky gelled hair and was wearing a vest.

"So, lads, who is going to be flicking the bean over the next two weeks, then?"

This was one of his openers. When he wasn't doing the airport shuttle run, he moonlighted as a DJ under the stage name, DJ Wank. I think that's all you need to know about Steve. After our welcome meeting where we signed up to go on a booze cruise and Billy expressed an interest in the jet ski safari, I was exhausted and returned to my room, which I was sharing with Rodney, for a nap.

I woke up at midday, put on a new t-shirt I'd bought from Dunnes Stores and headed poolside to find most of my friends drinking Mythos beer by the bar. They had just finished a game of water polo/rugby and were animatedly discussing the match highlights. It sounded like a glorious battle and I regretted my nap. Aside from seeing a gecko climbing on my bedroom wall, I had no tales to tell from the past two hours whereas I could tell that this water polo game was going to get a lot of airtime over the coming days (and, as it has since transpired, years.)

The first night out was as exhilarating and chaotic as you could hope for. With power in numbers, gone was much of the intimidation I'd felt in Malia and we had a terrific time working our way down the strip, drinking, dancing, shouting and branching off into subgroups, trying to find romance and 2-4-1 drinks deals. Drunk, delirious and drained, I shared a sunrise nightcap with Rodney, before heading to bed at 7am. Night mate.

Unlike in Malia, our accommodation was on the main strip this time around, which meant you could hear thudding club music all day, every day. I did not enjoy this but pretended I did, often dance-walking around the complex to prove that I was having a great time all day, every day.

I tended to peel myself out of bed circa 1pm, then go and discuss the previous night's adventures with whoever else was loitering around the pool, before returning to the room in the late afternoon to recharge. After two days, the bedroom floor was covered in beer-soaked clothes and broken glass, but I still spent large chunks of my holiday in there, lying on the bed, talking nonsense and listening to music on Rodney's phone. This was the first time I'd seen that music could be played through a phone. I was amazed. The only album he had was Back to Bedlam by James Blunt.

Dinner tended to be KFC or Pizza Hut, but we'd soon work this off with nightly games of beach volleyball, which is great fun although I have never played it since. My favourite nightclub was Rolling Stone, Kavos' only rock music venue, which was seldom more than half-full. At the time, I liked the Strokes, the Libertines and all the identikit indie bands whose careers were short-lived. I wonder what the lead singer of the Rakes is doing now? Customer Service Adviser? With its sweaty, dingy atmosphere, Rolling Stone reminded me of Bassment and, unlike many of the other clubs in Kavos, it was rarely frequented by men who wanted to either pull, have a fight or both. This despite the fact that you could buy a drink called the Headfucker for 5 euros. The only downside was that the ration of males to females was unfavourable but what does that matter when you are hugging your friends and dancing to "Can't Stand Me Now"? Besides, Rolling Stone also boasted a literal Rolling Stone outside its entrance where, every night without fail, a man would attempt to run on it and fall over.

**

"What the hell is her story?" Jim asked me, furrowing his brow. We were sat in Buzz Bar, overlooking the opening scenes of a new night's frolics.

"Who?"

"The woman who runs the penalty shoot-out competition. How has she ended up on the Kavos strip, running a penalty shoot-out competition? She can't have planned her life to work out this way, can she?"

I was stumped. What *was* her story? The woman in question was in her late-forties and from Derbyshire. Whether she was happy with where life had taken her or not, you could not deny that she had a sound business model. It cost 2 euros to take three penalties against a cat-like local goalkeeper. If you scored all 3, which was nigh-on impossible, you won a bottle of Spumante. You could buy this very bottle Spumante in any supermarket for 1 euro. I had no qualms with this fleecing as, if you did win the bottle, popping the plastic cork was nothing short of euphoric. One of the best bits of the holiday and, arguably my life, was when all 36 of us descended on the hallowed turf and danced wildly to a remix of "Poison" by Alice Cooper which was blaring from the nightclub next door. Happiness epitomised.

I did perhaps spend too much of my time hanging around the penalty shoot-out competition, which was reflected by my poor success rate with girls. Some of my friends – and not just the sleazy ones – were enjoying purple patches of romance in the bars and bedrooms of Kavos but, one week in, I had not so much a kissed a girl. I knew all the words to "You're Beautiful" at least.

After a typically boisterous night at Rolling Stone, Eddie and I got talking to some girls from Shrewsbury, who had been singing along to, and sitting down on the floor with us when "Sit Down" by James came on. I told the girls that I had been to Shrewsbury and thought it was a nice town, which went down so well that they invited us to join them at a pool party back at their hotel.

I got on particularly well with one of the girls – she hadn't been to Leeds but said she'd like to – and we arranged a date the following evening. A dinner date. In Kavos.

We met at a "nice little place" she knew on the strip which sold, she boasted, potato skins to die for. The date went well. I took her up on her recommendation and we also shared a pizza. She had two mojitos and I had three bottles of Mythos. We shared a lot in common, admitting that we found Club Sex's foam parties to be a bit over the top and preferred the atmosphere at Rolling Stone.

Midway through the date, I heard a familiar laugh behind me. I turned around to see that five of my mates were sitting in a nearby booth, hiding behind menus. They'd followed me and had eavesdropped the entire date.

The girl did not baulk at this and found it funny, saying it was the sort of thing her friends in Shrewsbury do "all the time." How many opportunities are there in Shrewsbury to do this sort of thing?

My pals had the courtesy to leave shortly afterwards as I tried to remember if I'd said anything during the date which would haunt me forever.

"What next?" I suggested as we walked hand in hand down the strip at sunset. I was hoping she'd suggest going back to her room. Mine was not an option. A further two bottles had been smashed and not swept up and when I left, Rodney was wearing a pan on his head.

"Well, my bus is coming in half an hour."

"What?"

"Oh, didn't I tell you? Yeah, we are leaving tonight."

"You're joking?"

"Sorry, that was why I suggested we meet up early."

"Oh."

"Will you come and wait with me outside the hotel?"

"I suppose so."

And so, I found myself sat on a kerb with her, three of her friends, fifteen or so other jaded holidaymakers and a pile of suitcases, waiting for a bus that I would not be getting on. We exchanged phone numbers and suggested we should meet up somewhere in between Leeds and Shrewsbury over the summer although neither of us could think of any towns which fit into this specification.

When conversation ran dry we started kissing while her friends, indifferent, discussed whether it was worthwhile deflating their Lilo and packing it up. To my horror, I noticed that the kiss had given me an erection. This was terrible timing and, given that we had roughly four minutes left together and we were sat on a kerb, unnecessary. I was wearing short shorts so there was no hiding place. If she noticed, she would be disgusted. I could kiss goodbye to a potential second date somewhere in middle England. I needed a plan.

"Right, I'm off," I said.

"What? Aren't you going to wait for my coach with me and give me a proper goodbye?

"No. Buzz Bar's happy hour is about to start."

I jumped up in a flash, turned my back to her and the crowd of people and walked off at pace.

"I'll text you," I said to the open air in front of me.

"Buzz bar is the other way!" she shouted after me.

"No," I shouted, not turning around. "It's definitely this way."

I continued walking in the wrong direction for fifteen minutes until I was certain that her bus would have left.

We would predictably never see one another again but this romantic misfortune did not dampen the rest of the holiday. With friends finding jobs and going to university, there was a sense that Kavos was a final hurrah and everyone had been hellbent on making the most of it. Even Vikram who'd crashed a quad bike and smashed his face in, Shaun who'd sliced open his leg and had it put in a cast by a cowboy doctor, and Dylan, who'd had all his money stolen from his room. On the coach back to the airport, jaded pals reminisced about the past fortnight and those who couldn't let go planned a night out at Baha Beach Club in Leeds that very evening. I looked out of the window and contemplated that I would never have a holiday like this again. It was something else.

19

My original plan was to go to Chester University to do education studies. However, this decision was based more on the fact that I watched Hollyoaks than a genuine desire to become a teacher, so I swerved and decided to take a gap year (it's impossible to say gap year without sounding annoying, isn't it?) where I'd work for six months and travel for six months with Eddie and Jack. It seemed everyone else was doing it so why not jump on the bandwagon? Besides, I'd made plans with Paul, a man from Bournemouth who I'd chatted to in the chill-out room at Stinky's Peephouse, to travel around Australia together. I hadn't heard much from him since the conversation, mind.

To start saving I went full time at Subway. As well as my former mugger, my colleagues were a diverse bunch ranging from Chinese and Indian business students to a semi-professional hockey player from Swindon and a nutter with an eyebrow piercing who claimed that he'd once pissed in the Southwest sauce and I couldn't tell if he was joking or not. I had also helped Jack get a job there, which was a bonus. Being a "Sandwich Artist" earned me status among my peers as I dished out free sandwiches to anyone I vaguely recognised. I'd also developed a fondness for a blond, freckled lady who worked across the road at Oddbins. We visited each other to get bags of change if we'd run out, something I ensured happened frequently if I knew she was on shift.

"Have you got anything larger?" I'd ask customers who tried to pay with a fiver.

I'm sure there was a spark between us but never acted upon it and bottled asking her out. Wearing a tiny, grubby cap and smelling of jalapenos didn't fill me with confidence.

During the summer, I also became acquainted with some of Headingley's odder characters. This included silver-haired man who always wore a leather jacket and jeans and, to the untrained eye, looked completely normal. During every shift, I would see him walk past the shop, stop to cross the road and walk back the way he'd come from. This could happen five or six times in a shift. I kept seeing this guy, he was everywhere. Whether I was heading home for a nightshift or starting early in the morning, I'd see him at a bus stop, a street corner or a pedestrian crossing. Always walking, never looking ruffled. How far did he walk in a day? Where did he go? What was his game? After a while he began to terrify me.

I also got to know Louie, a man who looked about eighty and wandered the streets of Leeds drinking spirits, sniffing shoe polish and talking gibberish. He walked with a hunch and his face was wrinkled like the skin on your elbows. He was deemed harmless and affectionately known as Screwy Louie. I never found out if his name was really Louie or whether he was so-Called simply because it rhymed with Screwy. Over the years, Screwy Louie had developed an almost mythical presence in the community with speculative rumours circulating about his story. The most romantic was that Louie was a talented boxer who had moved over from Ireland in the seventies to pursue his dream to become a prize-fighter. Allegedly, he'd bulldozed his way through the semi-professional ranks until he was just one fight away from turning professional and embarking on a glorious career. After a bruising battle, Louie lost and, thus, hit the bottle.

He frequently came into Subway and I'd give free coffee to him and his mate, a towering Welshman who was once spotted wearing a pirate hat. During these exchanges, Louie was always polite although much of what he was said was indecipherable. There was a mischievous side to him; my friend and I once saw him approach a group of student girls and deliberately drop some coins on the floor. When one of the girls bent down to pick it up for him, Louie stepped back before smacking her arse with a rolled-up newspaper. The girls were appalled. I was, in all honesty, a bit impressed by his ingenuity. A clever trick. Harmless? Nearly.

During a quiet shift one morning, Louie came in on his own, without the Welshman. He seemed different. Fresher faced, like some of his wrinkles had been ironed out. Was he sober?

"Good morrow, fine sir," he said. "Could you fix me a latte, please? I am in need of caffeine."

I gave him his drink and he went to sit by the window. After a couple of thoughtful sips, he pulled a small pen – the type you get from William Hill – from his pocket and began scrawling on a napkin. Thinking nothing of it, I returned to chopping onions. Subway give you special goggles for this, which you must wear.

After a few minutes, Louie stood up, put his coffee cup in the bin and handed me the napkin. On it was a metaphorical poem comparing the ageing process with the seasons. It was eloquently written in neat, curvy handwriting. It was beautiful. I have no idea whether this was his own work or a famous poem. I like to think it was his own. After I'd read it, Louie pulled a huge wad of twenty-pound notes out of his pocket and peeled one off.

"I'd like to pay for my coffee today."

I was left stunned. Had Louie had an epiphany? The encounter led me to consider the story behind this enigmatic character and that night I couldn't sleep. Endless questions were flying around in my head; was Louie really a talented poet? A tortured genius? Why did he have all the money? Had he always been rich? Was everything an act? What was the meaning of all this?

The next time I saw Louie I was with Jacob and Cameron, walking through Headingley. Louie was wearing a black Santa hat, which said Bah Humbug on it and holding a half-empty bottle of White Lightning.

"Hi Louie, how's it going?" Cameron asked.

Louie seemed to take offence to this, pulled a tin of shoe polish from his pocket, whacked Cameron over the head with it and walked off. The money and the poetry felt like a hazy dream from another lifetime.

***

While I enjoyed working at Subway I disagreed with Jack's theory that £5.80 an hour was going to amass enough money to travel the world so I cut back to weekends and evenings and landed a nine-to-five call centre gig at a big bank. Workhorse. After four weeks of training which was unnecessary and comprised of immaterial role plays, we went LIVE. The team leader's pep talk before our first call was comparable to Al Pacino's in Any Given Sunday and I was terrified. I needn't have been. We were taking inbound calls, simply asking people a couple of security questions before transferring them. No problem. It soon transpired that we were not going to be snowed under. There were between five and ten short calls per hour.

This left a lot of time to piss around with the guys on my team, most of whom had just graduated from university which should have been an eye-opener as to the value of the modern degree but wasn't. I looked up to these worldly-wise men in awe, listening to tales of foam parties, promiscuity and "I had this mate at Uni who..." stories. I held my own with them but fear my popularity was based entirely on the fact that I dished out stamps so they could get free sandwiches from Subway.

We played stupid games where we each wrote random, unusual words on slips of paper. They were put in a hat and distributed and players had to incorporate their word into the next call to win a point. We held table football competitions which spanned throughout the whole week and set up an eight-player chess tournament, crafting boards and pieces from coloured card. I won. If this was what working life was like, sign me up. This is fun. I might not bother with that round-the-world trip after all.

For those of you who haven't worked in a call centre, a floorwalker is someone who has been there for a while and had a promotion. They don't have to be on the phone permanently and spend some of their time, as their title alludes to, walking the floors. What they do while floor walking, I never found out. One of our floorwalkers, Nazim, was a handsome Asian guy in his late twenties. He was impeccably dressed, drove a nice car and bounced from pod to pod, flirting with the women and talking to the men about football and cars. He was loud, confident and charismatic and I admired him. A call centre celebrity. Towards the end of a staff night out, I was pleased to find myself sat next to Nazim in a bar. An attractive girl from the mortgages department was out and I hoped she'd be impressed by the company I kept. Nazim bought a round of drinks and we chatted about 5-a-side football. After he'd told me with typical verve about a spectacular volley he'd scored recently, we slipped into a silence accentuated by the clinking glasses and laughing women surrounding our booth.

"It's all a front, Andy," Nazim said, eventually, looking at the floor.

"Say again?"

"This. The big guy act, it's not me. None of it, I put it on."

Swilling whisky around his tumbler Nazim revealed his struggles at school and battles with self-confidence. He had no idea where his life was going. He wasn't happy in the call centre, he told me. Not anymore. I was stunned. The next morning, I walked into work, concerned about my colleague's wellbeing. Should I see if he wants to go out for lunch? Get him a free Subway, perhaps? Nazim arrived a bit late, wearing Evisu jeans and a Von Dutch cap. It was dress down Friday. He bounded over to my pod.

"How do! Some sore heads today, lads and lasses? Good night, eh? Bloody hell, Andy. You were fucked up last night, mate!"

Everyone laughed. I joined in.

***

As well as the mortgages department knockout, I'd also noticed a girl in another team; a more important team than my own who didn't have time for chess tournaments. She was a few years older and thus, I presumed, unobtainable. After a few weeks, however, it seemed that she didn't mind me occasionally staring at her and started to smile back. I even caught her looking over at me a couple of times. Was I imagining this? Out of all the cool guys on my team, why was she interested in me? I was pushing the boundaries of dress code, wearing a baggy black hoodie over a tie-less shirt so perhaps she liked this rebellious side? The office bad boy. Maybe word had got around about my performance in the chess tournament?

One afternoon, a middle-aged team leader who claimed to be a hypnotist (I don't think it was paying the bills) approached me.

"Are you single?" She asked. "I think my friend Donna likes you."

This was fantastic. Although the last time someone had said, "my friend likes you" I was at a school disco, arguably a more appropriate setting. The team leader gave me Donna's phone number and after a few long-thought-out texts, we arranged a date the following Wednesday.

I was wearing a freshly ironed shirt underneath the lucky black hoodie and after chomping on three pieces of chewing gum and popping into Boots to pilfer a generous spray of the Calvin Klein tester, I was ready. Donna was wearing a blue frock and had a headband in her hair. She looked good. After an awkward walk through the drizzle to get to a fancy bar she had chosen, we settled into easy conversation. We ordered a couple of cocktails and chatted about our colleagues and work; something in common. A solid ice-breaker.

"You did what?!" she said, chuckling after hearing about our word in a hat game.

After a couple of drinks, we moved to another trendy venue called Snake's Bar. I'd been here a few times with my pals and the nights always seemed to follow an intriguing pattern. The bar was always empty until around 1 am, at which time floods of attractive girls wearing classy dresses would arrive, as if from nowhere. I'd never had much luck with any of them but that didn't matter tonight. When we arrived, it was – true to form – empty so the only female in the bar was with me, flashing smiles at me while swirling a straw in her Mojito. Hurray. With an older woman on my arm and a buzz from the cocktails, I felt like quite the man about town. I realise now that, at eighteen, I didn't have many stories to tell or indeed hold many interesting opinions, but it didn't seem to matter as Donna was happy to chat away as I chucked in the odd witticism and subtle compliment.

"Your telephone manner is fantastic. You really put the customer at ease."

It was soon midnight and with rain falling outside, we ordered a taxi to share. I still lived with my parents so inviting her back was out of the question. I'd ambitiously hoped she may ask me to hers but it didn't materialise and we bid one another farewell as the taxi pulled up on my street.

On my way to work the next morning, I felt groggy but pleased. My first date with an adult woman had been a success. I opened my wallet for bus fare and found nothing but a crushed Airwave and a receipt from an ATM stating a hefty cash withdrawal. Had I paid for those cocktails? Did we split the taxi fare? Whatever, it doesn't matter, I told myself. It was a good night.

I arrived in the call centre to see Donna sat on a table surrounded by a gaggle of captivated women, including the hypnotist. She was talking about our date. I was the centre of call centre gossip. I felt famous. The guys in my team called for an impromptu morning session of table football so we could discuss how the date had gone at length. I seem to remember saying, "I think I'm falling for her" which was, with the benefit of hindsight, ridiculous.

My reckoning that the date had been successful was confirmed when Donna and I arranged to meet up again a couple of nights later. We went to a pub near her house and again, got along well.

"Really? You beat Kalpesh at table football?!"

At the end of the date, I walked her home and was about to call a taxi, but realised I was out of cash. I rang Will and he agreed to come and pick me up. On the drive, I boasted of my romantic endeavours but he was unresponsive. He was very stoned. Every Friday I'd been paying half my wages into Leeds Building Society but it wasn't going to be possible this week. I might not even need to save anymore though. If I had a girlfriend would I even want to go travelling? Was Donna my girlfriend? What are the rules?

The following Monday I got into work, feeling on top of the world. It had been an exciting time. During my break – which essentially lasted the entire shift – I strutted over to Donna's pod to have a chat. The word pod is too cheery for a group of tired people sat around staring at computer screens.

"Sorry, I'm on a call," she said. She wasn't on a call.

I tried to brush it off but sensed something was awry. I texted her that evening and got no reply. The next day I gave her a smile but she turned away. Apart from a couple of call transfers, the girl and I didn't speak to each one another again after that.

It was over as soon as it had begun.

To rub salt into the wound, another couple began dating which created a buzz and dominated the call centre gossip. I was yesterday's news.

It took the managers a couple of months – far too long – to realise that my team were getting paid for doing nothing and we were disbanded, retrained to do a proper job and chucked into new teams where we had to speak to people all day, every day and do things.

My illustrious start to call centre work became a distant memory as I found myself fading into the scenery of my new pod, separated from my old pals, the chess gang. Here I was nothing special; no longer a free sandwich provider, no longer the chess champ, no longer a romancer. Just a bloke, wearing a headset and getting paid £6 an hour. Crushing.

20

As the countdown crept into its final month, my excitement levels were becoming unbearable. I couldn't concentrate on my work and scrolled through pictures of exotic places while amending people's standing orders. With Thai beaches on my screen, my failed romantic endeavours mattered little.

An emo colleague with a swept fringe and flesh-hole earrings had been to Southeast Asia the previous year and I listened eagerly as he told me of his adventures. He was a good guy but our travelling conversations abruptly ended when he was sacked. It emerged that he'd been looking up the personal details of footballers on the database and prank texting them. I'd been aware of this and hadn't discouraged him so it was perhaps a lucky escape that I'd clung on until my final day where I received a farewell card, complete with predictable ladyboy jokes inside, and left the call centre one last time, walking on air.

My mum helped me pack my bag – a giant red backpack which represented excitement and opportunity now but would soon become a sworn enemy. My mum is good at this sort of thing – thorough and organised – but one thing still rankles; she said I shouldn't take any trainers, assuring me all I needed was a pair of hiking boots. Why I didn't question this, I don't know. My parents took a farewell picture of me on the drive with the big bag on and I met my companions, Eddie and Jack. Eddie had saved up by working four hours a day in a call centre which was both lazy and impressive while Jack had worked sixty plus hours a week in Subway. We only worked together a handful of times but that was no bad thing for Subway. On one occasion, we put a sign on the door saying, "Out of Bread" and went for a few beers, returning for the last hour of the shift, tipsy and barely capable of chopping peppers. I'm not proud of this.

Prior to our departure Eddie and Jack had shaved their heads as a sort of symbolic beginning to the trip. I declined the invitation to join them as I was worried we'd have looked like racists. Besides, I don't suit skinheads. My head is too long and my ears stick out. I'd bought a notebook to chronicle my adventures and jot down the e-mail addresses of all the beautiful women I would no doubt meet over the next six months. On the flight from Manchester I sketched a front cover which gives a fair representation as to my character at the time. It had *Andy's Travel Book!!!* on the front in 3D bubble writing surrounded by a wacky spider web design. Underneath it, I'd scrawled LUFC alongside a cartoon sketch of a Rastafarian smoking a joint.

Our first stop was Bangkok where we'd booked a hotel for a few nights to find our feet. We took a taxi to Koh San Road where we plodded along, weighed down by our bags and I stared wide-eyed at my surroundings trying to take it all in; the searing heat, bursts of colour, spicy smells, bustling streets and grinning Thai folk filled me with pure joy. On our first night, we sat on a rooftop bar watching the rowdy crowds below and discussing our plans and Eddie and I had a conversation about what the best course of action would be if we saw the silver haired guy who roamed the streets of Headingley, on Koh San Road.

"You'd have to kill him," Eddie said, stony-faced. "There would be no other option."

A barman in an Iron Maiden t-shirt claimed that the percentage of the Chang beer we were drinking was random with some as strong as 8.0% and I had no reason to disbelieve him as Eddie, Jack and I staggered back to our hotel in the wee hours, arms around one another, stuffing our faces with spring rolls. It had begun. The biggest adventure of my life was underway. The world was our oyster! I celebrated by being sick in the toilet.

We'd planned to spend a couple of nights in Pattaya but on arrival were overwhelmed by the seediness. I'm not one to get on my high horse about these things and, of course, you expect it in Thailand but seeing guys in their sixties and seventies with teenage girls on every street was a bit much and we left within hours, heading to the one of the islands, Koh Samed. The beaches were stunning – white sand, turquoise sea like the images I'd scrolled through at the call centre. On the first day, we predictably burned to a crisp after falling asleep on a floating raft in the midday heat sans sun cream. Jack, the experimental sort, was keen to test the theory that Thai energy drinks are laced with amphetamine so we spent one evening ploughing through a range of syrupy, sickly sweet liquids, ending up dizzy and sick with an aching jaw. With red itchy skin, the three of us crammed into a double bed in a beach hut (a prearranged money saving masterplan) to endure a sleepless, thoroughly unpleasant night of tossing, turning and regular trips to a basic outside toilet. Perhaps there was some truth in the amphetamine rumours although maybe it was just the vast quantities of sugar and caffeine? Either way, it wasn't fun.

We took a boat to the nearby Koh Chang and spent a week in a bamboo bungalow. Brian, the man who ran the accommodation was your typical expat escapee, leaving a chequered past in East London behind him to start afresh in a tropical paradise. I didn't mind him until he referred to himself, without a smile, as the Ginger Ninja and bragged of his romantic exploits since moving to Thailand. Also staying in the bungalows were an affable Scottish couple in their late twenties called Simon and Lydia. Simon, a lean guy with David Luiz-esque hair was one of those people who can function perfectly while exceptionally stoned and we shared beers together in the evenings. We thought he was beyond cool and clung onto his every word as he regaled us with tales, one of which mirrored my own about the bedside cabinet and top shelf magazines. We burst into wild laughter until Lydia stormed off, claiming we were disrespecting women and that Simon was a shit guy. This seemed a bit over the top but Simon didn't care. He'd seen this footage before.

"Snorkelling tomorrow, lads?"

Our next move was to take a night bus up to the Cambodian border. Freezing air-con, karaoke videos all night and no toilet – the stuff dreams are made of. Well, if you can sleep. I couldn't. A frisky hippy couple were sat behind me, whispering sweet nothings and smooching. When I finally felt myself drifting off, I heard a rustling noise and turned around to see the girl giving him a hand job under a towel.

From the border, we took a minibus to Sihanoukville where the ugly city centre is juxtaposed with the beautiful shoreline surrounding it. This was another arduous journey where we were significantly over charged and shared the minibus with a pair of middle-aged German sex tourists in alarmingly short shorts. I was quickly learning that the travelling part of travelling wasn't great. In Sihanoukville, we stayed in rooms above a bar on the beach, which was owned by a worse version of Brian in Koh Chang. A scrawny man in his thirties with lank, greasy hair and yellow teeth, he proudly informed us that he could never return to England as he had racked up tens of thousands of pounds of debt and fled the country. He had a Cambodian wife who "allowed" him to sleep with prostitutes at the weekend and he wore a t-shirt saying, *I do my own stunts.* We spent the next few days trying not to make eye contact with him and lounging, drinking lager and tossing a frisbee around in the shallows. Eddie launched one throw, which caught a gust and soared straight past my outstretched arm. Time slowed to a standstill as the frisbee arrowed towards an Australian woman returning from the bar with a tray of drinks.

"Watch out!" Jack screamed but it was too late. The disc clattered into her, glass and liquids flying everywhere. Jack, a kind-hearted soul, was devastated and ran over to apologise on Eddie's behalf. Thankfully there were no serious injuries and once she recovered from the shock, which took a while, she saw the funny side. Kind of.

We spent a few days in Phnom Penh, a frantic city where your senses are assaulted and motorbikes manically whizz past you on potholed roads. Employing the classic travel tactic of saying "Disco please?" to a tuk-tuk driver, we spent our first evening in The Heart of Darkness, the only nightclub I've been to where you have the option of leaving your gun in a locker and receiving a ticket to pick it up when you leave. We bumped into a couple of Dutch girls who we'd met earlier in our travels somewhere – it was all becoming a bit of a blur already. I'd assumed that this coincidence meant it was acceptable to try it on with one of them, Anna. Just as I was getting to the punch line of Jack's misplaced frisbee shot, a curly-haired Canadian with a winning smile walked over and introduced himself.

"This is Alan, he's my boyfriend," she said.

"Right. Hi, Alan."

Boyfriend? In the Heart of Darkness? What are you playing at, Anna? With the benefit of hindsight, Alan may well have been an actor, deployed to halt my Angkor beer-fuelled advances. Romantically things hadn't got going/nothing whatsoever had happened and this was causing angst. I was nineteen, single and travelling the world. If ever there was a time to be getting together with girls, surely this was then? Was it the hiking boots?

After leaving Phnom Penh we visited the Angkor Wat temples. They are, of course, spectacular but our day there was tarnished as Jack and I had fallen upon unspoken bad terms. We'd been grating on one another which is to be expected when staying in such close proximity, although I think much of my hostility towards him stemmed from pathetic jealousy. He had gone home with a girl he'd met at the Heart of Darkness and I hadn't. I'd taken a tuk-tuk back with Eddie.

Our subsequent plan was to cross into Laos but this was not a smooth bit of admin. We found ourselves stranded in a hostile border town after giving our passports to a Cambodian man on a scooter known only as Mr T and entrusting him to get a Laotian visa for us. He claimed it would take a day but it ended up taking seven. Whilst waiting for the visas, Mr T advised we stay with his pal, Mr Leng who owned a hotel near a lake

I sensed Messrs T and Leng had profited from this visa charade before but didn't hold it against them. Mr Leng had a winning smile, an impressive moustache and wore a white suit. Outside his modest hotel, he had his name up in large flashing lights. Who can't admire that kind of confidence? At his hotel, and against my mum's advice, we hired scooters. Five seconds after getting on I'd driven mine straight into a small wall in the hotel grounds and flipped off, cracking my knee and severely bruising my ego. Mr Leng rushed over and doused me with Tiger Balm before pleading that I didn't mention the crash to anyone. Something about insurance I gathered.

21

The opening riff to "Where is my Mind?" by the Pixies was booming out of loudspeakers in a packed wooden bar by the side of the Mekong river. The sun was glistening on the slow-flowing water as I bobbed along in an inflatable rubber ring, a chilled beer in one hand, my pals either side of me and pretty girls everywhere. This was why I'd wanted to come travelling.

We were in Vang Vien in Laos, having as much fun as nineteen-year-olds can have. After eventually getting visas sorted, this was our third stop in Laos following brief stints on Don Det Island and Vientiane, where we'd formed a brief alliance with three guys from Didcot. They were the same age and doing a very similar trip so all the signs suggested we should hang around together. The hitch was that we didn't really like them and they didn't really like us. They spoke like they were gangsters – "sick mate," "safe man," – despite a private school background in Oxford's suburbs, and conversation never really clicked. They weren't bad guys but we certainly didn't want to spend more time than necessary with them and after hushed conversations and hidden signals, we adjusted our travel plans so as to avoid bumping into them again. They were probably doing the same thing. I was learning that dodging unwelcome travelling companions is something of an art form. You should be allowed to be blunt, shouldn't you? "Sorry, I don't want to hang around with you anymore," would save everyone a lot of hassle.

Vang Vien was my favourite place so far. Tubing was an excellent way to spend the day and the town itself was quaint, although much of it was under development. The main road through the town was still being built and rumours suggested that they were two years behind schedule. This wasn't surprising as everywhere you looked – in the back of their tuk-

tuks, in their diggers, by the side of the road – were sleeping workmen. A dirt track leading down to the river was lined with bamboo bars and happy cafés ("happy" an easily-cracked code meaning drugs are on the menu). One afternoon, Eddie, Jack and I drank some mushroom shakes in a café run by a cheery local man with a slick side parting. My only previous experience on magic mushrooms hadn't been a roaring success but I trust a man with a side parting and told myself everything would be fine. And it was. Fun even. The three of us ended up sitting by the Mekong as the sun set, a much more appropriate setting than a hostile nightclub in Leeds city centre. While not hallucinating, I felt delightfully fuzzy as we skimmed stones into the orange water. When we got back to our bungalow, a storm started and as thunder crashed and rain pounded on the roof, I stayed up for hours sketching a picture of a clown riding an elephant. I was pleased with it.

The following morning, the dirt tracks had turned to mud, with the holes in the unfinished road overflowing with water which was streaming down towards the river. We went to see our pal with the side parting but were saddened to see that his café had been destroyed by the storm. The walls and ceiling had caved in completely, a tarpaulin was strewn on the floor and wooden planks smashed through tables. From under the rubble, he emerged with dust on his face and a hammer in his hand.

"Hello, my friends!" he said, grinning. "Look, it's all fallen down!"

"How terrible, are you okay?" Eddie asked.

"This happens all the time," he said before giggling. This was baffling. His livelihood had crumbled, why was he so happy about it? As his chuckles grew louder, I looked at Eddie and Jack and we couldn't help but join in. He lost it and began howling with hysterical laughter.

"All fallen down!"

"Seriously though, what are you going to do?" Jack asked him when he'd finally calmed down.

"I'll just build it again. No problem! Do you guys want a beer?"

What a great attitude.

***

We returned to Thailand and Chiang Mai, where we planned to go on a jungle trek but became side-tracked by a riverside bar offering two-for-one on towers of Chang beer. On the way back to our hostel, Eddie and Jack began play fighting. It was one of those play fights that turns into a real fight and they ended up grappling on the floor, arms and legs flailing. The next morning there were bad heads and bruises but no hard feelings. This was, perhaps, an indication that the cracks appearing between us were widening.

Belatedly we did a short jungle trek but the only other people on it were a couple in their thirties, who were arguably the driest people in the world. Stingy complainers who were scared of elephants. The man worked at Curry's. Why my brain has stored that piece of information is anyone's guess.

Our next stop was Pai, a hippy backpacker place full of bamboo bars playing Clearance Clearwater Revival. In Pai I began to lose my mind. One evening I met a young Thai man who was wearing lipstick and a singular hoop earring. The progressive, liberal guy I am, I thought nothing of his appearance and accepted his offer to play a drinking game based on Rock Paper Scissors. It was not a challenging game – the loser takes a glug of whisky. It was, however, quick-fire and I was on a different planet when the bar threw us out in the early hours. Eddie and Jack had long since left.

"Lift back to your place?" my new mate asked, unsteadily clambering onto his scooter, earring jangling.

"Sure."

I sat on the back, clutching onto his shoulders and swaying as the stars in the night sky swirled and we weaved along the bumpy road.

"Thanks," I said when we got to my hut, "see you later."

"Later?" he looked hurt. "Can't I come in with you now?"

How had I been so naïve?

"Sorry, that's not my thing," I slurred.

"No problem, can't I stay over though?"

"No."

Our accommodation was cheap so we'd treated ourselves to our own huts as a break from the three-in-a-bed routine. Eddie emerged from his, bleary eyed to see what the commotion was. The Thai man was on his knees, pleading with me.

"But why can't I come in? I gave you a lift?"

"What is going on here?" Eddie asked.

"Can I stay with you?" the Thai man asked Eddie.

Eventually we got the message across that he was not going to be staying in either of our huts and with tears forming in his eyes, he powered up his scooter and disappeared into the night. Such was the amount of strong whisky I'd had, I wrecked my room when I got in, clattering around and ripping the door from its hinges before passing out on the floor.

I arose at 1pm with a sandpaper throat and a head like thunder. I had flashbacks of the night's events – what was the significance of the man in lipstick? – and my heart sank when I saw the door to my bungalow separated from its hinges, lying in a puddle of beer on the floor. Had I done that? I got up and staggered out of my hut in search of water. Dripping with sweat in the afternoon heat I walked along a dusty path for a few minutes in search of a shop but had no joy, instead of arriving at a building site with skips full of rocks and splintered wood. I rubbed my eyes.

Is that Jack? Why is he carrying a wooden plank over his shoulder? He dumped it in a skip then walked over to me, looking exhausted.

"Morning, Andy," he said, wiping his brow.

What the hell is going on?

Eddie emerged from behind a wooden hut, carrying a large rock.

"Hi."

"Why are you doing manual labour?"

"The owner of our accommodation said we needed to work a shift to pay for the damage you caused last night so we are helping him to clear this site," Eddie said.

"He wants to build some new huts," Jack added cheerily. "We've been working for four hours."

Neither of them seemed angry.

"Sorry," I said. "Do you want some help?"

"No, it's okay. We're nearly done. Just got a few more rocks to move."

"Thanks, I appreciate it."

I felt awful. A drunk, entitled kid committing mindless vandalism in a developing country. Everyone's favourite kind of guy. At least, Ryan Lochte, I'm honest about the error of my ways.

While in Pai we were reacquainted with a couple of girls we'd met in Vang Vien, Keri, and Kirsten. Eddie and Keri got together leaving a direct head-to-head between Jack and me to win the affections of Kirsten, a slightly mad Canadian. After slugging it out for three consecutive nights in the bamboo bars, where fortunately the lip-sticked subject of my unrequited affection wasn't sighted again, Jack ultimately won the battle and I sadly became the fifth wheel. In case there was any doubt in Kirsten's mind, I made the decision for her when I took to the stage at an open mic night and chose to play a little-known and aggressive NOFX song. Given that the performances preceding me had comprised almost entirely of Bob Marley and Jack Johnson numbers, my song selection was wildly inappropriate. A middle-aged Australian guy cut me off halfway through to the notable relief of the dreadlocked crowd.

"Okay, thanks, Andy from England. That's enough now."

The romantic quandary was no fun and the morning after my impromptu gig, humiliated, hungover and sunburnt, I decided that Pai wasn't for me. I needed to leave. The answer to my woes was to get a solo bus back to Bangkok, on which I poured my heart out to the six-foot elven Dutchman sat next to me. He lacked empathy and kept trying to steer the conversation back to football.

"I just don't understand what I did wrong? Why would Kirsten not pick me?"

"Hmm. I suppose you feel like Dirk Kuyt when he wasn't selected for the national team."

My solo globetrotting didn't last long. I spent one night in a grubby hotel and in the evening, went for a wander along Koh San Road. Last time we were here I was so happy and now, without my pals, I just felt lonely and frightened. I didn't speak to anyone, had a Subway for my dinner (they didn't accept the stamps I'd brought with me, the bastards) and slinked back to the hotel where I desperately e-mailed Eddie and Jack saying I missed them. They left the girls and got the next bus to Bangkok.

The following afternoon my pals arrived at my hotel as I was laying on my bed listening to Taking Back Sunday through speakers on my I-pod. I'd bought the I-pod from the guy with the swept fringe at the call centre. He'd sold it at a good price but I hadn't had the chance/didn't know how to put my own music on it and was stuck with nothing but angst-ridden emo music. I was elated to see my friends again and we hugged one another, laughing.

"We can't listen to this shit any longer though," Eddie said once we'd calmed down and we headed to Koh San Road again where we bought a knock-off CD player and each picked an album. I went for the Arctic Monkeys, Jack, a Motown collection, and Eddie questionably opted for the Top Gun soundtrack. I bought the pair of them some postcards and spring rolls as an apology for my behaviour in Pai and all was forgiven.

***

I'd long been keen to get to the party islands in Southern Thailand and was delighted to arrive on Ko Pha Ngan, home of the full moon party. They really milk the moon for what it's worth with our first night out occasion-worthy because there was no moon – a dark moon party. Nonetheless, moon or not, being on Haad Rin beach for the first time was spellbinding. The stunning cove is bordered by cliffs with the white sand beach packed full of bars and nightclubs. Dance music was blaring, show-offs were doing fire poi and lanterns were being released into the night sky as thousands of partygoers frolicked on the beach. This was it. The stuff of nineteen-year-old dreams.

Shortly after arriving we'd been accosted by Bronson, a short, stocky Australian, who was travelling alone. His hair was shaved apart from a long rattail tied into a plait which came halfway down a chubby back which was covered in a tattoo of his family tree. A literal tree. A neon cartoon tree.

We stayed in Coral Bungalows where trendy house music played by the pool all day and, even in the mornings, the atmosphere was akin to being in a pretentious nightclub. It was full of slightly intimidating folk who were all just that bit older and cooler than us. The women were mostly Scandinavian and beautiful and the men stood around drinking vodka-based drinks, nodding their heads. I've never been able to pull off this look, although large biceps are a prerequisite, aren't they? Bronson and the three of us sat on the margins and I felt that familiar knot in my stomach which ties when I feel out of place. I should be having fun, everyone else is? Would anyone care if I wasn't here?

A couple of days later my despondency lifted. Four girls who we knew from home – Joanna, Abbie, Sophie, and Hayley – came to stay at the bungalows. I'd known the girls since primary school and it was great to see some familiar faces in a foreign land. It was just a shame that Bronson kept trying it on with them. The girls were all attractive and cool and as soon as it was established that we were friends with them, our stock around the pool skyrocketed. The men nodding their heads wanted to shake our hands and buy us drinks. A Swiss man with an afro offered me a drag of a large joint that he'd spent nearly an hour crafting. Even the Scandinavian girls no longer looked straight through us and asked what are plans were for the evening. It was comical really.

Being in a larger, mixed group boosted my confidence and one evening on Haad Rin, I got chatting to a Norwegian girl and we sat down by a campfire to share a bucket of whisky and red bull. Curly blond hair and a winning smile, I thought she was beautiful. I'd found myself in that rare level of inebriation where confidence is raised but sloppiness has not yet reared its ugly head. I listened to her travelling tales and she laughed at my jokes. It may have taken a while but this had to be it. My first taste of travelling romance was imminent. With my heart pounding, I prepared to lean in for a kiss.

A stout man bundled into the corner of my eye and tumbled onto the sand beside me.

"Andy, ya fucking cunt!"

It was Bronson. His face was covered in neon paint and he was beyond drunk.

"Why the fuck won't your mates pull me, man? For fuck's sake!"

"Is this your friend?" The Norwegian asked as Bronson began slurping from our whisky bucket.

"Um, sort of."

"Right. I'm going to find my friend, Ingeborg. I might see you later."

Frustrated by my luck, I was resigned to the idea that I would not find love on my travels. It just wasn't going to happen. What did it matter anyway? I told myself. I was in a tropical paradise, knocking around with my pals. And Bronson. Life was good. The following night, I drank too much, lost everyone and stumbled the mile or so back to Coral Bungalows, alone. The walk was too much and I passed out on a hammock outside a stranger's beach hut. Some time later, I was awoken by a hand shaking me awake. Disorientated, I expected the hand to be either the irate occupant of the hut or perhaps Bronson. I was surprised to see a freckled brunette with green eyes. I didn't recognise her but she claimed to have seen me around. I hoped she'd spotted me as I was stood with a vodka-based drink, while the Swiss man offered me a drag of his joint.

"Shall we go for a swim?" she suggested.

"Yes, great idea."

And so began a magnificent night of romance with Jessica, a girl from somewhere near Portsmouth. Not quite as exotic as Norway but I was ecstatic the following morning, irritating Eddie and Jack by being far too talkative for a hungover breakfast. After numerous futile nights of trying to catch the eye of girls in bars, I'd finally got lucky by passing out on someone else's hammock. Where's the logic in this life?

Having stayed on Ko Phangan for thirteen long nights, Eddie, Jack and I said goodbye to the girls and we left on the morning of the world famous full moon party. As party ferries of revellers flooded towards the island with dance music blaring, we sat on a small, near-empty boat heading the other way. Awful planning.

In Bali we met Rodney, Patrick, Noel, Dylan, and Chris. The five of them were on a similar round-the-world ticket and it was delightful to be reunited with old friends. Eddie couldn't contain his excitement but chose a peculiar way to express this, putting his hand in a ceiling fan and badly cutting it. While the atmosphere in Bali was a touch subdued following recent terrorist attacks – Australians had been advised by their government to stay away – it was a beautiful place. The group of us chatted about our adventures so far and enjoyed long days on the beach where we played football and tried, with limited success, to surf. We spent our evenings in the quiet bars and clubs on Kuta strip, usually ending up in Bounty, a vast, empty nightclub where, in an original marketing gimmick, the barmaids balanced drinks on their heads.

One of my fondest experiences from our travels was a night walk up Kintamani volcano. We arrived at the peak at sunrise to see pink clouds breaking to reveal breath taking views of the island. On the way down, one of our tour guides lobbed a pinecone at Eddie and a fight began. Ducking behind trees and chucking pinecones at Balinese men while they do the same is fun. Great fun. It represented one of those rare moments in life where you appreciate how good a time you are having, while it is still happening.

Back in our room, Jack had an epiphany.

"Perhaps we don't need to drink all the time?"

I nodded in agreement. We were halfway through our trip and all we'd really done was booze on different beaches. Had the volcano climb been the inspiration we needed? Would we spend the rest of our travels climbing mountains, trekking through jungles, learning new languages and visiting historical landmarks?

No. We went to Bounty that evening.

22

Shit, I can't look like that? My hair was greasy and had grown unevenly, with thick curly clumps bunching around my ears. I had spots all over my forehead and on my chin and my sunken eyes were puffy and swollen. I'd put on weight but exclusively on my stomach, a pot belly sticking over my board shorts looked silly with such thin arms. I looked awful. Australia had ruined me.

After a few days in Darwin where we'd befriended and quickly unfriended, Idan, a stingy Iranian man who we'd met in a jacuzzi, Eddie, Jack and I flew to Cairns. By chance, we bumped into Morgan, Aiden, James, Sean and Peter, some pals from home on a volleyball court. This was a sizeable coincidence. It's one thing bumping into someone in a shop in Leeds but chance meeting familiar faces on the other side of the world is something else. (In fairness, scores of people we knew were travelling the world in 2006 and we'd all booked pretty much identical trips from STA.) Cairns was fine if not inspiring. A lady who worked at our motel was also on the payroll of a Heaven and Hell-esque club called the Woolshed and persuaded us to give it a go.

"I call it the Pullshed," she said. "Y'know, because you always pull when you go there."

In four consecutive nights there, I didn't pull. I did eat an awful spaghetti Bolognese one evening though. Why was a nightclub selling spaghetti Bolognese?

On my final night at the Woolshed, I can have few complaints about the absence of romance. During the day, I'd picked up a nasty ear infection in the hostel swimming pool but, unwilling to let a small issue such as searing pain ruin my plans, headed into town. Midway through the night, I looked down at my t-shirt and noticed that a trail of ear wax was seeping from my ear, dripping down my neck and onto my clothes, glowing luminously under the strobe lighting.

The primary selling point of Cairns is the Great Barrier Reef. We booked to go on a trip but it was a 7am start, so I didn't make it. Everyone else mustered the strength and had a memorable day out as I stayed in a dingy room watching The Life Aquatic on an old TV.

Eddie, Jack and I left our pals as they were putting on shirts to head to the Woolshed again, taking a night bus to Brisbane. I liked Brisbane so much that I made ambitious plans to emigrate there after university. Quite what I'd do there, I didn't know but this was of little concern as we walked along the riverfront with the bright sun glimmering off the shiny skyscrapers surrounding us. In a park, a couple of local guys in their twenties came and sat with us. They worked in an abattoir killing pigs and were enjoying their first days off in months. They were easy company if a touch crass, and generous with their weed and beer. We shared a pleasant hour together until they started shouting appalling abuse at a black guy who was walking past, minding his own business. I felt guilty by association and was desperate to tell the black guy that we weren't their friends although this would have been a tough sell when we were sat together on a bench with empty cans surrounding us. We made our excuses and left our racist companions, claiming we were busy that evening and hoping that they wouldn't turn on us and beat us up.

After Brisbane, we reconvened with Rodney et al at Byron Bay. Our accommodation was their camper van, parked in a car park on the outskirts of town. Occasionally, a man in a uniform would ask us to move so we would have to drive a couple of laps of the town before returning to our spot. Eight men crammed like sardines into a van for four people was not ideal. Far from it. The giant multipack of crisps which I was living off, doubled up as a pillow one evening to the chagrin of Chris who was sleeping next to me.

"Just get out, Andy. I've had enough. You're not even paying to stay in the van."

This was a fair point so I left the van and slept on the beach, waking up face down in the sand, having been bitten savagely by midges. The following afternoon we were mindlessly slinging pebbles at a signpost, the kind of affordable entertainment we were now consigned to. Eddie picked up a large stone, released his grip far too late and watched in horror as it smashed through the front window of the van. At least it let some air in. With all the men in there, it was getting fusty.

Eddie and Jack were desperate to head to Nimbin for the Mardi Gras festival but I wasn't so keen. Leeds had reached the play-off semi-final and I was concerned it would be difficult to find somewhere willing to show a lower league English football game at 5am in a small town renowned for its cannabis counterculture. Besides, Eddie and Jack couldn't give less of a shit about football whereas Rodney and Dylan were big fans who I went to games with back home. After discussion, we agreed I'd live in the van for a couple more weeks while we headed South before meeting with Eddie and Jack in Melbourne.

Dylan and Rodney had passed their tests so they did all the driving, including some arduous overnight hauls along the desolate long roads. We kept spirits high by playing Blink 182's greatest hits on repeat and drinking inordinate amounts of coca cola, something I was finding worryingly moreish. On the long drives, there were a couple of close calls. Ten hours into one leg, a giant kangaroo bounced straight in front of the van and Rodney swerved at the last second, avoiding a smashed windscreen and a dead marsupial by inches. On another occasion Dylan fell asleep at the wheel and began to veer off road. Fortunately, Chris was still awake and noticed this. He snapped Dylan out of it, fed him more coca cola and urged him to continue.

"You can do it mate, it's only six hours until Sydney."

We lived in a multi-storey car park in Soho, Sydney's red-light district, for over a week. This was too long. We did, at least, find a bar which agreed to put on the Leeds game. They won and we celebrated with a 7am drinking session, accompanied by an overweight Leeds fan in his fifties. He was wearing a Leeds shirt but I don't think he was a huge fan.

"What are you doing for the final?"

"I'm not watching it. I'll be in Thailand. Shagging away."

"Oh."

***

As we arrived in Melbourne, our final stop in Australia, we had all gone slightly mad. Living in a van, spending every waking moment together, eating badly, drinking too much and barely sleeping is a cocktail detrimental to your sanity. Who knew? Somewhere along the way, we had acquired a furry toy possum which we took with us wherever we went. I was a keen Neighbours fan (this was in the BBC, Boyd and Skye heyday) so visiting Ramsey Street was a highlight. We also went to a rugby league game although I spent the entire second half sitting on a metal toilet courtesy of a bout of food poisoning. Apparently, it was a great game.

We flew to Christchurch in New Zealand, the country I had been looking forward to the most. Some mountain air would do me the world of good. Rodney had found himself a girlfriend of sorts, who he'd met in Asia and was on a similar trip to us. While we were lounging in bed in our dorm rooms talking to the toy possum and acting weird, he was going on coffee shop dates in town. It later emerged that the girl had given herself a fake name. She'd wanted to reinvent herself while on her travels.

One afternoon we found ourselves at a loose end.

"Let's get tattoos," Jack suggested.

"Ok."

Rodney was, I imagine, sipping a Frappuccino with the fraud at this point and Patrick already had an impressive tally of three tattoos. One of which says: *I fear no man but God* in Latin across his stomach. This left Eddie, Jack and at the parlour. With little planning, Jack flipped through a laminated booklet and identified the tattoo he thought would best represent his round-the-world experiences; a cartoon man with no face, carrying a balloon. On his right triceps. Obviously. Eddie went next, opting for the face of a black man with swirling eyes. On his left calf.

"I might not get a tattoo, actually," I said, having seen my friends wincing with pain and immediately question their decisions. To celebrate/commiserate the tattoos, we bought some legal ecstasy impersonations from a Seven Eleven and went out with Rodney and Patrick. The pills blew my mind and we danced the night away in a near empty nightclub with a flashing dance floor. I did kiss an American woman at one point but she claimed to have a flight early the next morning and showed little interest in returning to an eight-man dormitory with a man who was talking gibberish and had saucers for eyes. When we got back, my friends and I sat in the hostel lounge and stayed up until sunrise having a sentimental conversation.

"The thing is, mate. I just think your parents would be so proud of you."

Right now? While you are gurning your face off and drinking neat spirits at 6am? After writhing in bunk beds with whizzing minds for a few hours, the comedown smacked and it was atrocious. The group dynamic was a million miles away from the heart-to-heart and we couldn't look one another in the eye. My stomach was churning and I was having dark, existential anxieties. At least I didn't have a bad tattoo. That would have been too much to deal with.

The depression lasted for a few days so, overall, not a fair trade off for approximately twelve hours of fun. Endorphins are like the timeframe for a debit card transaction – you can take them out and use them up in a flash but putting them back in takes 3-5 working days. Quite how they were allowed to sell the pills in convenience shops is beyond me. Worse than an ecstasy comedown.

When we'd recovered we took a Greyhound bus to Queenstown, which is surrounded by stunning scenery. With towering snow-capped mountains and crystal-clear lakes, it's a more dramatic version of the Lake District, my favourite spot in England. Queenstown is home to the Nevis bungee jump, which was the highest in the world at the time. Patrick, Jack and I booked it even though it was, quite possibly, the last thing I wanted to do. Peer pressure is awful. And it never stops. Taking the rickety cable car over to the launching platform, which hangs over a 200-feet gorge, I was close to tears.

"Right, you're up," said a muscular Maori after he'd tied the rope to my legs. "Just look at those mountains over there and fall forward. Once you've stopped bouncing, pull the lever and you'll be in a nice seating position for me to pull you back up."

My heart pounding, I shuffled towards the edge. If I looked down, I'd certainly bottle it so I did as the muscular Maori said and fell.

It was incredible. Exhilarating.

Until the lever bit. I didn't pull it hard enough so the mechanism didn't work properly. Rather than shifting me into a comfortable, dignified position, my legs were skewed at awkward angles, one horizontal and the other vertical. With the blood rushing to my head reddening my face and my hamstring pulling, I was dragged, upside down back onto the platform, shouting "Ow. Ow. Ow." Not quite the heroic return I'd hoped for.

We said goodbye to Dylan and Noel who were coming to the end of their travels and had decided to relax in Queenstown for a few more days. They'd joined a gym which I deemed a bit odd. Chris, who was on the same ticket was not keen on his travelling finale being leg day and came with us to explore Franz Josef, a magnificent glacier on the West Coast. After an excellent day, we returned to our hostel where my pals mocked me for a fruitless attempt to chat up a girl in the lounge.

"So, um. Have you been to the glacier?"

We slept in on the morning of our departure so packing our bags was frantic. I did my usual irritating trick of letting everyone else work through the detritus of clothes on the floor before simply sweeping up the remains, which would, logically, all be mine. Eddie was getting wise to this.

"It's selfish and annoying, Andy. Stop doing it, you dickhead."

With bags stuffed, we bid a final farewell to Chris who was having a lie-in before his own bus back to Queenstown.

"New Zealand is great, isn't it?" I said as our minibus bobbed along the country roads, with stunning scenery on either side.

It would later transpire that concurrently Chris had not been quite so content. In my minesweeper packing technique, I had grabbed his only pair of trousers, leaving him boxer short-clad in a glacial town. In this state of undress, he went to the hostel reception which was bustling with the day's new arrivals. He explained his dilemma and waited among baffled travellers while they checked lost property, eventually returning with a pair of tiny baby blue shorts. Skin tight. He would later tell me that, if he'd been presented with a button which would kill me, he would have pressed it without hesitation or guilt.

We took a ferry to the North Island, arriving in Wellington at midnight where our Greyhound bus to Auckland was due at 7am. Short of cash, we decided against accommodation and stayed up, roaming the streets, spending a large chunk of the night stood outside a high-street Footlocker watching a LeBron James highlights reel on repeat.

On our final night in Auckland there was a blackout in our hostel. Stubbly and looking rugged, I was determined not to let a small issue such as complete darkness stop me from shaving and cut my face to ribbons, with blood streaming down past the sporadic stray hairs I'd missed. As we never learn, we took some Seven Eleven pills again before going to a nightclub where we befriended some towering Maoris, one of whom had a face tattoo, and danced to repetitive techno. On returning to the hotel I called Alfie in Leeds, who was holding his annual birthday barbeque. Given my energy levels and the excitement of speaking with long since seen pals, the conversation went on for a while and racked up a bill into the hundreds. I was starting to miss home.

23

We slept for a couple of hours before a long flight to Chile. I'd arrived in New Zealand, jaded, hungover, smelling musty and looking like shit. I was leaving New Zealand, all of the above – with the addition of fifteen shaving cuts on my face. The flight to Santiago was thoroughly unpleasant but the worst of the hangover had ceased when we arrived and exhaustion made way for fresh optimism as we embarked on the final continent of our trip. Wide-scale student protests were in force across the city – something to do with politics, I gathered – so the atmosphere was a touch frosty and roads were at a standstill. We decided to take it easy for our first evening. A chance to recharge batteries. We had planned a table tennis tournament in our hostel games room but, during the knock-around, the two available balls were trodden on and broken. Eddie and Jack decided to go out but Rodney, Patrick and I called it in and went to bed early, shattered.

At 5am I was snapped out of a deep slumber as Eddie and Jack burst into our room, visibly shaken.

"We got kidnapped!" Eddie shouted.

"It was terrifying," Jack said.

Once they'd calmed down, we learned the full story. They had got talking to a man on the street and got in his car, just as your parents advise. He'd seemed genuine and driven them to a nice restaurant he knew. It was filled with the man's extended family who were sat drinking and eating fine food. Eddie and Jack were introduced and pulled up seats, joining in the festivities. The language barrier hurdled by beer and wine, my pals were well-liked and had had a jolly old time. An evening with the locals, all very authentic. No problem so far.

After the table was cleared, the man asked for a quiet word out the back with Eddie and Jack. He took snort of cocaine from a canister, then glared at them.

"You pay the bill."

"Okay, how much do we owe?"

"Not just you. For everyone."

"We can't afford it."

The man smashed his bottle on the wall and waved in their faces. When a crazed, cocaine-fuelled Chilean pulls that trick out of the bag – in Chile – you should comply, shouldn't you? Jack handed over his credit card – intended for emergencies, of which this probably qualified – and the man paid the hefty restaurant bill with it. He sounded something of a Jekyll and Hyde-type as he then gave Jack the card back before giving them a lift back to our hostel. A bizarre hustle. Had he pre-planned it or just gone a bit mad? Kidnapping may be a slight overstatement but, nonetheless, they'd had a rough introduction to Chile.

This first instance of a hostility was just one of many we'd go on to experience throughout a turbulent ten days in the country. We took a coach up North, renting an old lady's apartment in La Serena, an out-of-season seaside resort, with empty hotels and boarded up shops akin to Morecambe Bay. The first bar we went to said, "No Gringos" on the door. We foolishly assumed this to be a joke. Walking in, the music stopped Spaghetti Western-style as a room full of angry drunk men shouted abuse at us. We kept our heads down for a few days after this, staying in the apartment, eating McDonald's and watching films. Just like the travel guides recommend. One evening, watching a bad Nicolas Cage film for the second time, cabin fever kicked in so we decided to man up and venture out to the bar area of town. It was fun. Early on, Eddie got together with a beautiful Chilean girl. She took his e-mail address and said she wanted to take him out on her boat the next morning before she headed off into the night with a winning smile. Delighted Eddie was in dreamland adding to a collective good mood as we drank and danced for the rest of the night.

"Perhaps we were wrong about Chile?" I said to Patrick. "Everyone's really nice."

"Yeah, we've just been unlucky. Must have been in the wrong places?"

Minutes later as we were trying to flag down a taxi, a gang of hooded yobs swaggered over to us. One of them whipped out a machete.

"Money, passports. Now."

Ready to hand over everything I owned, I was stunned to see Eddie's beautiful girl and her pals walking towards the melee. She had words with the knifeman and successfully discouraged him and his gang from mugging, or indeed killing us. As they slinked off, she flagged down a taxi and bundled us in.

"Not safe. You must go home now."

Our saviour.

"Let's leave Chile," I said back at the hostel and everyone vehemently agreed. Except Eddie, that is. He never did go on the beautiful heroine's boat.

Our next stop was La Paz, the highest capital city in the world. I learned that altitude sickness is real and felt nauseous and light-headed as we slogged the steep streets, eventually finding the hostel where our friends Will, Clarence, Lee, and Mick were staying. They were midway through a two-month tour of South America and over beers recounted tales of their trips to Macchu Pichu and the salt flats. They'd made friends from all over the world, eaten exotic cuisine and learned basic Spanish. None of this was relatable.

La Paz is a chaotic, dizzying city with buildings seemingly toppling down the sides of the steep mountains on which it is built. We explored a bit before finding refuge in a fairly crap expat café bar called Oliver's Travels. We spent a full day here watching the opening round of world cup fixtures and trading football stickers with other Brits, many of whom were progressively wired on cocaine which you could buy at the bar. Seeing wild-eyed grown men clenching their jaws while saying: "Got, got, got. Need!" is an unusual and not altogether pleasant sight.

Football fever had kicked in and the following day we took part in a well-organized 5-a-side tournament. For some, this was the greatest day of their travels. For me, it was among the worst. While my mates were put in a team together, I ended up on my own on an awful team, where our only good player was a cocky Londoner who didn't like me and refused to pass the ball. We lost every game and I played terribly and hated every second. My pals won the whole thing and Will was player of the tournament, basking in the glory of minor celebrity stardom during the post-tournament drinks back at the hostel bar, while I glumly sipped a beer on the balcony staring into the distance and thinking about what might have been.

By the time we'd got to Mongo's, a lively nightclub playing Latin dance music, I was still in a foul mood and as my pals danced, I stood by the bar contemplating the many misplaced passes I'd made.

"Hello mister, you dance?"

In front of me stood a pretty, petit black lady with tight curly hair and superb hips. Superb hips *and* she didn't know what had happened on that fateful football pitch earlier in the day. She represented a fresh start. Life after the football tournament had to start somewhere, why not now?

She told me her name was Matilde. Her English was passable, my Spanish not so much, but we got along well and danced, drank tequila and smooched. I was having a great time.

"I go now mister," she said after an hour or so, "phone por favour?"

I handed it over and she punched her number in.

"Call me manana, si?"

"Uh, si."

The following evening, Will's Rosetta Stone Spanish came into use as he called Matilde arranged a date on my behalf. I had *ni Buenos ropas* so turned up for my first date in months wearing combat trousers, hiking boots and a creased San Jose football shirt. Slick. It didn't matter though. She wasn't the pretentious type; we went to a fast food restaurant and shared a bucket of fried chicken and chips before wandering the streets for a while and ending up at our hostel, where my pals had kindly vacated our dorm for the evening. They'd returned to Mongo's.

It was a wonderful night. However, the romance would not last long and in another case of bad timing, we were clearing off to Argentina the next morning. Matilde and I exchanged e-mail addresses before saying our goodbyes outside the hostel the following morning. While short-lived, we'd shared a magical few hours together, and there was a lump in my throat as I turned to walk away.

Bolivia also marked the end of our short stint with Will et al and more significantly, it was time to say farewell to my one of my original travelling buddies, Jack. He was extending his trip and heading to Caracas to meet our school pal, Tino, who had returned to live in his native Venezuela. With all these goodbyes, I was emotionally crumbling and stared out of the window as another long coach ride began, already filling with nostalgia about times just passed. I could feel that our trip was nearly over. The end was nigh.

***

Buenos Aires, or BA as the travelling aficionados/dickheads call it, is arguably the coolest city I've been to. Leeds notwithstanding of course. Cosmopolitan with wide European-style streets lined with designer shops, fancy steak restaurants, and fascinating architecture all around. Argentinian people are a beautiful, sophisticated and well-dressed bunch. Well, most of them anyway. On our first day in the city, we had a run in with Argentina's answer to Screwy Louie who was not so dapper. We'd just watched Argentina vs Holland in a local bar – awful game, electric atmosphere – and were walking back to our hotel. An elderly man with one eye began following us. He was glugging a non-specified spirit out of a small clear bottle and carrying a plastic world cup.

"Gringos," he said just in case we hadn't noticed him. We stopped and turned to face him.

"What's your problem, man?" Rodney asked.

"Puta gringo!"

He raised the plastic world cup above his head and hit Rodney on the shoulder with it before waving it at us like a whirling dervish. We began walking briskly and fortunately managed to lose him.

Back at the hotel, baffled after the bizarre encounter, we headed to our room for a nap. We left the lights and the door wide open with all our valuables sprawled across the floor and, surprisingly enough, got burgled. A man – I assume it was a man – had pinched some loose cash and Rodney's camera, which had the entirety of his travelling photos on it. This was pre-Facebook and an upsetting thing to lose at the end of a long trip. Our pal, Morgan had had his camera nicked on a bus in Asia but the thief had a conscience and left his memory stick. A kind thief. Rodney, however, was not getting the breaks in Argentina, and he and Eddie spent the following day hanging around at the police station to no avail.

We visited the Boca Juniors stadium where an obese Maradona impersonator did keepie-uppies and went to a nightclub one evening. Well, I say evening, the Argentinian approach is to sleep for a few hours, get up after midnight and head to the club circa 2am, staying out until breakfast. We learned this, and much more, from an arrogant ginger-haired Israeli man who worked at our hostel and knew everything about everything. Despite his irksome presence, the nightclub was fun, although slightly daunting owing to the beauty and style of the locals who were unimpressed by my hiking boots and dirty shirt combo. We returned to the hostel at 9am and sat in the outdoor courtyard with the Israeli man whose energy hadn't wavered as he continued to dominate conversation with worldly-wise tales.

"I'm going to grab another beer," he said, before jumping up and – with a sickening thud – whacking his knee on the side of a table. I glanced over at Patrick and there was complete silence. For about two seconds. Then Patrick exploded, beginning to howl uncontrollably with laughter. It was impossible not to join in.

"Hey, guys, c'mon?" the Israeli man said. "Anyway, it didn't even hurt."

With tears in his eyes as he hobbled to the bar, he was fooling nobody. The Israeli's knee whack represented the end – and possibly highlight – of our time in Argentina.

And then it was on to our final stop, Rio.

24

After rereading the e-mail several times, I sat in stunned silence as the knot in my stomach tightened. I turned off the computer monitor – because that would solve everything – left the hostel and stood outside in the searing morning heat. I hunched over, putting my hands on my knees. Sweat was dripping down my forehead and my heart was pounding. A pair of American guys who I'd spoken to briefly a few days previously strolled past without noticing me. They were chatting animatedly and one of them was holding a giant beach ball. Presuming that neither of them had recently found out they were going to be fathering a Bolivian love child, I greatly envied them. Just two friends on holiday, having a good time. I longed for the days – yesterday, for example – when my life was that simple. If I could push a button and swap lives with the American guy holding the giant beach ball, would I do it? Probably.

I paid for three more nights at the hostel and retired to my former dormitory, where I lay down, staring at the sagging rungs of the bunk above me, for the rest of the morning. This achieved little. Early afternoon, the men from the Midlands barrelled into the room.

"Andy? Why are you here?"

I explained how my day had gone.

"I wouldn't worry about the e-mail, mate," said the drug dealer, coolly. "She'll be bullshitting, just be after some money. They are all at it."

I wasn't sure who he meant by "they" but felt a measure of relief at his sage words. Perhaps he was right and she was lying?

"We're going on a favela tour later," the accountant said. "Do you want to come?"

I wasn't enjoying being alone and agreed. A smiling tour guide took us through the bustling labyrinth of a hillside shantytown, cheerily assuring us – in case there was any doubt – that these people were "very, very poor." Stood outside a young mother's hut, gawping at her while she was trying to boil a pot of rice for her kids, I felt spectacularly uncomfortable. As far as tourist attractions go, this was one of the more intrusive ones.

Afterwards, we went for a few beers and, for a couple of hours at least, I managed to push my predicament to the back of my mind. Being in the company of others, especially people I didn't know very well, was a useful distraction.

When we returned to the hostel, I replied to Matilde, saying: "Are you sure?"

I finally contacted my mum, as I'd planned to do hours previously, opting to withhold from mentioning that she may soon be a grandmother to a Spanish-speaking child. I lay tossing and turning in damp bedsheets that evening, my mind racing. Would I have to emigrate to Bolivia? I was nervous about moving to Lancaster University, let alone La Paz. What would I do there? My child would be unusually tall for a Bolivian. Would that be a good thing or not? Was Alfonso or Rogerio the better name?

I went to the hostel's internet cafe the next morning to find a new e-mail from Matilde.

"Yes. Is true. What now?"

I replied telling her that this was not a problem I'd faced before and I was therefore unsure what to do now. I admitted that I didn't quite feel ready for fatherhood.

My patient mum had, at least, got back to me. There was a flight to Heathrow in three days and she'd booked me a seat. I spent the remaining days with the guys from the Midlands, sitting around on the beach, playing pool and revisiting Sugar Loaf Mountain. While these days were pleasant enough, two or three times an hour, I would remember that a Bolivian woman who I'd met twice thought she was pregnant with my baby, feel like I'd been smacked in the stomach and go quiet. The time went quickly though and soon enough I was bidding my new friends farewell for the second time and taking a minibus back to Rio airport once again.

***

Gladly I hadn't thrown my passport in a bin this time and there were no delays. I'd envisaged the flight home to be a time of reflection, where I would review all that had happened – the adventures we'd had, the places we'd been, the friendships we'd made over the past few months, but his was not the case. I nodded in and out of consciousness, having unsettling dreams about being kidnapped and worrying about what my future held.

Arriving back in your home country after months on the road is surreal and it was all a bit overwhelming. Everything was so familiar yet I felt detached and disorientated. On the train from London to Leeds, I was acutely aware that I could understand all the conversations going on around me. Hearing a heavily-perfumed woman talking on the phone – loudly and in detail – about a disappointing evening at Frankie and Benny's, I wished this wasn't the case. I stared out of the window through dozy eyes. It was a typically drizzly day and as green fields, rolling hills, industrial estates and nowhere towns sped past in a blur, I felt relieved to be back.

In the 10-minute taxi ride from Leeds train station to my house, I noticed that the city looked more-or-less the same as when I had left. Life, it seemed, had gone on without me just fine. At home, my parents greeted me with a welcome hug. I was delighted to see them again.

Before the kettle had even boiled and without even thinking about what I was saying, I blurted it out.

"A Bolivian girl says she is pregnant with my baby."

Going through photos and telling travelling tales was put on the backburner for a while.

***

I was honest about the turn of events and showed my mum the e-mails. The old problem shared, problem halved adage didn't quite ring true but I felt approximately 15% better once I'd got it off my chest. My parents were understandably alarmed but did a good job of pretending to be calm. After mulling it over, my mum replicated the thoughts of the drug dealer from the Midlands, suggesting that I could be the victim of a scam. This made me feel better, although the e-mails that continued to come through from Matilde, seemed legitimate enough. In one of them, she expressed, over several paragraphs, her happiness about bringing a child into a world where Evo Morales was going to be the first indigenous Bolivian president.

Sitting around stewing all day would achieve nothing. Besides, I'd got into some hefty debt on my travels; I needed a summer job. Rodney had recently started a catering gig at Headingley Stadium and suggested I joined him in working in the restaurants and on the bars. The interview process was not rigorous: "What apron size are you?" and I started a couple of days later.

It quickly became apparent that silver service is not a talent of mine. On my second shift, I dropped a pork chop on a woman, watching in horror as it swirled through the air, bounced off her expensive-looking coat and smacked onto the floor. Luckily, the woman was locked in conversation and didn't seem to notice but instead of coming clean, I fled the scene, hiding in the kitchen, where I spent a deliberately long time picking up the next set of plates from an irate chef, called Steph. Steph the chef.

As well as struggling in the restaurants. I also worked shifts behind the bar. Working at Headingley Stadium did not represent the most challenging version of bar work. Using a six-pint dispenser, we had to press a button and wait for the lager to pour into plastic cups, before selling it at extortionate prices. For £1 punters could buy a cardboard four-pint holder, although the product was structurally flawed and, on numerous occasions, I saw the holders disintegrate leaving cricket fans covered in Carlsberg. When this happened, I'd dart back into the stock cupboard to check that we had enough crisps while my colleagues apologised and handed out kitchen roll to livid, lager-soaked men.

During one shift, a nozzle on the six-pint dispenser malfunctioned so one of the pints came out head-heavy. This sparked a game between my colleague, a cheeky chap called Ryan, and I where we took it in turns to serve pints with increasingly large heads. Ryan won after managing to maintain a straight face and successfully sell a cup filled almost entirely with froth to an inebriated man wearing a sunhat.

When Rodney and I were put on the bar together or in the same restaurant, we had a good time. We'd spend the shifts pissing around and trying, with little joy, to flirt with our female colleagues. Innumerable blond-haired students, most of whom were studying Sports Science at Leeds Met, worked there but Rodney and I lacked the pizazz to charm them and they gravitated towards the more senior staff members, including Rodney's older brother, a team leader and prolific womaniser.

I was picking up any shift I could, which helped to keep my addled mind occupied but one night in Bondi beach club, I was reminded of my quandary. Making the most of the £10-all-you-can-drink offer, Noel and I were holding six bottles of Fosters each and heading towards the revolving dance floor with intent, when my phone rang. The number had +s and 0s in funny places. Putting a finger on my left ear to block out the final chorus of "Summer of 69" I picked up the phone.

"Hello."

There was a crackle and a delay. I could only make out a few words.

"Ola…"

"Hello?"

"Mister Andy?"

"Yes, who is this?"

"…Bolivia."

"What, I can't hear properly?"

"….El Presidente Morales!"

"What?"

"...La Paz"

"I CAN'T HEAR YOU. I'M IN BONDI BEACH CLUB."

"…Bambino."

The line went dead.

How had she got my number? Had I given her it? I couldn't remember. After the barely decipherable conversation, I reconvened with Noel on the dance floor, but I could no longer enjoy my evening. Six bottles of Fosters or otherwise, the phone call from La Paz was preying on my mind. Hearing her voice had made it all seem very real.

The next morning, I wasn't feeling too clever. I arose at midday with a foggy head and a sinking feeling. Initially, I was unaware of the cause of my anxiety. Oh yes, Bolivian baby. That should do it. The fear didn't stop there, though – there was something else. I looked at my phone to see seven missed calls from Rodney. My shift had started at 9am. Shit. I splashed some water on my face and pace-walked the half mile to work, arriving in the Long Room – a bar and restaurant overlooking the cricket pitch – to find Rodney dragging a stack of chairs. He looked exhausted. And furious.

"What are you playing at, dickhead? I've had to stack and move two hundred chairs on my own."

"Oh, sorry mate. I slept in."

"Well, I've finished now."

"Do the managers know I didn't come in on time?"

"No, I haven't told them. They think you've been here with me."

"Thanks, man."

"No problem."

He was scowling. It was a problem.

When we left – two hours later – I lied on my timesheet saying that I had arrived at 9am as anticipated. This angered Rodney even further and we walked home together in silence – it was the only time we've fallen out and, I must concede, it was fully deserved.

I felt guilty about this charade but when I got home, things took a turn for the better.

"Andrew?" my mum called from the back room. "Come here."

I walked into the backroom where she was sat at the computer.

"Now don't get annoyed…"

"Why? What have you done?"

"Well, I logged on to your e-mails."

"Why? How do you know my password?"

"It's written on a post-it next to the computer. Anyway, as I said, don't get mad, it's good news."

"What? What's good news? Why are you going on my e-mails?"

"I just wanted to read the e-mails from the Bolivian girl again."

"For god's sake, why? I showed you them."

"Well, as I was checking, a new e-mail came through."

"It did?"

"Read it."

I looked at the screen. It said:

"No bambino. Falsa alarrma. ¡lo siento mucho!"

For now, fatherhood could wait. I was in the clear.

25

"Everyone seems alright, don't they?" I said to my new housemates, Rowan and Julian, as we stood at the Student Union bar.

"Yeah, I'm just glad I wasn't put with any Christians," Rowan replied. He was a slim guy with floppy brown hair. He was wearing a worn green hoodie.

I considered saying "me too," not because I have anything against Christians but because it was my first day at Lancaster University and I was keen to appear agreeable. I decided against it and didn't reply. We stood in silence for a few seconds.

"Well," Julian said, scratching his neck, "I'm a Christian. I'm in the Christian Union."

Rowan looked to the floor.

"Ah shit, I'm sorry. I didn't mean it like that…"

I laughed. Mostly down to relief that someone other than me had made the first faux pas. Fortunately, Julian didn't seem too offended and it acted as an icebreaker; a better one than catching a ball and saying an interesting fact about yourself.

My independence was four hours old. After an uncomfortable journey from Leeds where the neck of my guitar had been digging into my back and I'd needed a piss since Wakefield, we had arrived at Lancaster. During the poignant unpacking of bags from the car, which was parked illogically far away, I took in my new surroundings. The picturesque campus is sprawled across a hilltop a couple of miles out of the city with buildings dotted around lakes and green fields. Not quite so pretty was my accommodation for the year; a tiny white box with a less-than-single bed, a coffee-stained desk and a large crack running down the window. I was living in halls of residence with seven other blokes.

When saying goodbye to my parents I'd thanked them for everything; a heartfelt moment, difficult for the twenty-year-old man to express. My mum responded with a firm hug while trying to hide a solitary tear rolling down her cheek. My dad said, "Give over, Andrew."

When I was sixteen I'd visited John at Nottingham University where he was studying law. He was living in a shared house, formerly a brothel, with a bunch of mates. They spent their days playing Goldeneye on the N64 and their nights drinking lager. My brother had grown an afro and was known as "Afro John." The lifestyle looked excellent. I couldn't wait.

After an opening weekend comprising of a painful Fresher's dinner where I'd sat next to a solemn man with an eyebrow piercing and an organised bar crawl which included chanting and forced frivolity, my expectations had waned a little and I started to worry. While Rowan and Julian seemed like good guys, I quickly established that my other housemates, who were all in their final year, were an unusual bunch. One had cosmic blue hair and allegedly kept a satanic bible while another spent much of his time on his computer, playing an airport manager simulation game. Of course, who you live with is a lottery, but I was concerned that not one of my new housemates so much as supported a football team. How had this happened? What would we talk about?

On the Sunday evening, my fears were allayed somewhat when the final room in our flat was filled by Pete, a six feet five giant from Halifax. He arrived carrying two crates of beer and apologised for missing the first weekend. He'd been in Edinburgh, gambling on fruit machines. He had a code which increased his probability of winning. The code, he told me, no longer worked in Halifax.

After settling in, the first term went as one would expect; drinking excessively, playing computer games and burning pizzas. I spent most of my time with Pete and Rowan. Pete and I spent entire days in bookmakers and arcades, squandering our student loans while Rowan's tastes were more sophisticated, with a fondness for niche music and foreign films. This created a nice balance ranging from fixed odds betting terminals to critically analysing City of God.

At twenty, I was quite old for a first year, although not as old as some. One morning, a balding, overweight guy in his late thirties started a conversation with me on the way to the shop. He was wearing a Scooby Doo t-shirt which was too small.

"Hello mate, how are you settling in?"

I assumed he was an ironic lecturer or a visiting parent, dropping off a TV that didn't fit in the first car load perhaps?

"Um, okay thanks. You?"

"Fresher's week has been mad, hasn't it?"

"Sorry?"

"Yeah, I've been out every night so far. Just need a couple of Red Bulls to power through tonight!"

That evening I saw him dancing alone on a raised platform in a nightclub in Morecambe with a sweat patch on his back and a blue WKD in each hand. This would become a common sight throughout the next three years and he wasn't the only one; there were quite a few of these men – always men. What was their game? An alternative mid-life crisis? I'm not ageist and all for continued education but would you not be a bit more reserved about it? Is it necessary to live in halls of residence and instigate Strawpedo tournaments with eighteen-year-olds? Each to their own, I suppose.

I was wary of some of the campus behaviour. Having travelled around the world, I probably thought myself wiser than I was, but still, much of the so-called fun seemed moronic. I was unconvinced by themed events and fancy dress. Why does dressing up as cops and robbers make a night more enjoyable? I was suspicious of student reps, social secretaries and DJs. Like 18-30 holiday reps, only with reasonable UCAS points as armour, these folks were desperate to be recognised – to gain status. They dominated group conversations with their opinions and exaggerated laughter but were difficult to communicate with one-on-one, not listening and easily distracted, looking over your shoulder for more interesting company.

Despite playing football (C team squad player) I found the university sports teams to be a pain in the neck. The "Hockey lads'" aggressive power in numbers, chanting and "banter" such as drinking one another's piss was particularly harrowing.

I couldn't understand the need to wear sports gear all the time; when you have training or a match, fine, but when you are going to a seminar and playing zero sport that day, was it essential? Would it make girls fancy you more if they knew you were on the lacrosse team?

Some of my grievances may have stemmed from jealousy (not the piss drinking bit) and trying to figure out what kind of guy I wanted to be. Thai beach party experience or not, my identity was not fully formed and I was still, in many respects, clueless. I didn't want to be a nobody but if being a somebody here meant dressing up in a toga, I was willing to make the sacrifice. Barring the addition of a risqué pair of neon trainers and an overplaying of my interest in hip-hop music, I wanted to stay true to myself. That sounds cheesy, doesn't it? The type of thing an American talk show host would say, or the generic advice offered by a friend towards the end of a lager-fuelled heart to heart.

My romantic endeavours did not run smoothly. Shortly into the first term, a good-looking blond girl delivered a note to my flat, saying that she'd seen me around and wanted to meet up. This was 2006, just before Facebook and Tinder etc. changed the course of modern romance. Letters and notes of this kind were soon-to-be-extinct and this may have been one of the last of its kind. It was exciting. Do you get the same excitement from swiping a mobile phone screen? I tried to play it cool and asked if she wanted to come to our flat for a cup of tea. In my mind, I was now a strong conversationalist and thought this would go well; I would impress her with travelling tales and fondness for Tupac, before inviting her to my room where I would woo her by playing a Radiohead riff on my guitar.

Of course, things didn't work out like that. For starters, at criminally short notice, she brought a friend along. Panicking, I knocked on Rowan's door, interrupting him watching The Garden State, and asked if he'd be my wingman.

"Uh, ok. I guess."

In my fluster, I'd forgotten to sort out background music in the kitchen so a haunting Evanescence track was seeping from the man with the Satanic bible's room and through the whole flat. The stark kitchen lighting coupled with a faint smell of vegetable oil in the air did not create a romantic setting. Far from it.

The girls arrived.

"Hi."

"Hi."

Rowan established geographical common ground with the girl's plus one and they settled into easy conversation. I, on the other hand, froze and couldn't think of anything to say.

"So, uh, where are you from?"

"Preston."

"Oh, I've heard it's a bit of a shithole?"

"I like it."

Silence.

I never recovered and within half an hour the girls had left, uninspired. As we lived so close to one another, I saw her every day for the rest of the year. For the first few weeks, we said hello. After this, it turned to flat smile and nod and, by the end of the term, nothing. It was as if we'd never met.

Time flew by. We'd befriended some girls – Karen, Hannah, Isabelle and Fiona in the flat above and had many enjoyable nights out in student haunts. On occasion I'd meet Jim, my old friend from Leeds who was also at Lancaster and we'd get stoned and drift in comfortable silence. I acquainted myself with the Megabus and visited friends from home in universities around the country, invariably having fun apart from one trip to Nottingham where I woke up under Cameron's bed to discover I'd lost my wallet, phone, passport, and keys. The big four.

Towards the end of the second term I was still not sure what to make of it all. I'd grown to like my housemates but most of them were leaving at the end of the year. What would second year be like? Was the university lifestyle for me? Was my degree worth anything? On the final night before Easter, I drank several Jägerbombs, felt uncharacteristically confident and got talking to a girl from one of my seminars in a club. She had blond hair, green eyes and a sprightly Southern accent. Very Southern. I followed her into the girl's toilet and we ended up kissing. And from that moment, everything would change.

***

I'd had two previous dates at university, neither successful. The first one was with a girl I'd met upstairs in Revolution at 2am. In the light of the day she looked so different to my nocturnal memories that I couldn't identify her and stood in her vicinity scouring the campus bar for a couple of minutes before she tapped my shoulder, startling me.

"Didn't you recognise me?"

"Haha, don't be silly. Of course, I did."

"I don't think you did."

The bad start was made worse when she spent the duration of the evening talking about a hockey player who lived in her halls, who she was almost definitely in love with. To change the subject, I'd asked her if she fancied a game of darts. She said no.

The second date was with a girl who wore a baseball cap backwards.

Third time lucky, I was feeling better about things. I, kind of, knew Louise already so wasn't flying in blind. Getting together on the last night of term had worked in my favour, providing the opportunity to think up well-crafted, twice-analysed texts throughout the Easter holidays and we agreed to meet up for a drink on our return.

We were meeting at a campus bar at 5pm. I picked out my favourite Carhartt t-shirt, wore some new H&M jeans and applied a touch of hair wax. My only concern was having no clean socks apart from a yellow football pair. When I arrived, Louise was stood at the bar and looked exactly how I'd remembered, which was a good thing, her shoulder-length blond hair going well with a stylish black frock. She was grinning when I arrived and there was a sparkle in her turquoise eyes. She looked beautiful. I felt my heartbeat accelerate.

"What are you drinking?" she asked.

"I'll get the first round."

"Don't be silly. I insist."

"Great. Kronenbourg, please."

She turned to the barman.

"Can I have a bottle of wine and a pint of 1984 please?"

"I'm sorry, 1984? We don't sell books. Did you mean 1664?"

Louise blushed and looked sheepish. I could see what she'd gone for – using the trendy name for a drink to appear knowledgeable – we've all done it. It was a minor – well, three centuries wrong – faux pas but it broke the ice and we both started laughing. I was also surprised and quietly impressed, that she'd ordered a full bottle of wine for herself. We sat down on tall bar stools by the window, settled into easy conversation and I found myself having a delightful time. She was confident, bright, bubbly and giggled almost constantly, which is helpful on a first date. We chatted about all manner of things ranging from embarrassing teenage tales to our plans (or lack thereof in my case) for the future. Time flew and by 8pm we went our separate ways as we had both plans to go out with housemates that night. After we'd kissed goodbye, I left the bar drunk and dizzy with happiness. It had been the best date I'd ever been on. Hands down.

I subtly convinced my housemates to alter our arrangements and crafted a plan which enabled our night to end in Toast, a low-ceilinged nightclub which played R&B and hip hop. This was to none of their tastes but I knew Louise would be there. Inside, I sacked off my friends almost instantly and found her on the dance floor, drinking a large glass of wine and shaking her hips to "Crank That" by Soulja Boy. 2007 was a golden age for music. We picked up where the date had left off and within half an hour ambled outside to the taxi rank. I wanted to pay but checked my pockets and found nothing but a pair of Asda receipts masquerading as notes. Embarrassed, I prepared an excuse but the stars aligned and something superb happened. In the backseat of the taxi, neatly folded into a perfect square, was a ten-pound note. With sleight of hand, I pocketed it without Louise seeing and gave the taxi driver a healthy tip as he dropped us off on campus. I stayed at Louise's and awoke the next morning feeling as though I had a new girlfriend.

The seminar we shared was in Psychology in Education, a minor subject I'd taken on a whim. I don't remember much of the content apart from one piece of research where we'd stood in the centre of campus keeping a tally of the different ways in which males and females held their bags. It was a cold day, I felt uncomfortable and never gathered the reasons for doing it. Was our tutor taking the piss? Psychology in Education was something we had in common though, and before announcing that we were going out – not that I imagine anyone cared – we could claim to be studying together. While people from our course assumed we were analysing why 22% of men at Lancaster carried satchels as opposed to rucksacks, we were drinking tea, holding hands and kissing. The recklessness of young love.

As is the norm in the bubble of a university campus, our relationship rapidly gathered pace. I met her friends, who were a lovely bunch and introduced her to my own housemates, something I was anxious about. I hoped nothing would happen that would reflect badly on me. Would Julian evangelise her? Would Iestyn talk about the airport manager computer game? Louise came to meet us in Walkabout and seemed completely unfazed about the occasion, working her way around the group introducing herself. As I stood at the bar with Winston, requesting that he not mention the extent of our gambling habit, I saw that she was stood with Eric, one of my oddest housemates and, in fact, one of the oddest men I've ever met. I kept an eye on the situation and saw that Louise was listening intently to what he was saying, looking genuinely interested and giggling. I had never seen Eric talking to a girl before and felt a surge of warmth. In fact, it was more than that. Louise laughing at the likely questionable jokes cracked by a man-from-Accrington-with-a-huge-quiff-and-indecipherable-accent was the moment I realised I was in love.

The ensuing two months flew by in a whirl of romance, wine and entire days spent watching Friends on an ageing laptop and I was as happy as I can remember being. Sadly, this wasn't to last as Louise slung a spanner in the works.

"So, I'm moving to Australia for a year."

Not London or even France. Fucking Australia.

As we were saying our emotional farewells in a carpark on a dank and windy afternoon, my pal Rowan walked past, wearing his green hoody. He didn't realise what was going on.

"Hi, guys."

"Hi."

"Sorry, am I interrupting something?"

"Well…"

"Andy, I was thinking we could get Domino's and play some Mario Kart tonight?"

"Sure."

"Have you got the two for one pizza code?"

I looked over at Louise who had a tear rolling down her cheek. Rowan noticed, gave us a flat smile and walked off briskly. After Louise had got in a car and I'd watched it disappear out of sight, I was crestfallen. The fairylike of the last two months was over in the blink of an eye and I was on my own again. As I was trudging back to the flat, I decided that the best way to get through this was to drink heavily, all the time, for the remaining ten days of the year. This elaborate self-destruction caught the attention of my housemates and they seemed concerned. Being an attention-seeking, love-struck idiot, I suppose this was all I was aiming for.

26

Upset with the world, a holiday was in order. That summer a bunch of mates from Leeds were going to Zante for what sounded like a similar/identical holiday to Malia and Kavos. Eddie and I were in The Shoes one evening, discussing whether we should go or not. After recalling a night in Kavos where we'd been chased down the street by a maniacal Greek bouncer, we decided to give it the slip and instead use our student overdrafts for something more sophisticated – an inter-railing trip around Europe. Like me, Eddie had found love in his first year of university which influenced our decision. 19-20 happened to be a plum age for romance as Patrick and Rodney also met their future wives around this time. Were we more desirable now we'd travelled the world? Or, was our success because the four of us now lived in different cities from one another? Either way, Eddie and I now thought ourselves better equipped for museums and cappuccinos than bucking broncos and fishbowls.

Our first stop was Prague, a beautiful city home to some fine architecture and some of the world's best beers. We stayed in the Golden Sickle Hostel and by complete chance (meticulous planning?), Eddie's girlfriend, Felicity and her pal, Danielle happened to be staying at the same place. Within minutes of arriving, my travel companion and Felicity had disappeared to the dormitory so I found myself sat in the courtyard with Danielle, a girl I'd never met.

"Cigarette?" she asked.

"Sure."

She was affable and we settled into pleasant conversation until a ruffled Eddie and Felicity joined us half an hour later. Prague was good fun. We ambled through cobbled streets and over the Charles Bridge, went to cafes by the river and spent an evening in an enormous building which claimed to be home to "5 nightclubs in 1!" 5 is a lot of nightclubs, let me tell you. The morning after, feeling a little jaded, something both harrowing and ironic happened. We'd planned to see Bodies, the science exhibition where real human bodies have been dissected and put in glass cabinets, which was doing the rounds at the time. However, on the way to the museum, we saw a dead man. I don't know how he'd died but he was lying on the floor on a street corner with policemen stood around shooing people away. We followed their instruction, left the scene feeling depressed and opted against going to the Bodies exhibition. This was the second time I've seen a dead man – the first was in Leeds. I was on the way home from a long shift at the call centre when a man jumped off a building and landed right in front of my bus, causing the driver to slam on the brakes. This shook me up so I called my dad, explained the situation and asked if he could come and pick me up.

"Well, not really Andrew. I'm about to put tea on."

"Oh, ok. I guess I'll walk then."

At the Golden Sickle, we befriended a pair of unlikely travelling companions; Tim, a posh ginger-haired cameraman from Bristol and Hugo, a short Portuguese weed dealer. They'd met at university but didn't seem to get on particularly well and looked relieved when Eddie and I informed them we had a similar itinerary for the summer and we agreed to meet them later in the trip.

Keen to get to a beach, our next stop was Split, a place I knew nothing about other than that the football team Hajduk Split often features in the preliminary stages of European competition. I was also looking forward to taking advantage of the pun opportunities that the city offered. "I'm sick of this place, shall we split?"

Felicity, Danielle, Eddie and I arrived at sunrise. With us being carefree and adventurous/disorganised and shit, we hadn't booked anywhere to stay and went with our first offer at the train station which came from an elderly Greek-Croatian lady who couldn't speak English. We gathered that she lived close to the station through her pretending that her index finger and middle finger were legs; universal sign language.

It was a scorching morning and it took us a while to get to her house as we were carrying massive backpacks. I still hadn't mastered the backpack look. Is it possible? I doubt a man has ever wooed a woman while wearing a backpack. On the way, I noticed a man selling fake football shirts by the roadside. This was the summer that Thierry Henry had moved from Arsenal to Barcelona and my tired eyes lit up when I saw a passable replica of the new shirt at the front of his stall. We got back to the lady's flat which was up a non-descript, cobbled side-street. It was bit mildewy but pleasant enough – what you'd expect from an elderly Greek-Croatian lady, I suppose. As she was showing us our room and how to use the keys, I wasn't paying attention. I needed to get the Thierry Henry shirt.

I chucked my stuff on a mattress, took out twenty Euros from my money belt – again, not a cool look – and said I was going to explore. Eddie suggested we freshen up, get changed and venture out together but I was having none of it. My mind was focused on one thing only.

"I won't be long, just going for a quick stroll."

With the elderly woman still showing my companions the knack to locking the bathroom door, I skipped out of the flat, excited. Now, where was that football shirt man? I went with my heart and took a left, back the way we'd come. Or so I thought. After another left, a right and a long stretch along a dusty street, I still hadn't found the man and didn't recognise anything. I felt the first wave of panic and tried to fend it off. It will be fine, I'll find the man, have a shower and be at the beach while Croatian ladies give my new football shirt admiring glances in an hour's time, I told myself. Easy. Today is going to be a good day.

I went back the way I'd come but must have made a subtle error as I found myself by the side of a busy dual carriageway. I know if you find a river, you are meant to be okay, how about a dual carriageway? If I follow it, will it take me back to the generic flat on in the winding back streets of a suburb of Split, a city that I have never been to? A city which I had spent more time thinking up puns about than looking at maps of?

Why didn't I get a card from the woman with an address on? At least then, a taxi means safety. I was annoyed with myself. What an idiot. The morning sun was beating down. I was dripping with sweat. I stomped along the side of the dual carriageway until I found myself at a grand building surrounded by wide steps. I imagine it held some historical significance but as a lost and scared twenty-year-old, this wasn't a priority. What the hell are you supposed to do here? With most problems, you can think; this is shit, but I know what I have to do to resolve it. There is protocol. Lost in a European city with just a twenty Euro note on you, no phone and no address to go to, what is the protocol? Is there one?

I sat down, put my head in my hands for a while and considered my plight. I was lost. With Louise in Australia and me unsure what the heck I was doing with my life, I was both figuratively and metaphorically lost. Right, pull yourself together. Don't be shit, just retrace your steps. It will be fine. I started walking. After what felt like an hour, I still hadn't seen anything that I recognised. This wasn't good. I changed my game plan. If I go back to that big, possibly-famous building and wait, someone will surely come and rescue me? This was, of course, flawed logic. Last time I was there, I'd felt so lost that I wanted to cry.

I turned again and headed down a side street, which I expected would take me back to the steps. More side-streets, dammit. The city was a labyrinth. My heart began pounding and sweat was rushing down my temples. I ran my hands through my hair and looked to the sky in despair. In the corner of my eye, a man was approaching. He looked like Eddie. Was this a mirage? No, it was him. Thank God. How had he managed to find me?

"Alright, Andy," he said. "You ready for the beach then?"

He was calm. Unfazed. Had I been overreacting? I was shaking.

"I got a bit lost I think, I was starting to panic a bit."

"The flat's just up there. You've been gone for about twenty minutes."

"Really?"

"Yes, I've just had a quick shower. Come on, let's go to the beach."

My heart rate dropped. I wasn't going to become homeless on the mean streets of Split after all. I wasn't going to

dehydrate and die on the side of the dual carriageway.
Everything was okay. Hurray. I turned to Eddie.

"I don't suppose you saw the guy selling football shirts?"

***

We had three good days on the beach in Split before splitting
from the girls once again and moving onto Solta, one of the
islands, with Hugo and Tim. Here we played football on a
dusty pitch and went net fishing with limited success. I've
never got fishing. Dylan, a keen fisherman once invited
Rodney and me to join him for a day out. We set off in
darkness and arrived to sit by a cold pond at 6am. Dylan told
me and Rodney off for talking and was angry at us for bringing
a flask of whisky.

"You're not taking it seriously, guys."

And so we sat, in silence, for eight hours. I think I caught
two small fish. Perhaps the appeal will come to me later in life?
After leaving the island, Tim and Hugo fell out although the
reasons were hazy – Facebook had just been invented and I
think a derisory status update may have been a flashpoint. Tim
headed to Italy while Hugo came with Eddie and I to Budapest.
We stayed in an old lady's spare room on the "Pest" side of the
Danube and spent a day at the royal baths, where attractive
European ladies were sadly outnumbered by hard-faced men
with militant hairdos in Speedos. Much alike my mishap in
Split, the three of us got hopelessly lost one afternoon as we
tried to get back to the flat, eventually spotting a familiar statue
which saved us from a night on the streets as dusk was falling.
For reasons unknown, we spent most of our time hanging
around at the Mammut centre, a generic shopping plaza. None
of us had much money and even if we did, we had little interest
in shopping. One evening I got chatting to a long-haired
Bosnian man in an outdoor bar. He was a nice enough guy, if a
bit intense, and conversation ranged from grim tales about his
war-torn country's past to Edin Dzeko's goalscoring record at
Wolfsburg. We left to move on to a nightclub on the top floor
of the Mammut centre but on the way, the Bosnian stopped in
his tracks.

"No! No!" He shouted.

"What's up, buddy?" I asked, fearing something was seriously wrong.

"I've left my phone in the bar!"

"Oh, okay. If you go back someone might have handed it in?" I helpfully suggested.

Despairing, he put his head in his hands. Was he crying?

"Go without me, I beg you," he said, as though we were leaving him to perish in battle, not heading to an Irish-themed bar. And so marked the end of a brief friendship.

We went to the Spirit of Sziget festival on a giant island in between Buda and Pest and saw an eclectic bunch of bands ranging from Razorlight, who were in their fleeting heyday, and Faithless who were outstanding. The festival was brilliant although we couldn't afford a tent and my master plan of staying up all night to save on accommodation was thwarted by a day of beer and goulash causing drowsiness circa 1am. As Eddie bounded to the dance tent I fell asleep inside a giant tyre.

We'd had grand plans to visit Italy and Germany but after checking our bank balances had to get a train straight through to Amsterdam, our final port of call. We brought our return flight forward and went home earlier than planned. Much earlier. The trip had been supposed to last five weeks but we were Leeds-bound after fifteen days. We'd celebrated our poor planning by spending a woeful final day in Amsterdam where we sat in a coffee shop and smoked a strong skunk joint early in the morning before spending the rest of the day, not talking to one another, a bit scared of everything. We tried to take the edge off by spending the last of our funds and concluding hours of our momentous, once-in-a-lifetime inter-railing adventure, watching Die Hard 4 in a multiplex cinema.

27

Instead of exploring Rome and Munich I spent the last few weeks of summer back at Headingley Stadium serving overpriced Carlsberg in plastic cups to inebriated cricket fans. I didn't mind it and it was fun working with Rodney, although he was much more popular among the managers and soon given a prestigious blue shirt, meaning he was effectively my manager, even though we'd started within days of one another.

In October, I returned to Lancaster for my second year. There had been confusion and controversy surrounding housing arrangements. I'd ummed and ahhed about moving into a shared house in town with Rowan, Karen and a couple of others, before pulling the plug last minute and opting to stay on campus with some friends from the C team. Karen joined us but following threats from an aggressive landlord with a receding hairline, Rowan had signed the tenancy agreement for the house and was tied in. The rooms in the house that Karen and I left vacant were taken by staunch Christian Union members. One of whom was thirty-four, balding and worked at KFC. He claimed to have several girlfriends concurrently which didn't seem conducive to his faith. Had he mixed Christianity up with Mormonism? Did the girlfriends exist? He didn't smell great so I thought it improbable. The other was also odd, once urinating in a bottle and leaving it on the kitchen table for days, Howard Hughes-esque.

I felt bad about selling Rowan out, although this had never been my intention. I'm just indecisive. He spent most of his time at our flat on campus anyway which eased my guilt, and we found ourselves in a small but strong group, going out most evenings and spending our days sitting in the kitchen, occasionally venturing out to play headers and volleys. Along with Jamie and I, our core group consisted of Duncan, a giant

Scot with a surreal sense of humour, Greg, a stocky gym-goer and talented cook from Blyth and Karen, who probably questioned her decision to live with us when, on the first night, we began a penalty shootout competition in the corridor. Our flat had occasional cameos from a pair of Charlton fans, one of whom had a chequered past including unconfirmed rumours of an arrest for arson. Spending so much time together, we became ensconced in our own world, rarely mingling with outside folk. With many of these hours spent drunk or in the discomfort, delirium and sporadic euphoria that comes with hangovers, we talked nonsense for hours on end, discussing anything and everything.

Despite the friendships I'd formed and the fun I was having, Louise lived in Melbourne. This was not fun. We spoke most days on Skype but this only made me miss her more and despise modern technology. The beeping of an incoming call on Skype still makes me shudder. The time difference was a hindrance; as I was arriving home from a centurion drinking challenge, Louise was strolling to her morning seminars. I was keen for a sentimental, Dawson's Creek-type chat or a raging argument but she wanted neither.

Similarly, when I was arising and she told me she was going on a night out, I found myself envious of her companions.

"Who are you going with?" I'd ask, through gritted teeth, feeling pangs of hatred if men's names were mentioned. I'd never been much of a jealous guy but now I was. Jealous of faceless names I would never meet, thousands of miles away.

I was unsure about our status. She was away for a year. A whole year. Was I single during this time? "It's complicated" on Facebook? (Did anyone ever use that?) At any rate, I wasn't sure how to behave. Late one evening, I was lying on my bed staring at my ceiling and listening to a reggae compilation, when a girl in first year knocked at my door with a bottle of rose wine asking if she could come in. She was attractive but it didn't feel right and nothing happened. It would have felt like a betrayal. I would later find out that the girl had a rare addiction to eating sponges so this was, perhaps, a lucky escape. I doubt I was mentally strong enough to have been able to deal with that. And I value my sponges – useful items.

Towards the end of the term Louise called saying that she had a surprise. I'm not one for surprises and just wanted her to tell me what it was. My guesses ranged from a Melbourne Victory football shirt in the post to a toy possum. It was neither. She was coming home for Christmas. This was magnificent news.

She arrived in the last week of term and I went to meet her at Lancaster train station. I showered, put on some aftershave, gelled my hair and, for reasons unknown, put on a baggy grey sweatshirt. As I waited at the station, my mind was racing. Excited and agitated. I couldn't keep still, pacing up and down the platform, guzzling a bottle of room-temperature Dr Pepper which brought on indigestion. What if she wasn't like what I remembered? What if she'd gone off me? Notwithstanding fuzzy pixelated Skype images, I hadn't seen her in six months and now she was going to be standing in front of me within minutes.

The train pulled in, hissing and screeching and, as I saw her getting off, I felt my heart fluttering. I was full of joy. I jogged over to her and we hugged and kissed, damp-eyed. I was exceptionally happy. After emotions had died down, Louise pointed at my jumper.

"You sure know how to impress a girl, don't you? What the hell is that?"

I needn't have worried about anything. Aside from bronze skin and lighter hair, she hadn't changed at all. How it was between us was, if anything, better than I'd remembered. All the angst, all the waiting, all the phone bills and off-kilter drunken calls had been worth it. It was all worth it.

We arrived back at my flat, where the girl who ate sponges had put bottle of imitation champagne on ice for us (she'd soon got over me and had been sighted at a recent party leaning on a fridge freezer with her hand down a friend's jeans). I introduced Louise to Greg and Duncan, who she didn't know, and they hit it off even if she thought I acted weird when in their company.

"You lot don't half talk some shit," she said to me having endured a long conversation between us as to who would be best equipped to win a footrace to the end of a rainbow. At the end of term came our Christmas Ball, a glitzy affair held at the

Hilton in Blackpool. Louise was wearing a new purple frock and had done something intricate with her ponytail. She looked splendid. Sat on the bus with an Asda George suit on, gel in my hair and a glamorous girl on my arm, I felt like the man. Sadly, moments of self-satisfaction rarely last long and just outside Poulton-under-Fylde, things quite literally unravelled.

Louise bent forward to grab some mascara out of her bag and, in a flash, her dress ripped down the back.

"Andy!"

She was scowling. Was she blaming me? I'd been looking out the window, drinking a can of Strongbow. Surely a sound alibi? A resourceful friend, who'd come well equipped for this kind of thing, had safety pins and Sellotape on her. This at least kept the dress together but with glimmering silver spikes, and large patches of skin showing, the effect was diminished somewhat.

"This has ruined everything," Louise said as we walked into the hotel. I disagreed, trying to make a joke out of it. There was no laugh. Annoyed, I foolishly used the word "irrational," which instigated some sharp words, and muffled bickering throughout a frosty dinner. After we'd eaten, a man in his fifties in a tuxedo crooned some old swing songs. He had a superb voice and as Louise and I were dancing, the magic of the evening was reignited. As long as I couldn't see her back, that is. Later, Duncan and I saw the singer wearing a hotel staff t-shirt, pushing a trolley with filthy plates and cutlery on it. What was that about? soul singer/pot-wash is an unusual job combination. Did it affect his hourly rate?

Towards the end of the night Louise and I went outside. Ever the cliché, I'd bought some cigars and wanted her to witness me smoking one. The fact your suit jacket is too small and the sleeves ride high up your arms is inconsequential when you are smoking a cigar. As I was lighting it, a tall man wearing trendy glasses shouted to his friend.

"Look, that girl's dress is fucked!"

I pretended I hadn't heard and said nothing. The man had a loud voice. I had definitely heard.

"Why didn't you stand up for me?" Louise said, red-faced, back in the hotel.

"What did you want me to do? Have a fistfight?"

Given the volume of port that had been drunk, the ensuing argument had little structure.

"Smoking cigars doesn't suit you. You look stupid."

"Who's that guy you always talk about in Melbourne? I hate that dickhead."

For a long time, we trawled the hotel floors locked in a passionate and incoherent dispute until, exhausted, we slumped down and sat on the floor in a lift.

"Sorry," I said. "It's not been our night, has it?"

"No, I'm sorry too."

We laughed. In the grand scheme of things, this wasn't so bad, was it?

"Hang on, what's the time?" Louise asked.

I glanced down at my watch to see it was 12.59am. The last bus was at 1am. We sprinted outside just in time to see the packed bus turning the corner and driving into the cold, dark night. Following a long, silent wait in the hotel foyer and a three-figure taxi fare, we made it back to my room from the Christmas ball at 3.30am, vowing not to let it ruin Louise's time back in England.

Ever the jet setter, Louise and her family spent Christmas in America. I missed her but enjoyed the festive period at home nonetheless. On Christmas Eve, as was tradition, I went to the Original Oak, which always hosts a nostalgic congregation of old friends, acquaintances and foes. As most people are in a cheery mood/drunk, you always find yourself talking to an interesting cross section of your past and present. Or being cornered by someone who you never really got on with as they tell you about how they have smashed their targets and earned a bonus, before waiting for you to get a round in.

"Grab us a sambuca as well, Andy, yeah?"

Christmas Eve is the only day of the year when I see Seamus, the dapper chin scratcher from primary school, and he and I have an odd tradition. Circa 1994 we used to play a crap football game on his Sega Mega Drive. Once there was a malfunction in his game and the commentator said some peculiar things that made no sense. When we see each other on Christmas Eve we repeat these commentator glitches, scratch our chins, then walk on. That's it. No small talk. I have absolutely no idea what he is doing with his life.

After the pub, despite not being religious – a fair-weather church goer – I went to midnight mass at St Chad's with my family. My brother had been in the pub since lunchtime. When the vicar told us to turn around and shake hands with the people on the row behind you and wish them a Merry Christmas, John took this seasonal cheer to a new level. Behind him was a young lady who smelt of mulled wine and, after shaking hands, they started kissing. He'd pulled in a church. Is that acceptable?

After a few shifts at Headingley cricket ground I was relatively flush and had bought some decent presents for my family, including a Leeds United shirt for John. In return, wrapped in A4 printer paper, he'd got me a can of Red Bull. I don't like Red Bull. Christmas Day was as you'd expect; eating and drinking to excess before playing the game where you put post-it's on your head for one too many rounds before slumping on the sofa, watching people die in EastEnders.

***

When Louise returned we booked Jet 2 flights to Paris where we stayed in a two-star hotel with a broken lift and damp wallpaper. It was my first holiday with a woman other than my mother and it was brilliant; a romantic four days in a wonderful city. The only hitch came on the final night when we went for dinner at a Michelin starred restaurant on the Champs Elysees. With our relationship still in its embryonic stage, I was keen to impress, so had worked a couple of extra shifts at Headingley over Christmas in order to fund a posh dinner. Sadly, I'd blasted most of my budget buying drinks for an American exchange student clad in a basketball vest on our first night and was left stunned when the bill came to 180 euros. I had a lot less than this.

"Louise, I don't suppose you've got any spare euros?"

After scrabbling around, between us we had 185 euros. I thought no tip was less insulting than 5 euros and was on the receiving end of filthy looks from the restaurant staff as I walked out with my head bowed, seven courses of rich food churning in my beer-bloated stomach.

Shortly after we got back, Louise was away to Melbourne again. Our time together had passed in the blink of an eye. These magical days together did, however, confirm that the long-distance tosh was worth sticking out and we decided that we were going to make it official. No ambiguity, no grey areas, no asking girls for their phone numbers then feeling guilty (on the rare occasions they said yes – was guilt necessary if the answer was no?) A proper relationship. And so it was, for the first time since I was fifteen, I had a girlfriend. If I could just hold on for five months I'd have a girlfriend living in the same hemisphere as me. With relationship status clarified, and the fact that her time abroad was halfway through, I was not quite so devastated as the first time she'd gone; crestfallen, just less so.

The second and third term at University carried on where the preceding one had left off. Rowan hosted a Sunday morning radio show and allowed us to co-host on occasion, which was fun. At the time, I thought we were witty, entertaining DJs although if I listened back now, I don't know if this would be the case. It would probably be similar to listening back to Falling with Superman's CD.

We became keen watchers of wildlife videos on YouTube and continued to spend most of our time sitting in the kitchen talking gibberish. On one occasion when we were discussing the world's first Liliger (a crossbreed between a Ligress and a Lion), Karen, who is patient and agreeable, stood up and said. "I'm going back to my room, I can't stand this anymore," giving the door a hard slam on her way out.

Our social isolation became apparent one evening when we were chatting with the guys who lived below us, who we sometimes knocked around with.

"What are you guys up to tonight then?"

"Quiet one tonight, lads. We're going to stay in and take it easy."

A couple of hours later we heard music and laughter blaring from their flat and at 10pm, taxis pulled up and they jostled out of the building, singing a Kaiser Chiefs song and drinking cans of Carling. We'd been shunned.

The only time that there was any hostility among the four of us came during the period after Greg had been called up to play for the A team. His promotion was deserved – he was the best football player among us by a distance – however, it didn't prevent Duncan and I sharing glances with one another when he gave us an extensive match report or talked about something funny one of his new teammates had said. Any fallout didn't last long though and as second year slipped into its final few weeks, I was aware that it had been a special time.

My exams went fine and were finished nearly a month before we broke up for summer, leaving a sweet window of frivolousness. During a beautiful summer's day, I enjoyed one of my greatest sporting glories; calmly converting a dubious penalty past a bespectacled goalkeeper in a 4-1 win over our rivals as hundreds of people gathered around the pitch. That the vast majority were drinking and having barbeques, showing zero interest in the match, is by the by. While these carefree weeks were great fun, there was a tinge of sadness as Greg and Duncan were going to France and London respectively for their third years and the Charlton fans were graduating. It had been a one-year wonder. Unlike many people you meet in your twenties where you promise to stay in touch knowing that you'll never see one another again, I knew that this would be different and was certain that the group of us would remain friends long after the end of term parties had finished. Besides, it wasn't all bad. My girlfriend was coming home.

I met Rodney and some of his university mates down in London for a couple of days before reuniting with Louise in Kent. One of Rodney's pals; a tall, odd Russian with haunting blue eyes was also getting the train to Kent to see his family. I liked him but didn't know him very well and for reasons unknown, he was wearing fake sleeve tattoos on both of his forearms. I just wanted to be alone, gather my thoughts and calm myself down before seeing my girlfriend for the first time in months. I didn't want to be making small talk with a Russian man wearing fake sleeve tattoos.

"Shall I get off at your stop and meet Louise?"

"Absolutely not."

"Oh go on Andy, it will be funny."

"Why will it be funny?"

"It just will. How about if you wear one of my tattoos. She'll find that hilarious."

"No, she won't. Please get off at your stop."

He reluctantly agreed and got off at Rye, leaving me alone for the reunion. I felt lightheaded with nerves and excitement as I got off the train and found a grinning Louise waiting for me on the platform. We were back together and this was excellent.

28

The summer that followed represented a rare period of financial responsibility. Louise had come to stay at mine in Leeds and we wanted to go on holiday together. Having barely worked during two idle years at university – six to eight hours per week of lectures left me far too exhausted for a part time job – I was cash poor. Louise, to her credit, had worked as a waitress but spent most of her wages on frocks and wine. Student loans drained, we needed to earn our holiday.

This was pre-credit crunch so fortunately jobs – albeit crap ones – were readily available. A bubbly recruitment consultant found a "great opportunity" for the pair of us; a customer service role for a bank. AKA: a call centre. The wounds from my call centre past had just about healed and with the prospect of lying on a lilo with a Pina Colada in hand at the end of it, we accepted the offer and started training the following Monday.

We'd decided it might be annoying if we were publicly a couple from the outset so sat a few seats away from one another, among our new colleagues. As is usually the case, the training group was a mishmash of fifteen-or-so folk who would never have been seen together in any other context. It included a nervous man close to sixty, a mouthy teenage lad and a handful of middle-aged ladies, one of whom was possibly-but-not-definitely pregnant. I sat in between a hooded rapper from Bradford and a dreadlocked oddball who I'd known, and actively avoided when we were in college.

"Hi, Andy, what you been up to?"

What, in the three years since we last saw one another? Did he want a précis? I didn't want to encourage him too much. We might end up as pod buddies.

"Oh, you know, this and that."

He told me, in depth, what he'd been up to; two tough breakups and lots of gigs. Metal bands I'd never heard of. The first couple of days of training were your standard online courses and group brainstorming sessions.

"What makes great customer service? In your groups, you have an hour to create a presentation."

An hour? Are you fucking kidding?

The training was punctured by agonising lunch breaks in the canteen.

"So, what did you make of the money laundering course?"

"It was alright. I see you like gravy with your chips?"

I found it difficult not to communicate with Louise at all and we found ourselves chatting to break the monotony. I must have looked like one smooth customer. Or did my peers see me as a sleazebag, homing in on the only woman below forty in our group?

On Wednesday, we discovered what our role entailed. We were going to be upgrading customers from telephone to online banking. Hurray. We learned the crux of the job through a series of laborious tutorials about the system – an eighties DOS-style nonsense. Our course leader, a rotund woman in her thirties and a ten-year call centre stalwart informed us there would be a test on Friday and handed out revision manuals to take home.

Homework? I didn't see the hourly rate as deserving of unpaid overtime and with an air of arrogance, boasted to Louise that I was not going to open the book.

"I'll still pass. How hard can it be?"

Louise has only failed one test ever – a French vocab test in Year 9 which still haunts her – and she diligently opened the book to write and re-write formulas using the AltGr button. What the hell is that button?

"I think you should look through it at least, Andy," she said, scribbling furiously.

"You've got to be joking?" I smirked, my eyes fixed on a Channel 5 Van Damme film.

"There's a lot to remember, it's quite hard."

"Don't be daft."

"Go on then, genius, how do you open the page to send confirmation letters to customers?"

"Fine, I'll look through it."

I was glad I did. We did the test before lunchtime. It was sat in exam conditions and tension was high. The papers were marked during our lunch break and when we returned, group numbers had visibly thinned. Six, including the mouthy teenage lad and the shy sixty-year-old, had not returned.

"So," the trainer began after five minutes of muted chatter and puzzled expressions. "You may have noticed that some of the team are not here. Unfortunately, they didn't meet the requirements and we've had to let them go."

Brutal.

"Looking at the positives, give yourselves a pat on the back. You'll be going LIVE this afternoon!"

Try as she might, her enthusiasm was not contagious. The empty space where Darius used to sit was too much. We got our test papers back and I learned that I'd passed by one mark. Had I not copied Louise's answers, I too would have been walking. I'd narrowly escaped humiliation. If I'd been dismissed, what would Louise have done? Leave with me? Leave me? Would the holiday have been off? It didn't bear thinking about.

The job itself was predictably dreary. Answer an endless flow of calls from people predominantly of bus pass age, and talk them through changing from telephone to online banking, to a flurry of fluster and frustration.

"Why do you need to know my mother's maiden name? What's it got to do with you?"

Once calls were complete we posted letters confirming the "migration." No need for such a fancy word. The target was to migrate eighty customers a day. With our relationship still a secret, Louise and I sat together, which made things bearable. The sharing of a glance or shaking of a head went a long way.

During the second week, there was a fight in the canteen. One of the participants – a well-dressed Asian guy with spiky hair – had been in my training group and seemed affable. Following a heated discussion about his professionalism – he'd been playing an online game, where you had to park a car in tight spots while on calls – a shoving match began with a balding guy who wore a sleeveless cardigan. He'd been at the call centre for a while.

"Yeah, start a fight," said sleeveless cardigan. "That just proves my point, doesn't it? Very professional."

That did it. My training buddy smacked him in the face, catching him below the eye. The fight was swiftly broken up by a retired policeman team leader, who clearly enjoyed a return to action. As my training buddy was escorted away, never to be seen again, sleeveless cardigan stood clutching his face.

"See what I mean?" he said, holding back tears. "I told you he was unprofessional."

It was hard to disagree. During the third week, it got out that Louise and I were together. How this had happened, I don't know. The way we looked at one another? A smoking area kiss caught on CCTV? A floorwalker discreetly motioned for us to remove our headsets and idled over.

"Can I have a word with you two in my pod?"

We obediently followed and pulled up seats.

"So, it's become apparent that you two are an item."

Apparent? Had someone seen us holding hands on the bus? A rat? Should I be treating my colleagues with suspicion?

"Don't take this personally but one of you is going to have to move teams."

"Really? But we've consistently hit our targets?" I pleaded. This was true. Indeed, the previous week, we'd topped the figures charts. That it later transpired I'd been doing the job wrong was incidental.

"It's not fair on your team," the floorwalker said gravely. "Andy, do you mind joining my team? There is a space now."

This was the space vacated by the well-dressed fighter. It was next to the annoying dreadlocked guy. I minded.

"Fine."

"Okay, great. Thanks for being reasonable." She said. "Teammate."

Louise was scowling and mouthed, "fucking ridiculous" to me.

"Also," the floorwalker began, "I think it would be best if you didn't take your breaks at the same time."

I've never understood the logic behind making a miserable job more miserable. Why? The days that followed were bleak. I sat in silence on the bus each morning, giving Louise short shrift if she wanted conversation. After work, we had nothing to say to one another. "How was your day?" didn't cut it. A team leader listened into my calls, one of which I handled badly – "people can hear a smile, Andy" – and lunchtime with the dreadlocked guy was considerably worse than lunchtime with a girl I loved.

"Fancy coming to a gig tonight, Andy?"

"No."

After four weeks, enough was enough and we called time.

"But you'd said you were in it for the long haul?" Our recruitment consultant said, seeing her commission – possibly a new dress? – slipping through her fingers. We had, at least, saved up the money for a week-long stay in Tenerife and barring an ill-judged bus tour of the island, where the average age was seventy, it was excellent. I remain unconvinced that four bad weeks for one good one is a fair trade off though. With that said, the 5:2 ratio of a working week is not much better, is it?

29

For reasons I can't remember, I arrived a few days late for my final year at Lancaster. I felt a knot in my stomach as my mum dropped me off to live in a small white box in student halls for a third successive year. With Greg, Duncan and the Charlton fans now departed, gone was the optimism of the past two years. Aside from Rowan and Julian, who were back like Louis Walsh and Sharon Osbourne on the X Factor, I didn't know who I'd be living with. You'd have thought I would have amassed enough friends by third year to avoid living with strangers, wouldn't you?

I bid my mum farewell and walked into my flat to hear music booming from the kitchen. I popped my head around the door to see ten or so strangers drinking and chatting animatedly. A kid in a backwards cap nodded at me as though he was doing me a favour. What was his game? Why were there so many people here? Why did they all look so young?

"Hi," I said. "I'm just going to…you know," I pointed towards my rucksack, as if this was an explanation, and hastily left.

Rowan must have heard my muted arrival and was stood in the corridor.

"What hell is this?" I asked.

"We've been put with Freshers," he said gloomily. "I've got some ales in the kitchen, will you go and grab them?"

"Can't you do it?"

I dropped my bags in my room then joined Rowan in his. He'd plucked up the courage to fetch the drinks and emerged from the party zone looking fraught.

"It's horrible, Andy," he said, taking a long sip. "They are all really young and giddy. And loud. Very loud."

This makes me sound a miserable bastard – perhaps I am? – but I just hadn't got the energy for this anymore. For the first time in my life, I felt old. I'm fully aware that, at twenty-two, this sounds absurd. In life terms, twenty-two is fledgling, but as an undergraduate on a university campus, it's over the hill. I was four years older than the Freshers. I no longer had any desire to say "safe," to guys in high-top trainers, listen to drum and bass, or play, "I have never..." in a futile attempt to show off to girls from Surrey.

I met my flatmates over the coming days and barring a thin, moping guy who didn't talk at all and ate nothing but cheese on toast, they were chirpy enough. In one of life's mysteries, a girl I lived with referred to the thin, moping guy as a "legend!" on a night out without a hint of irony. St George slew a dragon to acquire legendary status, what had this guy done? How was this so? What changed? Or did he just feel no need to impress me? I didn't dislike any of these lot, they were just significantly younger than me. I'd done some calculations and worked out that when I was going to Dust, they were still in primary school. We were never going to be friends.

At football trials, I was nutmegged by a kid who looked twelve and when we ventured to The Sugarhouse nightclub, I stood in a corner with Rowan drinking beer after beer and romanticizing the time when we were bright eyed and bushy tailed, although, after discussion, we concluded that perhaps this had never been the case.

I'd had a niggling feeling I would feel this way but felt under pressure to enjoy the year which was potentially my last of little responsibility. The call centre had been a worrying glimpse into what post-university life held in store and even if I secured a 2.1, I was aware that my degree was unlikely to catapult me to instant megabucks.

"Did you say sociology and criminology combined honours, sir? What are your wage demands? What kind of company car are you after?"

It wasn't all doom and gloom as Louise was back. In her first year, she'd landed in a dream hall of similar-aged, likeminded girls, and she effortlessly resumed her friendship with them. They were a nice group and didn't say things like:

"He literally shit in my face!" which we overheard one of my flatmates saying during a drunken spat about tickets to a bar. I spent much of my time at Louise's which may have been to the chagrin of her housemates at times. Post football, sweaty shin pads and shorts strewn on the landing while I used their shower must have been irritating. I like to think we got on well regardless.

In my first term, some friends from Leeds came through. Merging different groups is always tricky – a skill I've never mastered – and these visits were not without incident. First up were Johnno, Dom and Kirk who lived together. All of them had gone straight into full-time work after school and decided to take a week off to tour the country, visiting as many friends' universities as they could although when they arrived at Lancaster, they were visibly jaded following a debauched night with Eddie in Manchester. After a few beers, Dom perked up and was in the middle of telling a fairly atrocious story when one of the freshers, a flamboyant drama student wearing pink pyjamas walked in

"Um, who are you?" she asked.

"More to the point, who are you?" Dom said, before continuing with his story.

Not dignifying him with an answer, she opened the fridge door.

"Where are my yoghurts?"

Johnno and Kirk had eaten her yoghurts.

"I don't know," I said trying not to make eye contact with the pair of them who were on the verge of exploding with laughter. She continued to potter around emitting that quiet anger that women are so good as Dom, oblivious to this, told the punchline of his story.

She was appalled.

"I'm going back to my room."

Slammed door.

Dylan came through for an evening and went down well with my housemates initially. However, we lost one another on the night out and he spent the early hours roaming corridors pounding on doors, which didn't go down well. The following morning, having had two hours of sleep and shaking life a leaf, I had my first ever driving lesson. It was terrifying.

Rodney and Matt were my final guests and were polite and friendly for the most part. I do, however, have vague memories of Rodney running around naked outside, claiming that he had lost a bet. It later transpired that there had never been a bet. There had been no reason for his nakedness.

***

During my final year I was a victim of identity theft. I'd got to know a guy in one of my seminars following a rapport built on mutual cluelessness about the module. While our peers held heated discussion about the pros and cons of communism, he and I would share comforting, "I also have no idea what is going on," glances. One thing led to another and we soon found ourselves going for lunch or a coffee together after the seminar to discuss important issues such as which girls on the course we found attractive.

On one occasion, we went for a pint after a late lecture. It was one of those pints that make you want to drink several more pints, so we decided to go for a night out. The only snag was he was wearing unsuitable clothing, even for a student haunt – a polystyrene running t-shirt, if memory serves me correct. Ever the problem solver, I devised a plan whereby we could go back to my halls of residence nearby and I could lend him one of my shirts.

A few others joined us and we had a standard night at the student union, drinking bright-coloured sugary drinks in plastic cups and struggling with the age-old conundrum of trying to show that you have a sense of humour but are also cool when the Baywatch theme comes on. Up until this point, all fine. A new friendship formed, nothing strange about it.

The next time the guy and I went for a pint after a lecture, "Last Nite" by The Strokes came on in the pub. He turned to me and said, "I prefer "Heart in a Cage." That's the best Strokes song, Andy." You'd be forgiven for thinking this a negligible comment – nothing too unusual. However, "Heart in a Cage" happens to be my favourite Strokes song and I was certain I'd told him this during our night out. I tried to brush it off. Must be a coincidence?

In the ensuing days and weeks there were more incidents, which may have seemed like nothing on their own, but together unnerved me; a subtle change of hairstyle, an impression of a lecturer straight out of my repertoire, ordering Kronenburg, not Carlsberg like he had the first time we'd been for a pint. Things escalated when me, the guy and a few others were talking about the computer game, Championship Manager. He addressed the group with a tale about his friend from home who had allegedly put on a smart suit when he had reached the FA Cup final. Everybody laughed apart from me. I felt a chill go down my spine. I'd told him this. It was my story. I know this because I'd stolen the story from someone else.

The final straw came when I was walking across campus and I bumped into him. He was wearing the shirt I'd lent him all those weeks ago. He didn't seem embarrassed at all, didn't even mention it. Not on. Give me my shirt back. The guy's collection of anecdotal tales is probably out now.

***

It wasn't such a bad year in the end. Different to my previous two in many respects but similar in others. I had fewer friends but still played football, went to the pub with Rowan and Karen and occasionally went out, though the three nightclubs that Lancaster offered were wearing a little thin by now. I spent most evenings with Louise whose job as a waitress at the campus hotel allowed us free access to the swimming pool and gym. With saunas and outdoor Jacuzzis, this was an undeserved treat for me although one afternoon I had a slice of bad luck. Louise had talked me into trying aqua aerobics and I foolishly agreed. The group was predictably dominated by women in their sixties and seventies while a middle-aged instructor, who still believed she was nineteen, roared out instructions over a too-loud Jason Derulo track. In spite of this, I found myself enjoying it and as I joined in the exercises, the weightlessness in the water gave me a great sense of wellbeing. Unfortunately, the girlfriend of a guy on my football team also worked at the hotel and, as I was jogging on the spot with my hands in the air, she walked into the swimming pool area.

"Andy?"

"Please can you not mention this to anyone?"

The year flew by and it was soon the Easter holidays. Without wishing to sound arrogant (pre-cursor to sounding a *bit* arrogant), I'd found my degree straightforward. My A-Levels had been more challenging and cost roughly £30,000 less. However, with dissertation deadlines and exams to revise for, as the final term loomed, I was feeling a bit of pressure.

To take a break from my study schedule I took the final Saturday of the holidays off to go to watch Leeds vs Tranmere with Rodney and Dylan. That morning I'd been awarded a £30 free bet by a generous online bookmaker and splashed it on a five-fold accumulator. Leeds won 3-1 and, as the rest of the scores came through on the vidiprinter, I realised that I was £350 richer. This instigated a day of wild celebrations and the three of us had a wonderful time hopping from bar to bar, drinking fancier-than-usual drinks. We ended the night in the Academy, a huge club that had taken over the premises of my old favourite, Creation, which had allegedly shut down after a man had been found inside with a shotgun. With this kind of story, the differences between truth and urban myth are often paper thin. If you believe the rumours, a man once snuck a crossbow into Stinky's Peephouse. I wonder if he had a dance?

I digress. It was a great night but by 2am I was exhausted and made a French exit, leaving Dylan and Rodney dancing to a Skrillex track while I snuck out the side door. It was chaotic outside and I couldn't hail a taxi, so made the decision to walk the three miles home, thinking it would clear my head and ease my impending hangover. It was, however, unseasonably cold and by the time I'd got to Hyde Park corner, the bitter bite in the air had become excruciating. The pavements were becoming icy but, desperate to get home, I broke into a jog.

Picking up the pace on a downhill stretch I lost my footing and took a spectacular tumble. My inebriation hampered my reaction times so much that I failed to put my hands out and face-planted a kerb, leaving me semi-conscious with a bust nose and my front two teeth no longer attached to my mouth. I lay shivering on the freezing pavement for a long time until a group of students saw me, helped me to my feet and assisted me in hobbling all the way home where I burst through the front door, covered in blood.

"I've lost my teeth!" I shouted.

A fun night for everyone involved. The next morning, I woke up with a splitting headache and touched the gap where my front teeth had been to confirm that this had actually happened. I looked at my battered, scabbed, toothless face in the mirror and was close to tears. How had I managed to do this to myself? What an idiot. My mum and dad consoled me while ringing around emergency dentists to see if I could get in.

Louise was already in Lancaster but, having spoken to my dad, she got on the next train to Leeds. She came up to my room and hugged me while, once again, I fought back tears. Apart from the teeth, which didn't grow back and required falsies, the wounds were superficial and soon healed and I returned to university. The final term was fine. I got a 2.1, Louise a 1st and three years at Lancaster came to a glorious end at a Graduation Ball headlined by Alisha Dixon and a band from Sheffield who had once supported The Arctic Monkeys. After twenty-two years, my education was over. Time to see what the world of work had in store. My expectations were lukewarm.

30

Louise agreed to move to Leeds and we had a stint back at my parents' house. Louise gets along great with my parents but trying to find our feet was tough. We soon discovered, if you excuse the overused graduate cliché, that "real life" was a bit shit. There was no round-the-world trip at the end of the tunnel, nor was there the university safety net. To rub it in, the recession had smacked so finding any kind of work was nigh on impossible. Degree in sociology or otherwise.

The walk around town – shirt and shoes and rucksack full of CVs – was bleaker than ever. In one recruitment consultants' office, we were greeted by an agitated man in a shabby suit.

"Can we hand our CVs in?" I asked.

"You can, but you won't get anywhere. There's a good chance I won't have a job by tomorrow morning."

As if we hadn't been scarred enough by our first experience working together, Louise and I wound up as colleagues once again, taking the first thing we were offered.

"It's an awful job but you can't be too picky in the current climate," the recruitment lady said, before looking to the floor. "In fact, I fear for my own job."

She wasn't lying about ours. For £6.50 an hour, nine hours a day, we stood around a shabby table, stuffing leaflets into envelopes and sealing them. You weren't allowed to talk to one another or sit down and the only treat was, if we hit our target – lots of envelopes – we could listen to an irritating local radio station for the last hour of the day. Louise's reward for a first-class degree in economics? Sticking first-class stamps on envelopes.

We stuck it out for a week before heading our separate ways, landing new positions in menial office jobs which seemed luxurious in comparison. My menial office job was brightened up by sitting next to a witty out-of-work pilot who charmed the girls in the HR department and had more dates in a month than I'd had in my life.

I moved into a rented semi with Dylan and Noel while Louise moved into a shared terraced house on a street full of bright-eyed students to remind her of times recently left behind. My wages were modest and paying my own rent for the first time was difficult. I was starting to think that maybe adult life in general was difficult. Who knew? I barely saw my housemates as they had already seen enough and were saving up to travel the world once again. They worked two jobs and put almost every penny they earned in their savings pot. We were all cash-poor, with little disposable income. Aside from the odd football accumulator, of course – we still found the money to lose heavily on those every Saturday, resulting in punched doors and long silences at 5pm.

After a couple of months of treading water, a position in a care home which I'd tentatively applied for months ago, got back to me out of the blue. The interview went well and I was offered the job. There were eight clients, aged between sixteen and twenty, each with severe disabilities. Although the personal care aspect took a bit of – okay, a lot of – getting used to and you would sometimes get kicked and punched, I enjoyed it. It was, without wishing to sound annoying, rewarding.

The home was split into two bungalows, one for male clients and one for females. Fortunately, my colleagues Mark, Neil and Dan were of similar age to me, and when working together we had a good laugh. The dream shift was working in the male bungalow with my pals. Once the clients had gone to bed and we'd sorted everything out, we'd sit around drinking tea, watching TV and placing football bets on our phones. We took the clients out bowling, around the park and to see Leeds United. During a match against Hull City, one of the clients, who had a propensity for random screaming, yelped at an opposition player as he was taking a throw-in. This caused him to jump out of his skin, terrified. The Leeds fans laughed and jeered at the Hull player. Our client an instant hero.

The rotas were random and at its worst, I'd end up on the late shift with one of the scary, middle-aged women with thick Yorkshire accents. I'd rightly or wrongly earned a reputation as lazy with the housework so they bossed me around for entire evenings. They simply couldn't bear the thought of me sitting around doing nothing, even when there was, literally, nothing to do.

"Will you just re-clean the door handles, Andy?"

At twenty-two I lacked experience in conversing with older people and found it difficult to establish common ground with these ladies. In fairness, they didn't always help themselves. I was once in the kitchen loading the dishwasher when one of them stormed in and glared at me.

"I'm sorry, but do you know what I mean?!" and left, slamming the door behind her. I had absolutely no idea what she meant. She'd given me very little to work with.

These ladies seemed to talk about either traffic or deeply personal aspects of their lives. There was no middle ground. I would walk into a shift not knowing whether I'd be greeted with: "The M1 was chock-a-block this morning," or "My bastard of an ex-husband is kicking off about custody arrangements again."

While I enjoyed most facets of the job, shift work is a parallel universe. Sometimes I'd be there from 2pm on Saturday to 2pm on Sunday. Days of the week became meaningless. I'd have the Friday feeling on Monday and the Monday blues on Friday night. This was affecting my relationship with Louise who was doing a nine-to-five. I'd go out and get slaughtered with my work pals midweek then call her at 1am spouting nonsense. I was developing a habit of drinking too much, gambling too much and being a dickhead too much. These are not desirable qualities in a boyfriend and we argued frequently. It was usually my fault, although I'd rarely admit it and go quiet for hours in the aftermath, mumbling muted responses and looking at the floor as though the world were against me. Living in different houses was unhelpful. It was never clear where I'd be sleeping – work, mine, Louise's or my parents. I was leading a nomadic existence, albeit within a six-mile radius, and I kept losing phones, wallets and keys. I enjoyed seeing Dylan and Noel when we were all in but this was rare. They now worked three jobs each, seven days a week, so when we were together having some beers or playing Pro Evo on the PlayStation, morale was low. Counting down to the next long day, which was always less-than-a-good-night's-sleep away.

To my shame, I still couldn't drive a car but was having lessons with a patronising posh lady. I stalled on a hill start once and she said.

"Oh, for god's sake boy. Concentrate."

When not shattering my confidence for £25-an-hour, she was an avid birdwatcher and our sessions always ended up on country roads where she could practice her hobby.

"Ooh, look at those red kites, Andy!" she'd say as I was skidding around a tight bend, petrified.

There was heavy snowfall that winter resulting in newspaper "Big Freeze" headlines and closed roads. During one shift at the care home, most of the staff couldn't make it in so I worked a 37-hour shift. Delirious and drained, with a three-mile trudge home through the thick snow to look forward to, one of the ladies with a thick Yorkshire accent eventually made it in to take over. I was expecting praise for my commitment and stamina but she shook the snow from her duffle coat and looked at me, annoyed.

"Do the door handles clean themselves, then? Can you do it before you leave?"

"Well, I've been here for a while. I was, kind of, hoping to clock off?"

Shortly after the big freeze thawed, my misery came to a head. It was raining and I was cycling to work along the main road past a crowded bus stop. Without knowing what had happened, I was sprawled on the floor with a cracked knee and a car behind me having to slam on the brakes. With the extreme changing of temperatures, the frame of my bike had weakened and snapped spectacularly in half. My injuries weren't serious but as a kindly long-haired man and I picked up the pieces of the bike while a sizeable traffic jam built up, I decided I'd had enough of this chapter.

31

"Why don't you move to China?" John said, his eyes not leaving the screen. He was playing Grand Theft Auto.

"Why would I do that?"

"Go and teach English or something. Have an adventure."

The more I considered it, the more it seemed a feasible option. Teaching English abroad, that's something people do, isn't it? Why not? I was fed up and, Louise aside, had nothing tying me down. Besides, I'd recently inherited a couple of grand from my grandparents so why not spend it on something good rather than see it whittle away unnoticed over a few months. Louise had no interest whatsoever in moving to China but was understanding and agreed to me giving it a go. It was settled that I'd work for three months before she'd join me for a bit and we would travel around Southeast Asia together. The only stumbling block was that to get on the next intake of a teaching programme which guaranteed a job and accommodation, I had to complete a 120-hour online TEFL course. The deadline was in three weeks, which, alongside a full-time job, was going to be a close call.

I was due a change in fortunes and quite literally got a lucky break. My 5-a-side team were playing against a team called Sick Memberz (yes, with a 'z'). The Sick Memberz were, it's fair to say, a touch on the physical side and I finished the game with a snapped metacarpal signing me off work for six weeks, full pay. Perfect. The injury also ruled out an upcoming driving test which was a relief such was the certainty that I'd fail and, perhaps, cry. My plastered hand meant I only had one finger on my right hand to tap at the keys so although the online course wasn't too difficult, it took a while. It consisted of short videos where a man with a ponytail taught English to a group of affable Eastern Europeans. You watched the video, answered a few multiple-choice questions, then tackled short essay questions about teaching techniques and lesson planning. The man with the ponytail was seemingly the standard to which we should aspire. You submitted your answers to "examiners" who passed or failed you. On each unit, you had three strikes.

I breezed through most of the questions, but there was one sizeable scare. On Boxing Day, I was at the pub, four-pints deep, when I was notified that I'd failed a unit. I shakily jogged home, re-sat the questions through blurry eyes and submitted it again. Half an hour later I discovered I'd failed again. Why? More to the point, why was the examiner working on Boxing Day? Last chance saloon, I drank a strong coffee, splashed water on my face, asked my dad to help me and scraped through. All a bit embarrassing. What would have happened if I'd failed? Booted off the course? It had cost nearly a grand, surely not? Whatever, I didn't need to find out. I was on my way.

The plaster came off a couple of days before I left, revealing stinking yellow skin and hordes of fine black hairs, making my hand look repulsive. My first stop was Beijing where everyone on the programme would stay in a hotel together for two weeks before disbanding and being placed anywhere and everywhere across China. There was an emotional farewell with Louise at the airport and, as we said goodbye through damp eyes, I felt like a selfish shitbag. She'd gone to Australia for a year though so I suppose this evened it up. That shouldn't be how these things work, should it?

After boarding the plane, which was unsurprisingly full of Chinese people, I noticed a tall ginger-haired man in his mid-thirties sat in the row in front of me. He was wearing a Gore-Tex jacket. I glanced at him wondering what his game was and noticed he was leafing through the paperwork the teaching programme had sent us. Shit, that meant I had to talk to him, didn't it?

I was aware that at some point during this Asian adventure I would have to talk to new people, I just hadn't banked on it being this soon. I'd hoped the flight would be time to drink a couple of glasses of red wine, contemplate how I'd miss my girlfriend and possibly watch an Adam Sandler film. This was a spanner in the works.

"Hi," I said, offering an outstretched hand. "Looks like we're on the same programme."

I flashed him my matching booklet to prove it.

"Uh, hi," he said. "Yes, it does." He spoke in a whispered mumble which was tricky to decipher surrounded by the jangling chatter of Chinese people. I strained my ears as he told me his name was Ernest. He was half-Paraguayan, half-Scottish, which I thought unusual. How had that happened? A gap-year romance? He wouldn't look me in the eye when he spoke and I soon deduced that he was painstakingly shy. Conversation fizzled out before the plane had taken off, leaving me on edge. Had I shot myself in the foot by striking up conversation? It was a twelve-hour flight. What are the rules? Was I now expected to chat sporadically to a timid man throughout the journey? Maybe I could recommend a film to him to take the heat off?

"Have you seen Titanic, Ernest? Great film."

It turned out it wasn't so bad. Ernest and I had a couple of brief discussions about plane food and I asked him whether it was true that jousting is still legal in Paraguay (it is). He only initiated one conversation during the flight, asking how I'd found the online tests. He had failed the course twice in the last two years, he told me with a solemn expression. He'd spent lots of money. At least he'd stuck at it I suppose, although perhaps he should have seen this as a sign that teaching English abroad wasn't for him?

At any rate, it was helpful to arrive in Beijing with a companion. A little less daunting. Within minutes I'd reassessed this view. Ernest left his rucksack on the plane and looked close to tears. It took half an hour to retrieve it while I wondered how on earth this guy was going to fare addressing a classroom of fifty Chinese teenagers. The pair of us were greeted in arrivals by a handsome man in his late twenties with floppy Hugh Grant-esque hair. I was relieved to have someone else to talk to and listened as he told us he'd been an English teacher himself for a few years and now worked for the programme, placing new teachers and, by the sounds of it, acquiring several Chinese girlfriends.

A crowd of seven others aged between nineteen and fifty gathered looking nervous and sleep deprived and we got on a coach to our hotel somewhere in the depths of the sprawling metropolis. When we arrived, there was a hub of activity in the foyer with flustered programme staff in neon t-shirts milling around while a group of sixty or so aspiring teachers stood around, confused. It was 3pm although I didn't really know what day it was or, indeed, what planet I was on. I stood next to Ernest until further instruction. Once again, he looked close to tears. A short, tanned man in his early twenties with severely gelled hair swaggered over to us. He was full of life.

"Alright lads. How we doing?"

Thick Essex accent.

"Hi, I'm Andy. Nice to meet you."

"Hi, my name's Ernest. I'm tired. Can we go to our rooms yet?"

"Nice one, lads. I'm Dave. Beijing looks fucking sweet. Who do you support? I'm a Spurs fan."

I liked his presumption that I was a football fan and felt happy with this topic. An effortless default for my tired, muddled mind and we settled into comfortable conversation.

"Leeds, eh? Your fans are fucking naughty, mate!"

"Yes, we've got a bit of a reputation, I suppose," I said. I didn't lie and say that I'd been involved in any football hooliganism but, perhaps tellingly, I didn't tell him that I hadn't. Ernest had strolled off alone and was staring out of a floor-to-ceiling window onto Beijing's smog-filled streets.

"Jesus, he's a fucking laugh-a-minute, isn't he?" Dave said. "So, where are we going tonight? I've seen a couple of bars. We need to find somewhere for the Spurs game on Wednesday."

I had a new pal. Sorry, Ernest. I would go on to spend nearly all my time with Dave, even though I was sharing a room with Nathan, a tall man with a shiny forehead who wore a silver neck chain over his t-shirt. On the first night, he'd barrelled in at 3am with a curly-haired Irish girl and they'd had sex in the bed next to me. While this was a traumatising experience, I turned it into a positive. On just the second day I had a story. A gambit. Depending on who I was speaking to, I adjusted the tale's tone. When speaking to caring girls, I could play the victim.

"I can't believe they did that Andy, it's so disrespectful."

Or, if speaking to laddish men, I could tailor more uncouth discussion.

"For fuck's sake, mate. I can't believe those grubby bastards woke you up."

This gained me instant popularity and the next two weeks in Beijing were unforgettable. It was Chinese New Year so, everywhere we went, whatever time of day, lunatics were launching fireworks on the streets. We visited the snow-covered Great Wall, went to Tiananmen Square and saw some temples. A temple is a temple though, isn't it? After three I'd got the idea. Enough temples. We went to Wangfujing food street and ate lots of weird food, however my overriding memory of this outing was not the exhilaration of eating snakes and scorpions, but of one of the stingiest acts I've ever witnessed. The food was cheap and everyone was sharing one another's, trying out new things. All good fun. When we were on the tube back to our hotel, a beady-eyed man wandered over to me.

"Andy, are we okay to settle up?"

"Excuse me?"

"Well, I couldn't help but notice that you only gave me three of your skewers, whereas I gave you three and you also shared a chicken one of mine with Dave. So that makes four in total."

We were talking less than 50p for four skewers. I was staggered.

"Are you joking?"

"No."

I handed him one Yuan, the equivalent of 12p, he nodded sombrely and stuffed the note in his money belt and slid off. Thank you, Reuben. You spoiled my trip.

Our evenings were spent drinking room-temperature Tsingtao and smoking in a late-night café near the hotel. It was so cheap to smoke that I'd decided to take it up for the fortnight. A bargain. Besides Dave, I got to know many of the other folk on the course. Dave and I shared similar opinions as to the type of people we liked, which was helpful. For example, when a man wearing an Alice-band began playing air guitar to show off to some girls, Dave turned to me and said, loudly.

"Who the fuck is this guy? What a prick."

The man pretended he hadn't heard but soon stopped with the air guitar. There were numerous good people on the programme though and we soon formed a circle with eight-or-so others. This consisted of a well-dressed Geordie and a reformed East London gangster, some heavy-drinking Irish folk, a couple of Canadians, a lovely Australian bloke and a Chinese girl who'd grown up in England. Dave had assumed she was a waitress.

"Hello. One. More. Beer. Please."

She responded:

"I. Am. Not. A. Waitress. I'm from Lincoln. You dickhead."

Throughout the week, we had a few seminars where experienced teachers – mostly Australian men who had moved out years ago and wound up marrying Chinese women – proffered pearls of wisdom about teaching and Chinese culture. This culminated in us forming small groups and teaching a mock lesson to our peers. It later transpired that how you performed in this dictated which school and city you were going to be placed in. The placements ranged from teaching toddlers in a rural Mongolia to working in an inner-city college in Shanghai. When we were doing our mock lessons, we weren't aware of their significance so many of the men – myself included – simply saw them as an opportunity to get cheap laughs and possibly impress girls. Some men took this too far by pretending to be a child when we were holding our lesson, which wasn't funny at all. Dave and I were paired with a zany Irishwoman and a loud-mouthed girl from Stockport. We opted for a simple lesson about directions, which went okay despite the fact I could feel my stomach ominously growling following the Wangfujing trip. I was very aware that I was wearing white chinos.

On the penultimate day, we found out where we were going to be placed. Our fate was revealed on a noticeboard in the foyer, reminding me of how my football team squad was announced at university. After first year trials, a guy called "Andy C" had been named in the starting eleven and I'd assumed it was me. It was not. I wasn't in the squad. This time it made more agreeable reading and I'd landed a placement in a middle school in Chengdu which was regarded as one of the best gigs.

Chengdu is a city of over fourteen million in Sichuan Province in the West of China, famed for pandas and spicy food. Who knew? Prior to getting a job there I was unaware of its existence. I scoured the Chengdu list and was pleased to recognise a few of the names. Notably the girls from Lincoln and Stockport and the nice bloke from Australia. Also, Nathan of shiny forehead fame and the Irish girl he'd slept with in the bed next to me. I was gutted to see that Dave had been placed in Harbin and have not seen him since, which is a real shame.

Over my short time in Beijing I'd met some good people and our farewell bash, a booze-fuelled evening in a dubious nightclub, was filled with emotion and empty promises.

"Yes, Andy. I will 100% come and stay at your family home in Leeds over summer!"

"And I will absolutely come and visit you in Shanghai for a weekend. Then you can come and stay with me in Chengdu!"

The following morning, I woke up on the floor and was awakened by a knock on the door from Ernest of all people. He'd been placed in rural Mongolia.

"Morning," he whispered, looking at the floor. "I think the coaches are leaving soon."

"Thanks, Ernest. All the best on your placement. We'll stay in touch."

I said my goodbyes to the rest of the party before the ten of us who were headed to Chengdu boarded the coach. I sat, staring out of the window, pale-faced and already nostalgic about my time in Beijing. On the flight, I was sat next to Niamh, a girl from Cork, who had secured herself a handsome Dutch boyfriend over the past few days. He'd been placed in Shenzhen at the opposite end of the country but they had made concrete plans to visit one another. More concrete than my plans to meet Ernest anyway.

We arrived in Chengdu mid-afternoon, where a minibus met us and took us to a posh restaurant. A private room had been hired with a large circular table in the middle and a spread of noodles, rice and ominous shiny food on small dishes. The idea of the dinner was for us to meet and greet representatives from each of the schools we were to be working in. I hadn't anticipated this and my hangover was in its ugliest stage; nausea, fear and anxiety. I was wearing Nike joggers and hoodie. Why hadn't we been warned about this?

I was sat next to a local lady in her late thirties who introduced herself as Ms Wang. She was, I learned, the head teacher at my school and made a point of her name being Ms, not Mrs, so I wondered whether she was a recent divorcee. Ms Wang was well-dressed and attractive but slurped her noodles as though she were alone, unconcerned with the noise and specks of sauce flicking on her chin. This was a distraction but her English was passable and I understood the gist of what she was telling me regarding my work rota. At one point, she said:

"The school is good but sometimes bad things happen."

Like what? I discovered I would visit the school on the Wednesday for a tour before classes started the following Monday. Just one commitment in the next week was music to my ears; I could get over this hangover. My flatmates were Niamh and Pippa, a tall nineteen-year-old from Melbourne who was intelligent and agreeable. Drained and bloated after the formal meal, which had lasted for nearly three hours – the courses, including duck skulls and chicken feet, kept coming – we finally arrived at our apartment at dusk. We were on the tenth floor of a thirty-storey tower block in a residential suburb. I remember standing in the courtyard staring up at the skyscrapers surrounding us and getting a wave of vertigo, causing me to go lightheaded and stumble backwards. For the first time since leaving England, it suddenly felt very real.

I lived in China.

32

I took an instant liking to Chengdu; bustling traffic and shiny skyscrapers as you'd expect in China, but also streams lined by willow trees flowing through the suburbs like veins and sprawling parks full of locals dancing, playing Mahjong and practising Tai Chi. The first week was fine. The girls and I wandered around, got lost, took buses to points of interest and bought foreign sim cards, a task which takes a full afternoon in China. Fortunately, Pippa could speak Mandarin which was useful as nobody spoke English. The locals did, however, stare at us everywhere we went. The girls found this creepy but I enjoyed it. It was nice to be noticed – an ego boost.

The residents of Chengdu are renowned for their laziness and this was quickly apparent. People sauntered along showing no urgency, and benches, pavements, parks and walls were constantly occupied by people sitting around doing little other than smoking or drinking tea. Sichuan women are famed for their beauty but had a reputation for being nutcases. The men who took on these beauties were known as "Soft Ears" because they would do anything their lady requested and bow to their every demand. Tired boyfriends carrying their designer handbags was a common sight, as was broken men getting shouted at on the street by hysterical women in stilettos. Angry yelling is well suited to the lively, up-and-down tones of the Sichuan dialect. Terrifying.

I contacted the local expat football team and arranged to attend training on Wednesday, which was turning out to be a busy day. My tour of the school lasted half an hour. I'd been met by Ms Wang who seemed flustered. Had her husband had enough of her demands over the years and played hardball in the divorce settlement? When I arrived, all four hundred of the school's students were in the playground, stood in lines forming a perfectly symmetrical square. A moustached man with a pot belly was shouting orders at them and they responded with shouts, stamps and salutes. If it weren't for the Chinese flag flying high, this could have been a North Korean training camp. What the hell was going on?

"The students have morning exercises," Ms Wang explained casually before leading us into the recently-emptied school for a tour. The décor was harsh; white and pale blue wallpaper, which was peeling at the edges. All straight lines and right angles. The classrooms were akin to Victorian England, with rows of wooden desks and bare walls, apart from the Chinese flag which was above the blackboards. I was horrified to learn that teachers shared communal squat toilets with the students.

My tour concluded at the same time as the morning drills and hordes of children were flooding back into the building. My presence caused a stir, with giggles, goggle-eyed stares and, "Herro, teacher!" shouted over and over. I smiled and waved, enjoying the attention. Ms Wang snapped at the students, ordering them back to their classrooms. A kid of fifteen or so, holding a basketball, stuck his hand out to give me a high five, which earned rapturous laughter from the swarms around him. The students' goodwill overrode my apprehension and as I said goodbye to Ms Wang at the gates, I was looking forward to getting started. This was going to be okay.

The following Monday and two minutes into my first lesson, it was not okay at all. I'd prepared a PowerPoint presentation to introduce myself and do some games and vocabulary exercises. With it being the first class, I'd spent large chunks of the weekend on it, poaching material from the ponytailed teacher of online course fame. I was confident. I was teaching sixty eleven and twelve-year-olds who were crammed behind their wooden desks, creating the illusion that the classroom was twice as big as when empty. They were delighted to see me and full of energy.

"Herro, teacher!"

"Welcome, teacher!"

"So tall, teacher!"

"You have girlfriend, teacher?"

"Hello," I said while setting up my laptop and plugging it into the projector. The projector didn't turn on.

"Sorry, one minute."

"Goodbye, teacher!"

Panicking, I ran to Ms Wang's office at the other side of the school.

"Ms Wang. I need some help."

"Why are you here? You must not leave the children unsupervised!"

"The projector doesn't work."

"It has been broken for a long time."

"Oh."

Sprinting back, I had no idea how I was going to fill the following hour. The kids remained cheerful, giving me another hero's welcome, reminding me of when you have a dog, pop out for a few minutes and return to jubilation. At least they should be an easy audience? I smiled again, although I was now forcing it. I turned my back to them, hated my life and began to draw some cartoon pictures on a blackboard with a stick of broken chalk. I made them repeat after me.

"Man."

"Man."

"Dog."

"Dog."

"Ball."

"Ball."

They were losing interest. Besides, by "boat," I was stretching the limits of my artistic aptitude. I needed something else. Pausing, the kids began to chat among themselves. Did they think I was a shit teacher already? Am I a shit teacher? I glanced at my attempted sketch of a horse. Maybe I am? Although horses are notoriously tough to draw though. Like bikes.

I was so stumped that all I could do was revert to what I'd initially planned. Projector or no projector. I opened the presentation on my small laptop and held it above my head. Of course, besides the front couple of rows, none of them could make out a thing on the screen. I was just some idiot holding up a computer, with sweaty armpits. It was awful. I'd got through all of the slides in ten minutes and besides two kids at the front who had listened to my every word with eagerness, I'd lost the class.

"Hangman?" I asked pensively. The two kids at the front nodded. That was enough. The remaining fifty-eight could ignore me for all I cared. I turned my back and was drawing the lines for my first word when there was a loud bang. I turned around to see two boys at the back of the class, rolling around on the floor, wrestling. As I ran over, the boy on top smacked the other hard in the face. I split them up but the one who'd been hit – a small, chubby kid with a round face – had a bust lip and was crying. I shouted at the aggressor and ordered him to stand outside while I tried to console the injured party.

His tears subsided and after he'd sat back at his desk, I returned to my game of hangman. What else could I do? With a couple of minutes of the hour remaining, Ms Wang walked into the classroom. She was holding the fighting boy by his collar, frowning.

"Why is he outside?"

"He was naughty," I said, choosing not to mention his impressive left hook.

"Never send children outside!"

Wonderful. My first class and I was getting a dressing down from the head teacher in front of sixty kids, one of whom was bleeding quite severely.

After this sticky start, the day picked up. If it hadn't, I would have quit before I was pushed. Ms Wang apologised for telling me off, saying I wasn't to know about sending kids out. She informed me that they were the worst class in the school; she'd wanted me to see the worst first, which I tried to understand the logic behind but couldn't. My next class was immeasurably better – the projector worked. At lunchtime Ms Wang introduced me to rest of the other teachers, none of whom could speak English, four of whom were smoking. I had one more class in the afternoon, before sitting around in the staffroom for an idle hour across from the PE teacher who had a free period, and was chain smoking. I wondered if I too should smoke? Would that help me fit it? At the end of the day Ms Wang called me to her office where she set up a PowerPoint presentation on her laptop and showed me her holiday snaps from a recent holiday to London. For over an hour.

Having got the measure of the place I settled into my routine. I was teaching sixteen hours a week although only four classes from each year group so I could replicate the same material and only had to do four lesson plans. Aside from the first class, who were irritating shits every time, most classes were fine. The majority of kids were hardworking, courteous and receptive. I was enjoying it.

The football team I'd joined, Chengdu Wanderers (the manager was a Bolton fan), were a good setup. There were about forty guys involved, split into a Saturday and Sunday squad. Most were from England but there were a decent spread of Europeans and a handful of soccer guys from the States who were too keen on pre-match huddles and fist bumps. I scored on my debut but that would be my only goal. A few weeks in, I'd been out drinking night before a match for the manager's thirtieth birthday. He and I had been last to leave and I'd slept through my alarm the following morning, arriving two minutes before kick-off. Given it was he who'd been keen to have about six "last one, mate!" drinks, I'd expected him to laugh this off.

"You've ruined our preparations, Andy," he said with a steely glare. "You're on the bench."

I never started a game again. I wasn't too concerned though. Joining the team had moulded my social life, with post-training drinking buddies ranging from directionless English teachers in their mid-twenties like me, to guys in their fifties who wore expensive watches and had important-sounding jobs comprising of words like "executive" or "analyst." Along with the group, I knew from Beijing, I knocked around with a good mix of folks. With expatriates making up just a few thousand of the city's fourteen million population, it was easy to make friends. I bet it would be much harder to make friends if I'd moved to, say, Ipswich. Everyone got on, even if it were apparent that back home, you would probably have made a conscious effort to avoid one another. Besides, there were only a handful of places for us to knock around in and if you went to these places on any night of the week, you would be able to find an acquaintance.

The football team drank at The Shamrock, your standard every-city-in-the-world Irish bar, and The Leg and Whistle, an English pub. For late-night drinking, we would go to Café Paname, a French bar with a free pool table and a disproportionate amount of middle-aged, scantily clad Chinese women. There was also The Bookworm, a bar with a large selection of books to enjoy with your wine. It was a good idea and I liked it, although it was oft-frequented by men with sinister intentions.

"It's a dead cert, Andy," one of the sleazier football guys had told me. "Sit there, pretend to read some Proust and wait for the birds to come over. Works every time!"

"Okay, I'll bear that in mind. Thanks, Clive."

Clive was one of those guys who started a conversation with a question and it almost always finished with him describing, in detail, an unlikely sexual encounter.

"Have you ever been to Tokyo, Andy?"

"No, I'd like to though."

"Last time I went, I had a threesome with two beautiful barmaids on a rooftop. You should go."

While I did, as expats do, spend much of my time in places not dissimilar to back home, I did, at least, get into the Chinese food culture. Aside from a couple of hungover KFCs I ate nothing but the local cuisine and fell in love with it. Previously, I'd never been anything close to resembling a foodie. This perhaps stemmed from childhood where my dad's specialities included chips and beans and pasta and gravy. Food had never interested me. I'd always seen eating as functional, not fascinating. Why spend two hours of your evening stressing over something that will be gone in ten minutes, leaving you with a shift in the kitchen? Why go to a posh restaurant and spend a tonne when you could go to a bar, not smell of garlic, buy fancy drinks and have a better time?

Living in Chengdu made me change my tune and I began to understand the appeal. In China, eating together is the main form of socialising. Whereas an evening out in a restaurant in Leeds would last Louise and I little over an hour (one Pizza Express trip was done and dusted within half an hour. "Now what?"), Chinese banquets stretch for hours. Once you've accepted the hygiene issues and are calm about the sharing of saliva with tablemates, dividing different dishes on a large, spinning table is a wonderfully companionable way of dining out. It helps that Sichuanese food is exceptional, well-deserving of its international fame. It took a while to grow accustomed to the spice – I shed a lot of tears over dinner and had to dash out of the classroom mid-lesson twice in the first week – but once I did, I was sold; sizzling hotpots, shredded pork in garlic sauce, sliced chilli beef, hot and sour eggplant, and my favourite dish in the world ever; kung pao chicken. Glorious.

***

Ten weeks into Sichuan living, Louise flew out to Thailand.

"If you're having an adventure, so am I," she'd snapped while we were out shopping in Leeds city centre one rainy afternoon before I left. She insisted we go to STA Travel to find her a suitable trip, which dashed my hopes of getting home for Final Score, and she booked a three-week stint looking after elephants in Thailand. Teaching English in China and volunteer work in Thailand; ground breaking stuff for the middle class, mid-twenties couple, eh? Phone signal in Northern Thailand was unreliable/dreadful but the odd text came through from Louise telling me that things were going well. The elephants were cute and the people were nice, apart from one dickhead. There's always one dickhead, isn't there? One evening, she rang me.

"Andy?" I heard a loud rumbling and the sound of distressed elephants roaring in the background.

"Hello, can you hear me?"

"Don't panic, there's an earthquake."

"What??"

"It's fine, the elephants are a bit scared but it's nothing to worry about..." The phone signal began to break up.

"Louise? Are you okay?"

"Oh shit, it's getting..."

It cut off. I rang back several times but it kept going straight to answerphone, leaving me hating the smug automated woman's voice and thinking that the earthquake was, in some way, her fault. I looked on the internet which confirmed that

6.8 magnitude earthquake had hit Myanmar, causing ripples through Northern Thailand. Buildings were toppling and people were getting injured. For the next four hours, I was a wreck, pacing around the flat and sharing a menthol cigarette on the balcony with my flatmate Niamh, although I think this was largely for attention and to emphasise my position as a worried man.

At 11pm my phone vibrated. It was a text from Louise.

"Sorry, the signal went. The ground really shook though. It was so funny! xx"

Funny?

Louise and indeed the elephants were unscathed and a couple of weeks later she arrived in Chengdu. I'd opted to wear a novelty jumper, sporting a wolf from a famous Chinese cartoon, which didn't go down well but it was wonderful to be reunited. Life was good. We were going to have a terrific time together in China.

Or so I thought. While Louise got on well with my housemates and pals, she wasn't so keen on China as a whole. Her issues were: the language barrier, the food, the traffic, the crowds, the staring, the toilets, the litter, the unpleasant odours, the pollution, the tap water, the lifts, the spitting, the eating-with-open-mouths, the warm beer and the plug sockets.

We still shared some good times going to see the pandas and spending a weekend away in the mountains. Louise came into my school and was a big hit with the students and we whittled away long afternoons playing cards in teahouses with Niamh and Pippa. I showed Louise the expatriate bars and, she got along with the guys in the football team. However, after six weeks and on the back of being served a duck's brain for brunch, I suspected she may have had enough.

"I want to leave, I hate China."

"Why? It's great."

"No, it's not, Chengdu is the worst place I've ever been."

"I thought you liked it?"

With a heavy heart, I decided it wasn't fair to stay here any longer. I'd initially said I'd only be here for three months and the time was up. I'd had my escapade. While I would gladly have stayed for a year, what would have changed? I'd got the gist. I handed in my notice at the school, having the courtesy to find a replacement in the shape of a rosy-cheeked Irishman. During my last week, I threw leaving parties in each of my sixteen classes. This was both lazy (Hangman and Oreos) and self-indulgent (throwing parties in celebration of myself). My favourite class was a top set, final year class and I made more effort for them, bringing in balloons, ball games and making a playlist based on their favourite music.

In the build-up to this I made a substantial faux pas. One of the girls in the class was intelligent but peculiar. Early in my tenure I'd been doing a standard role-play activity, where you interviewed a celebrity. I asked her which celebrities she liked and she said Michael Jackson. Reasonable enough, I'd thought.

"So, what would you ask Michael Jackson then?" I asked.

She started at me, glassy-eyed.

"Michael, what is it like on the other side? Can you still hear my voice?"

I needed to nip this in the bud quickly.

"Okay, thanks." I shot my head to a student sat at the opposite end of the classroom where the kid who liked basketball was sat.

"So, Kenny, what would you ask Yao Ming if you met him?

Days before my final class, the weird girl said she had some great ideas for the party. Sacrificial offerings perhaps?

"Can I have your phone number, teacher? I want to text you my plans."

"Can't you just tell me?" I said.

"I want to surprise my classmates."

"No, I'm sorry. I can't give out my phone number."

She stared at me again and her eyes began to well up. She was on the brink.

"Okay, fine," I said, writing down my number. "Text me your ideas."

As soon as I'd got home, I'd seen the error of my ways. What had I been thinking? I'd given my phone number to a sixteen-year-old student. Even worse, a bat shit crazy one. Sure enough, that evening she texted me with some suggestions for the party. Thankfully there was nothing untoward: a couple of ideas for games and a selection of Michael Jackson songs, including the one about his pet rat. Relieved, I replied saying good idea and forgot about the matter.

A few hours later, my phone rang. It was her. I ignored it but she was persistent, ringing over and over again, each time the ringtone cutting through me and inducing queasiness. What had I done? What if Ms Wang found out I'd given my number to a student? I already had her down as a bit of a man-hater, what if she thought I was a scumbag? I didn't want to end up in handcuffs. It would have put a real damper on my time in Chengdu. The next day the party went well and nothing was ever mentioned. Thank God. What an idiot.

Across the school, the students wrote me kind cards and gave me presents and, as Ms Wang thanked me for my efforts at the school gates, I felt a surge of emotion. I'd had a good time working here. I'd enjoyed my job and, for the most part, I'd been good at it. Having now had a positive teaching experience, I also felt a touch of relief. If at forty-five, I'm broke, single and hate my life, I could always max a credit card and teach English abroad; a viable plan B.

Louise and I hired out a bar for a leaving do which was well-attended. All the pals we'd made came and we danced and drank long into the night. There was a poignant moment where we stood in a huddle, arms around each other, singing along to Justin Bieber and I scanned the happy, drunken faces of the people who'd made my last three months, knowing that there was little chance I'd ever see any of them ever again.

We left the next day. Heeding his own advice, John had moved to Shanghai, where he'd met his wife-to-be Tomoko, a glamorous Canadian-Japanese lady, and we'd arranged to stay with them for a few days to commence our travels. We took a train, which was packed to the rafters and found ourselves crammed into a tiny cabin, shared with a family of four who ate an inordinate amount of prawn-flavoured pot noodles. Eleven hours in, I was intensely uncomfortable and desperate to get off.

"There's only an hour left," Louise consoled me as I glared at the slurping kid below my tiny bunk bed.

Three hours later, we still weren't there so I dug the tickets from my pocket. They clearly stated that we would arrive in Shanghai at 6am.

"Why aren't we there yet?" I asked Louise, blaming her for the delays.

Another hour passed so I asked the conductor what was going on, pointing at my ticket aggressively to bridge the language barrier. His English was minimal but I made out the keyword.

"Tomorrow."

It wasn't a twelve-hour journey but thirty-six.

"Do you know what, Louise?" I said, trying to massage the deep knots out of my neck with sweat-drenched hands. "I think it was the right decision to leave. I've had it with China too."

33

"It was incredible! I met so many amazing people!" is common analysis when people come back from long travelling trips. In my own experience, sure, you meet some nice people and make a few mates who you get along with for a few days and promise to stay in touch with but never do. But amazing? So many? I'm not convinced.

Having spent a few enjoyable days with John and Tomoko in Shanghai and five days in Hong Kong, Louise and I headed to the Philippines. Here we met a guy who was definitely not amazing. Like many people you meet in popular Asian travelling hubs, he was, in fact, a complete pain in the neck. We were getting picked up to go on an excursion to some underwater caves, which I'd been looking forward to until his unwelcome emergence. He was balding with tufts of unkempt brown hair and was wearing baggy blue yoga pants with a money belt strapped around his waist. He was holding a massive camera.

"The problems with the infrastructure of the tourist industry in the Philippines are down to government corruption."

Whoa, whoa, whoa. Let me stop you there, pal. It's 9am, too hot and we haven't met before. Are you really going straight in with this? What's wrong with a polite introduction that slips into a comfortable silence until the beer with lunch? That's what I'm looking for.

"How long have you guys been travelling?"

This question again, hmm? I'll be polite.

"Not long, just…"

"I've been on the road for two years now," he interrupted. "To start with, I did South America, then I moved on to Asia. I've done Thailand, Cambodia and Laos."

Can you *do* a country?

"I intend on travelling for as long as I can. I don't believe in getting caught up in the rat race of capitalist society."

That's controversial, you prefer pissing around on a long holiday than going to work?

"Can you take a photo of me?" he asked.

Click.

"No, not like that. You need to catch the sunlight on the water. Try again?"

On the short boat trip to the caves I predictably wound up next to the annoying man and listened to him talking about religion being the cause of the world's problems. Cheery. When we arrived at the caves, a group of twenty or so other tourists were there. A grinning Filipino told us we were going to be split up into groups of four to go on the boats. A chance to escape the annoying man, thank god. Louise and I subtly shuffled away from where he was stood, feigning interest in a wholly uninteresting tree. It was in vain. An unusual numbering process was employed by the Filipino guide and we ended up grouped, once again, with the annoying man.

"Hey, long time no see," he joked.

I crammed my legs in our narrow boat and the annoying man sat behind me, his sharp knees digging into my back.

"Can you hold my camera while I sort my life jacket out?" he asked. The water was shallow and life jackets strictly optional. Out of the entire group, he was the only one wearing one.

"Don't drop it, it's expensive."

"I'll try not to."

"Hey, can you just hold my legs? I'm going to lean out of the boat to get some close-up shots of these stalagmites."

I held his sweaty legs, which confirmed that my excursion was ruined.

After we'd returned to dry land, we were told that we could either get the return boat back to the beach or walk back via a five-km route through the jungle. The annoying man was peppering the tour guide with questions about the Filipino government so we saw our chance and bolted before he could tag along. We'd been walking for twenty minutes when the path became overgrown and unclear. I assured Louise that it was fine until it got to a point where it definitely was not as we'd got to the edge of a large, vertical rock with no way down. We had to turn back.

Sprinting towards us was the annoying man.

"Hey guys, bit lost? Didn't you bring a compass? Don't worry, I've got mine."

Yes, a compass might be a useful tool but also, just piss off.

We stomped along for a few minutes while the man told us about what software he used to edit his photos.

It was hot and Louise and I had run out of water.

The annoying man had not run out of water. He had a large bottle and was glugging it down.

"Could I have a sip, please?" I asked him but it was too late. He was already pouring the remainder of his water on his head. We fell into silence and wrestled through thick shrubbery with green insects chomping at our feet for the next twenty minutes. Eventually, the woods cleared out and we found ourselves on the right path to the beach and our guesthouse. The man crouched down on the path and started looking at something.

"You two go on ahead, I'm going to take some shots of this colony of ants."

That's the last of him at least, I thought as we left the annoying man lying on his stomach, clicking away. Two hundred metres down the beach, we were stopped in our tracks by a deep stream about ten metres wide, leading into the sea. There was no ostensible way around it, so we decided to swim through. Sweating buckets and covered in insect bites, it was refreshing and once I'd splashed to the other side, I'd cheered up. Was this the turning point in the day? The annoying man had ruined the morning but perhaps the afternoon could be salvaged; maybe I could buy a frisbee or try to beat my underwater swimming record?

Not far from our guesthouse, we heard a faraway voice.

"Guys!"

I looked around to see the silhouette of the annoying man in the distance. He was stranded on the other side of the stream, waving his camera and money belt above his head. Distressed. In order to get to the other side with his valuable possessions, he would have to leave an item behind and make two trips, which was risky as the item left behind could get stolen. You could argue that someone waving a camera and money belt above his head in a developing country deserves to have his things stolen.

His conundrum was similar to that fox and chicken icebreaker activity that someone always gets too aggressive about at the office teambuilding workshop. I was facing my own conundrum; do you help an annoying man to get his valuables across a stream? It was a tough decision. In the cave, the idea of chucking his camera in the water had genuinely crossed my mind. Was I now going to help save the thing? After thinking long and hard about it (ten seconds) I plodded back. With no hint of a thank you, the annoying man barked directions at me as the best way to solve what was, with two people, a simple problem.

"If you swim over with that piece of wood, I can use it as a raft," he said.

Are you kidding me? I get soaked again and you use a raft?

My mind flashed back to images of his lifejacket on the boat earlier and I felt a pang of guilt. He can't swim, the poor guy. Of course I'll help him out. What was I thinking? I waded back through the water with the plank of wood and handed it to him.

"Can you take my camera?" he said. "Don't get it wet."

I swam, one-handed with the massive camera held high above my head. Not an easy task. Meanwhile the annoying man slung the money belt over his shoulder and paddled across with his hands.

"That was fun, wasn't it?" he said when we finally got to the other side. I was soaked.

As we walked the final mile along the beach, any soft spot I'd felt for his inability to swim evaporated as he told that the stalagmites earlier had been nothing special and showed me his dozens of photos of ants. Eventually, we got to our guesthouse and exhausted and relieved, turned to go to our room.

"See you later then," I said, thinking, hopefully never.

"Sure. I'm going swimming. See you guys in the pool."

***

The annoying man aside, Louise and I had a wonderful time drifting around Southeast Asia. We spent a couple more weeks in The Philippines, the highlight being five days on Malapascua, a paradise island not yet overrun by tourism. It's a bit hypocritical when tourists talk about hating touristy places, isn't it? We befriended Daniel and Francis, a pair of locals who spent their days fishing, playing basketball and smoking cannabis. Daniel was married whereas Francis, a long-haired cad with a winning smile, was not. When he flashed Louise a grin while simultaneously smoking and hammering a nail into a wooden hut, she started giggling.

"What's the big joke, guys?" I asked, through gritted teeth.

On our final night Daniel hosted a karaoke party where his wife cooked a chicken for us and he drank obscene amounts of rum. It was a great occasion although Francis was dismayed when Louise, an animal lover, could not be talked into watching a cockfight.

We flew to Ho Chi Minh in Vietnam and did something stupid which I'd managed to avoid on my first travelling trip. You'd have expected five years later and now with a reasonably sensible woman by my side, the ship had sailed, alas it hadn't. We got tattoos. We'd had a few vodkas and, in scenes resembling the open mic night in Pai, I was booed off stage in a bar after attempting to play "Save Tonight" by Eagle Eye Cherry. This should have been a strong indication to call it a night but stumbling through the narrow streets, I was lured in by the lights of a 24-hour tattoo parlour, something which should absolutely not be legal. I tried sketching my own design – our names in bubble writing – but the topless tattoo artist advised I might regret the decision. Instead he suggested we get AL tattooed on our backs in italics. Great idea. At the time, we were friends with a heavy-drinking gay guy from Sheffield, called Al. Why not have his name etched on our backs for the rest of our lives?

Louise fell asleep while getting hers done and I don't remember mine. The following morning, I woke up with a banging head, aware that all was not well. What was it? What had happened? Ah yes, that's it. I had a mild panic attack and started crying. Louise thought the whole thing was hilarious.

We worked our way up the country on long, winding bus rides and eventually I got over the tattoo trauma. It helps that much of Vietnam is stunning and, barring a tyre puncture and seven-hour stop by the main road, the rest of our time in the country was great. We stopped at Da Lat, a former colonial town in the hills, which could be in the French Alps. Here we hired a tandem bike, climbed a mountain and drank lots of coffee. Tip: Vietnamese coffee is the best in the world. This wholesome activity was, no doubt, a kneejerk reaction to the tattoo decision. Playing it safe for a bit. You are not likely to end up in a tattoo parlour after a daytime stroll around a lake, are you? We moved on to Hoi An, a quaint riverside town where a man was foiled in his attempts to steal our laptop, and we hired scooters and drove out to "Vietnam's answer to Angkor Wat" which was a misleading title for a few piles of stones and a ramshackle café.

In our final stop, Hanoi, we met Will and Noel and took a three-day tour around Halong Bay which is stunning; thousands of limestone rocks jutting out from the turquoise sea with the surrounding islands containing tropical rainforests, picturesque beaches and extensive networks of spectacular caves. We went on a three-day boat tour with twenty-or-so other travellers. These things can be risky. If you are lumbered with a dickhead – the annoying man, for instance – there is no escape. We got lucky and the group were excellent. One of them, a tattooed Texan Called Kyle, could throw a frisbee over 200 metres. What more do you need from a shipmate? We swam, kayaked, explored the caves and mucked around by day, spending the evenings eating freshly caught seafood accompanied with whisky and beer.

We concluded our trip with a fond return to Thailand. I took Louise around some of the old haunts on Koh San Road, although I imagine my constant reminiscing became tiresome. Going with a girlfriend is, of course, completely different to going with your mates. With a girlfriend, you can't relive the excitement of being inebriated, getting in a Tuk Tuk and shouting "Disco!" to the driver, but you eat better food, do things during the days and walk along beaches at sunset, holding hands, something I never felt comfortable doing with Eddie.

We went back to Ko Pha Ngan, where the two types of trip collided. Will, Noel, David, Dylan, Harry and Mike were there on a lads' holiday. They were tanned, wearing Beer Laos vests and in high spirits. It was good to see them. On our first night on Haad Rin, we sat on the sand drinking whisky and Red Bull buckets and I considered momentarily what the Norwegian girl was doing with her life. I decided she was probably a social worker in Oslo but didn't mention my ponderings to Louise. I couldn't hack going out the following night and was relieved when Louise suggested we stay in and watch the Karate Kid. I'd also broken my little toe at some point, which was bad luck with the inaugural Ko Pha Ngan 5-a-side tournament taking place later in the week. I couldn't run and we lost every game.

This time around I did stay long enough to go to the Full Moon Party. Midway through the celebrations and to Louise's chagrin, I drank a magic mushroom shake and lost my head, believing that the sand was the sea and the sea, the sand. She had to stop me from drinking out of an ashtray and I was unable to speak sense, bursting into fits of laughter for little or no reason, to the bewilderment of her and my pals. From a selfish viewpoint, I had a great time.

We spent a week unwinding on Koh Samui before glumly accepting that we needed to return to Leeds, live with my parents, find jobs again and attempt to become responsible adults. You can only escape for so long, can't you?

34

It turned out that this escape was to last much, much longer. With nepotism aiding our cause, Louise received an e-mail from her mum saying she had a contact in Hong Kong who was looking to recruit a financial adviser. In the grimy dorm room of a cheap hostel just off Koh San Road, I stood, wearing a vest with a picture of Barack Obama on it (a bargain at £4) not knowing what to do with myself as Louise toiled with a poor Wi-Fi connection and spoke to the CEO over Skype. The call went well and she was invited to a face-to-face interview. We flew to Hong Kong two days later, Louise impressed, and she was offered the job. A whirlwind chain of events. My mum was surprised about this development.

"So, just to get this straight. You're not coming home and you now live in Hong Kong?"

"Well…"

Hong Kong is like nowhere else. Towering skyscrapers, neon lights, mountains, beaches, peculiar smells swirling through the opaque, smoggy air and a mishmash of people from all over the world milling around on the bustling, raucous streets. I liked it immediately. The price of accommodation in the city is obscene so we moved into a one-room, serviced apartment in Wan Chai. When the estate agent, a Filipino Called Mardin (not, he corrected me several times, Martin) showed us around, there were flies swarming around the property, a musty ambiguous stench coming from the bathroom and holes in the walls. He pretended this wasn't the case and grinned while pointing out our picturesque views – a main road, teeming with cars honking their horns on one of the busiest streets in the busiest city in the world.

Dylan, who was still on his travels – although he is almost permanently on his travels – came to visit shortly after we'd arrived. As Louise had just started a high-pressure new job and I was flat broke, this wasn't the best timing, but we enjoyed ourselves nonetheless. I showed Dylan some of the sights but we spent most of our time sat in my dank apartment, doing quizzes on the Sporcle website on his phone.

"So, what have you two been up to today?" Louise asked after returning from an eleven-hour day.

"Well, I can now correctly spell Kyrgyzstan."

Dylan left and I slung my CV around schools and language centres. After days of soul searching and long walks where I exhausted my iPod shuffle playlist, which for some reason contained every album by The Streets and little else, the interviews started to trickle in. My first was a bizarre meeting in a kindergarten where I was interviewed by an overweight Chinese man while we sat on toy plastic stools. The second was in a tiny, undecorated room in a shopping mall which was supposedly a thriving language centre, run by a camp English guy in his early twenties who had a Reading Festival wristband on. I didn't want, nor was I offered either of these positions and felt nervous and frazzled when I arrived at my third shot, Times Square Institute, which does not sound like an English school.

"So, Andrew. What do you know about the Times Square method?"

Shit.

"Sorry, nothing. I haven't had the chance to look on your website."

In stunning scenes, I landed the job, with the manager later telling me that she had admired my honesty.

While my debut novel was fiction, much of it was based on my time in Hong Kong and working at Times Square, which in a thinly veiled guise, I'd called Super English. Assuming you've read it – are you one of the lucky few? – I won't rehash my old material too much. I will a bit though. Plagiarising yourself is acceptable, isn't it?

I was teaching thirty classes a week. Most of these were "encounters" – small classes of 1-4 students which lasted an hour. Encounters were numbered from 1-70 with 1 being students who couldn't speak a word of English and 70 being fluent speakers supposedly. The sweet spots were 25-45. These

guys could speak decent English so I wasn't pulling teeth –
"My. Name. Is." – nor were they proficient enough to question
my methods.

"Why have you used the second conditional in this example,
sir?"

"Well done, Lam, I see you've spotted my deliberate
mistake."

"It wasn't deliberate, was it?"

On top of the encounters, I was expected to hold 4-5 "social
clubs" and "chat cafes" per week, which would be for students
of all levels and could have anything from 10-60 people
attending. These were a mixed bag. My first one – a chat café –
was a fucking disaster. I was advised by Harold, a tall
colleague from Derby, that all I needed to do was write down
some discussion topics on slips of paper and distribute them to
the students.

"The rest will take care of itself," he assured me, with a
wink.

I walked into the vast social club classroom to find 20+
students of differing ages sat around tables in silence, eagerly
awaiting the new teacher. What masterclass did he have up his
sleeve?

"Hello, I'm Andy. Nice to meet you all," I said, pulling up a
chair and trying to look cool.

I divided the class into groups of four and distributed my
slips. They said things like: holidays, TV, sport, and music. It
had taken all of ninety seconds to plan the class. A few people
looked at their slips but nobody said anything.

"Okay, let's talk in your groups!" I said, trying to muster
some enthusiasm.

Ripples of conversation began in a handful of the groups but
I was very aware that most students were just sat, staring,
waiting for me to do something. After a few minutes, it was
silence again.

"Right, swap your slips with the group next to you and talk
about something else!"

The same thing happened. When I suggested passing the
slips around for a third time, a woman in her sixties interjected.

"So boring! Tell us about you, Mr Andy!"

"What do you want to know?"

"Where you from? How old? You have girlfriend?"

A few of the students nodded encouragingly but the majority continued staring at me, glassy-eyed.

"Really?"

"Yes," said a man in his thirties in a baseball cap, "tell us everything about yourself."

If I were a social secretary at university or a woman on her third glass of wine in a Wetherspoons, this would have been music to my ears. As I'm neither, it was a living hell. In an unrehearsed soliloquy, I droned on for twenty minutes about my life, going off on some curious tangents. At one point, I was telling them about Sheldon, my old manager at John Filan's. Reminiscing about how unreceptive the students were to my anecdotal tales, it is difficult to imagine this book flying of the shelves. I wrapped up the lesson early to the relief of my audience. A painful experience all round.

Times Square Institute also offered "VIP" packages which cost an extraordinary amount but gave students the privilege of one-on-one tuition from an underqualified teacher like me. Every Monday from 8-9pm I had a class with a VIP Called KC. He wore Gucci suits and had a twinkle in his eye. With this being the final hour of my working day, I tended to get a second wind and KC was fortunate to find me in a bright, often caffeine-delirious, mood most weeks. KC was rich. I knew this because he told me several times. Whether we were working on a lesson about prepositions, tenses or colours of the rainbow, KC would seamlessly shift the conversation onto his wealth. I informed him that I was not educated in the world of stocks and shares, but this proved no deterrent.

"So, Andy. How is your portfolio doing this week?"

"I don't have a portfolio."

"I do very well this week. Good week for me."

KC had a wife and children on "the mainland" but said there were more opportunities in Hong Kong. Not just financial opportunities either.

"Many beautiful women in Hong Kong," he informed me, smiling.

Before one class, I met KC in the reception area. He was reading South China Morning Post and looking forlorn. The front-page story was about a bunch of brothels being raided and shut down in Guangzhao.

"Very bad for business," he said, shaking his head.

"What has it got to do with business?"

"I have many business meetings in Guangzhao."

"In brothels?"

"Of course."

"Of course?"

"Whisky and ladies are a fine way to build up trust with new business partners."

"Right."

For all his questionable ethics, I quite liked KC and was sad when he told me he was moving back to the mainland.

"Are you moving back in with your wife?"

"No, don't be crazy. There is a major development in Shenzhen. Big opportunity."

After our final class together, KC offered to take me and Ronan, a silver-haired Scottish colleague, out for a farewell dinner. We went to a posh restaurant where he ordered a bottle of Baijiu which cost more than I earned in a month.

"Very good," he said, taking a sip and wincing. "Almost as good as a beautiful woman."

He poured Ronan and me a glass and ordered a mountain of food; prawns, squid, fish and a lobster.

"So, Andy, why don't you move to Shenzhen?" he asked, cracking the lobster's legs with pliers.

"I'm happy in Hong Kong, thanks."

"But there are many beautiful women in Shenzhen."

"I'm sure there are but I have a girlfriend, KC."

"Oh, such a shame. How about you, Ronan? Are you married?"

Ronan was obviously gay.

"No."

"Why don't you move to Shenzhen, Ronan? There are many beautiful women in Shenzhen. Many."

"I might visit sometime."

"Fantastic. We meet up in Shenzhen. I show you a good time, Ronan!"

"Maybe. How's the squid, Andy?"

As KC drank more Baijiu he became increasingly passionate about the idea of Ronan moving to Shenzhen as his womanizing companion.

"No wife, no problem. We find you many new wives!"

KC settled the hefty bill and was very drunk by the time we left.

"So, where to now, Andy?"

It was 10.30pm on a Monday and drizzling. I was full of seafood and Baijiu.

"I'm going home."

"Home? Are you crazy? Let's go to a nightclub. I know a very good nightclub. Many women."

"Bye, KC. Thanks for dinner."

As I turned to walk away, KC was trying to convince Ronan to join him for a nightcap in a massage parlour called Wild Cats.

Another one of my VIP students was a different kettle of fish altogether, although I imagine KC would have approved. One Wednesday morning I crawled in typically bleary eyed (Tuesdays were $10 for double vodka and mixers at Carnegies) and was greeted at reception by my manager and a stunning Latino woman in her mid-twenties. Wearing a designer leather jacket and tight ripped jeans, she looked like an A-List actress.

"Meet Gabriella, Andy," my manager told me. "You will be her personal tutor for the next two weeks. All of your other classes will be taken care of."

Gabriella was very nice. She was from Sao Paulo and was spending a month in Hong Kong visiting her "friend" – a middle-aged Frenchman who looked as rich as KC. We got on well and she stormed through the encounter classes as well as digressing to talk about Sao Paulo's nightlife and films that she liked. She was a big Scorsese fan. When the four weeks were up, I felt pleased with myself that I'd maintained my professionalism throughout and, perhaps even come across as quite a cool guy. A hip teacher. When we said goodbye, Gabriella went to hug me. I went the wrong way and headbutted her. So close.

***

Louise and I settled – if that's the right word – into the Hong Kong lifestyle; working long hours, eating too many takeaways, drinking in Wan Chai and Lan Kwai Fong and venturing out to the outlying islands, Lamma, Lantau and Cheung Chau at weekends, where we'd stroll in the hills, eat seafood and feel pleased with ourselves for living abroad.

I joined Corinthians, an English football team who played in the esteemed Yau Yee League, although this happened by mistake. I'd been e-mailing the manager from another club who told me to come to training one Wednesday evening. I arrived at the pitches late to find several different sessions going on simultaneously. Tempted to turn and walk away, I bit the bullet and opted for the team nearest to me, nervously jogging over and joining in the stretches in silence while the guys chatted among themselves and shot me confused glances. It worked out well in the end and I managed to get into the squad. They were a strong team and a good group of guys, ranging from early twenties to early fifties with a mix of teachers, recruitment consultants, bankers, pilots and a Russian whose profession was both vague and sinister-sounding. On my debut, a mild evening fixture on a floodlit pitch surrounded by glowing high-rise buildings, I remember thinking; this is brilliant. I live in Hong Kong, I'm playing football, we'll have drinks afterwards. Life is good. We won 3-0 and I scored but such was my excitement after showering and changing, I left my rucksack at the pitches and lost my kit within two hours of receiving it. The good times never last long.

I spent much of my free time with Marvin, a long-haired rugby player from St Helens who I'd half-known at Lancaster University. Marvin went out almost every night of the week and on Fridays, I would meet him at Carnegie's, a small, sticky-floored bar on Lockhart Road, where Coronas were $10 and, sometimes, girls clambered on to the bar and danced. Coyote Ugly is Louise's favourite film but she never warmed to Carnegies, which I thought inconsistent.

With the Sevens and an impressive amateur setup, there is a huge social scene based around rugby in Hong Kong and Marvin, who had been in the city for a couple of years before we'd arrived, seemed to know every expatriate on the island. This was beneficial as, on nights out, I could hang onto his coat-tails and feel as though I too was established. Marvin's rugby teammates were good guys and they welcomed me into their group, thankfully not judging me on the size of my biceps. I've never played rugby. When we were kids, Craig's rugby team were once struggling for numbers and he asked if I could fill in.

"Just go on the wing, Andy. You'll be fine."

I reluctantly agreed. On arriving at the pitch and seeing an opposition full of bearded, tattooed brutes, I pulled out a minute before the game, leaving Craig's team a man down but my bones unbroken.

While I liked the rugby guys, the sport's drinking culture took some getting used to and could be trying at times.

"Ooh, Buffalo, Andy! Down in one, lad!"

I'd just paid £7 for my pint.

"I'm sorry?"

"You can't drink with your right hand. Down it!"

"But..."

"Buffalo's Buffalo, mate."

"Oh."

My old school friend Joanna also moved over to Hong Kong with her boyfriend Ally, which was great. Ally expressed an interest in playing football so I invited him along to Corinthians training, where he played well. When the next squad was announced, he was straight in the starting line-up and I wasn't in the sixteen. I spent the Sunday skulking around, replaying a skewed finish at training over and over in my head, providing great company for Louise. In the evening photos went up on Facebook of the post-match drinks at the Queen Victoria. They'd won, Ally had got man of the match and in the pictures, some of the veteran squad members were picking him up on their shoulders as he drank tequila from the bottle.

Experiencing the true essence of living in an Asian city, I went to watch a Leeds game at Trafalgar, a British pub one Sunday evening. Alone. The pub was empty apart from a middle-aged guy in a Leeds shirt so inevitably we got talking to one another and, after several lagers, made tentative plans to start a Leeds United Hong Kong supporters club. Based on our current figures, we needed a big recruitment push. Leeds got battered but this is nothing unusual and I left the pub having found a new mate, Ken.

You'd be forgiven for thinking that, despite moving to the other side of the world, my lifestyle was much the same as back in Leeds. Louise and I did try to learn Mandarin but it was ultimately unsuccessful. Our tutor was a maverick and often went off-piste, talking about the history of Chinese emperors in-depth. While this was fascinating, it wasn't going to help me achieve my grand plan of becoming rich by expertly communicating with Chinese businessmen.

I did, in fairness, befriend some locals. One of my students, Percy, was a good-natured civil servant in his early fifties. He and I developed a friendship and he became the inspiration behind one of the lead characters in my novel. Is there a greater honour?

Percy regularly invited me to play in football matches between the Hong Kong civil service and the Hong Kong police force. Like the Sri Lankan cricketers at my primary school, I was seen as exotic and enjoyed the attention I got on the pitch, even if most of it was simply shouting "Gweilo! Gweilo!" at me. This means Ghost Man.

Most of the players were over forty and while some still possessed a silky touch, it was the first time in my life that I could outpace defenders. The games were held at bizarre times, ranging from 8am on a Monday morning to 10.30pm on Fridays. Shortly after kick-off one week, a typhoon hit and rain started lashing down. We were playing on the old-school Astroturf and within minutes the pitch was flooded.

We continued playing until we were wading through a shallow lake with water up to your ankles. The ball itself became increasingly irrelevant until it was eventually rendered redundant. A game of sorts continued though. I surmised that the rules were: find a man on the opposing team, chase him and kick as much water as you can on him. After a few minutes one of the opposition players, a grey-haired guy in a 1998 Juventus shirt, stumbled and fell over. Percy's eyes lit up and he shouted something in Cantonese. Giggling and splashing, adult men, fathers and high-ranking police officers sprinted over to the unfortunate and jumped on top of him in a huge pile on. Men just never grow up, do they? I like this.

A squad of local housewives came to Times Square every day and I got along well with them. When they asked if I'd like to play badminton in between my classes one day, I gladly accepted. I assumed it would be a bit of fun and a light workout but the ladies, some of whom were in their sixties, had other ideas. They were decked out in full kit including sweatbands and wearing scowling game faces.

"Morning, Patricia."

"No time for chat, Andy. Now we play."

They were all excellent players. Shuffling around the court at speed, smashing, slicing, chopping and lobbing, beads of sweat swirling under the bright lights of the sports hall. When we played doubles, if I made a mistake, my partner shook her head and shouted, "Aiya!"

It was brutal.

After we'd finished they insisted I join them for Yum Cha – the Chinese equivalent of brunch. While we ate dumplings, spring rolls and weird indeterminable goo, the badminton fanatics returned to their placid, relaxed natures and asked me about phrasal verbs. Normal service resumed.

One of the housewives, a loudmouth, was not a sportswoman and grew jealous when she heard of our badminton outing.

"You come for Yum Cha with me next week, Andy?"

I didn't want to get into a habit of this.

"Fine."

We met at the MTR station at 8am. She was stood with two men of around my own age. I recognised one of them as a student from Times Square Institute, but I hadn't seen the other guy before. He was wearing fake eyelashes and nail varnish.

"Good morning, Andy. My friends have joined us."

"Righto."

"I have surprise for you."

"What's that then?"

"We go karaoke!"

For fuck's sake.

And so, at 8.30am, preceding a ten-hour shift at work, I was eating noodles in private karaoke room while the flamboyant gay guy stood on a sofa belting out "Poker Face" by Lady

Gaga. When asked to join the lady for Yum Cha again, I politely declined.

***

I'm one of those people who moans about the modern celebrity culture and claims to hate the talentless idiots on reality TV shows. The reason for this? I'm jealous. I, like pretty much everyone else, would like to be rich and famous. Surely it would be fun? I try to conceal my celebrity yearning by saying things like:

"I'd hate to be famous anyway. Imagine not being able to go out for a loaf of bread without being hassled. No thanks. Not for me."

"I wouldn't be star-struck by anybody. They're just people, aren't they?"

Really, I know full well that if I met Leonardo Di Caprio in the flesh, I would be spellbound. In my thirty years on this planet I've had a couple of dabbles at the fame game. The first time was when I was ten. Danny's mum was one of the producers for Byker Grove, and managed to pull a few strings to get four extras roles in an episode. I was delighted. Imagine the status in the playground when I'm a famous TV star! The joy was short-lived. My mum had selfishly booked a family holiday to Majorca which clashed with the day of filming so I missed out. The extent of my pals' part was a blink-and-you-miss-it shot of them chucking pebbles into a pond. Still, they were on TV and therefore famous. Much more famous than me anyway. I still think of what might have been if I'd had the opportunity. Would I be writing this from aboard a yacht while George Clooney fixes me a whisky?

My second stab at the big time came in Hong Kong. I was asked whether I'd like to take part in a promotional video for Times Square Institute which, if it went well, might be put on YouTube. I'm almost certain that I got offered the gig because I was the only tall, white person available on the day but this didn't bother me one iota. I'll quite happily be a victim of positive discrimination.

I accepted in a flash and spent half a day filming the video alongside some amateur actors pretending to be students and more excitingly, a pair of pop star twin-brothers from Macau. The premise of the video was that Times Square Institute was excellent and I was an excellent teacher. The pop stars proved this by being in the classroom, looking handsome and happy. All I had to do was stand at the front of the class and appear thoughtful whilst a Chinese girl, inspired by my excellent teaching, delivered a perfect presentation.

I enjoyed hanging out with Asian pop-royalty (maybe a touch hyperbolic) for the day and was pleased with the video apart from a close-up action shot of me nodding my head which went on for far too long and drew attention to my oversized bottom lip.

The video never made it to Hollywood but I'd done enough to land another gig, this time for a photo shoot. The premise of the photos was much the same as the video only this time all I had to do was stand still and smile, surrounded by a bunch of Chinese people and the pop star twins, who were now close to being my actual mates. I didn't think much of the photo shoot, expecting the pictures to feature on our website and possibly in a brochure that nobody would read at a push.

A couple of months later I was in Causeway Bay, a flashy, hectic area crammed with shiny skyscrapers and designer shops. As I was wandering along, something caught my eye on a nearby building. I looked up and saw my own face on a gigantic billboard. A photo of me with my arms around the pop stars with the Chinese students was covering three stories of the building. Incredible. Redemption for missing out on Byker Grove all those years ago. I ran to our flat and got Louise to come and look at my crowning glory, before asking her to take photos of me in front of the massive me. Narcissism at its finest.

My fame did not pay the bills. I pocketed the equivalent of £42 for the photo shoot. I wonder how much the beautiful lady on the Gucci billboard next to mine got? I imagine she got more. The cow. Sadly, I did not earn city-wise adulation from the billboard either. I got the piss taken out of me by my football teammates and the only time I got recognised in the street was when a drunk man from New Zealand approached me.

"Hey, you're that fuckin' guy, aren't you?"

Here we go! I wonder if he's brought a pen for my signature?

"I recognise you," he said, while smoking a cigarette and blowing smoke in my eye. "You're on that fuckin' poster, yeah?"

"Guilty."

He grabbed his mate, a massive rugby player-sort.

"Look, Rick, it's that guy. From that billboard."

Rick looked at me dismissively.

"This fuckin' guy? I don't know who the fuck he is."

They walked off.

Shortly afterwards the billboard came down and, along with it, my short stint in the world of celebrity. What a ride.

35

Returning home from Hong Kong after three exhilarating years was a testing time. Obviously, it was great to catch up with family and pals but it doesn't take long – three beers? – until people have heard enough of your exotic adventures and you crash back to reality feeling as though you've never been away. I'm not complaining about this, it's natural. If you weren't there, there is only so much you care about someone else's adventures. When you look through people's photos, you are much more interested when you are in them, aren't you? God knows why this is, I see enough of my own face.

The homecoming was comparable to moving back in with my parents after university but, with me being older and even more clueless as to what life lay in store, roughly four times as bad. Directionless becomes less exciting as you get older. People do not find a free spirited thirty-year-old endearing. My book had just been accepted by a publisher, which was exciting, but it wasn't due out for another six months so was irrelevant for now. Besides, I was aware that the chances of it catapulting me to international stardom and financial freedom were slim. I needed to sort my life out again. I needed a job.

"You've got to treat unemployment as a full-time job," the internet advice guides told me and while I could see their point, let's be realistic. It wouldn't be possible to spend eight hours a day on recruitment websites without topping yourself and what would that do for your career prospects? I settled on treating unemployment as something a bit more casual; a part-time job-share with flexi-time, where you are allowed to have The Wright Stuff on in the background. Having been burned before by ambiguous job descriptions, I tried to avoid anything that was potentially a door-to-door gig or aggressive recruitment position. My tactic was to do one "proper" application a day ("proper" = filling in an application form) and scattergun my CV to other companies on the off chance.

Due to an increasing desperation regarding employment, after a while I found myself agreeing to attend any meetings or interviews that the innumerable recruitment consultants offered me during their continual bubbly calls. They had names like Ruby or Hayden and most conversations went like this.

"Hiya, Andy. What have you been up to? Time for a quick chat?"

Stop trying to be my mate.

"Yes."

"Okay, fantastic!"

It's not, nobody thinks this is fantastic.

"So, a great opportunity has come up at one of the fastest growing companies in the city!"

Shit job, small company then?

"Okay, what's the job?"

"Well, they are a market leader, offering exciting career progression."

"I'm still none the wiser."

"I think you'd be perfect for this role. It's crying out for someone with your expertise."

What the hell is this job?

"What are your movements like tomorrow morning? Can you swing by for an informal chat with a team leader?"

"Fine."

"He's a great guy. Very punctual though and big on first impressions. I suggest you wear a tie. Make sure your trousers are ironed."

Only slightly humiliating being told how to dress by a girl who is, by the sounds of it, fifteen.

So, at 9am on a Tuesday morning – it's always Tuesday; the grim realities of life are magnified on Tuesdays – I ironed my shirt and went to a new office block at the bottom end of town. It was next door to a strip club.

I was buzzed into the reception area where a heavily made-up woman welcomed me with a scowl and told me to sit down. She was eating a McMuffin. I could hear thumping club music in the background. I assumed that it was coming from the strip club until a black guy in a smart suit came out of the main office and the music flooded through the doorway. Why is club music playing in an office on a Tuesday morning? Again, what the hell is this job?

"Greetings, Mr Carter."

He had a winning smile and a firm handshake. Amiable. Perhaps this job, whatever it is, might be the start of a great new career after all?

I followed him down the corridor and into a tiny meeting room with two chairs and a whiteboard in it.

"Right, let's get started," he said.

On what?

The man turned to the whiteboard and wrote what I think said; Coca-Cola, Samsung and Google. His handwriting was unhelpfully small and his marker pen was on its last legs so the word Google was barely decipherable.

"What do you see here?"

Is this a trick?

"The names of some big companies?"

This was evidently the correct answer as the man then launched into a lengthy diatribe about the business model for each of these companies. He began drawing a diagram on the whiteboard but after a couple of boxes, his marker had completely run out. Undeterred, he acted as though the marker still worked and continued to write on the board. Nothing was showing. Even when he pushed the tip of the marker down really hard. It had clearly run out. Did he know this? I wasn't sure what to do. Was this a test?

After finally putting the marker in his pocket, which was a relief, he began talking about his friend, a qualified doctor from Ghana. This caught me off guard. Apparently, his friend had been a successful doctor in London but decided to give it up after hearing how much money could be earned in this company, which at this point I still knew nothing about. The conclusion of the tale was that his friend was pleased with his decision to quit being a doctor because he had recently been on an all-expenses paid trip to Dubai. The man showed me proof of this on his phone. His friend was stood near the Burj Khalifa and in fairness, he looked happy.

I noticed the clock on the wall and realised that I'd been in the room for twenty minutes. As uplifting as his friend's story had been, we weren't making much progress.

"So, what's your geographical location like, Mr Carter?"

"Do you mean, where do I live?"

"In which geographical locations do you think you could really excel in the field?"

Finally it clicked.

"Is this job a door-to-door sales position?"

He looked at the whiteboard and picked up his marker pen again to try to draw something.

Stop. Stop trying to use the marker pen.

"Is there a basic salary in this job?" I asked him.

"Well, my friend from Ghana..."

"Okay, I don't mean to be rude but I don't think this is for me."

I shook his hand and left the man, looking at his marker pen, forlorn. Outside a pair of pole dancers were stood around smoking. Presumably, it was the end of their shift.

My phone rang.

"Hiya, Andy. What have you been up to? Time for a quick chat?"

36

"If you could be any animal, what would you be and why?"

I'm sorry, what? What kind of a question is that? Until this, the interview had been normal; standard questions answered with feigned confidence, an overplaying of my importance in previous jobs and not knowing who to look at or what to do with my hands. Slightly excruciating and a bit shit. What you'd expect, it's a job interview. They are not meant to be fun. I am firmly against trying to make things that are not, and never will be fun, fun.

I'd been caught off guard.

"Um, a penguin."

Shit. Is a penguin even an animal? Is a bird an animal or just a bird? Is a fish an animal? My mind was racing.

"Why?" Jasmin, the interviewer and business owner asked. She was a well-dressed Indian lady not much older than me.

Oh god.

"Um, I like them I suppose. Everyone likes penguins, don't they?"

What the hell was I talking about? I'd bought a new tie for this and now I was making sweeping generalisations about the popularity of penguins.

"Okay, but why would you be a penguin?"

Make this stop.

"Well, they always seem to be having a good time, don't they? And they are cute."

Did that sound like I was calling myself cute? Why hadn't I composed myself, said "Lion" then spouted some bullshit about strength and leadership? Damn.

"Okay, thanks, Andy. We'll be in touch."

I was stunned when, a few days later, Jasmin called me back and I was offered a job with Jazz Solutions. The other candidates must have been weak. Or non-existent. I accepted. The job was in recruitment. If you can't beat them, join them. It's always "in" recruitment. Jazz solutions was a tiny company with my only colleagues being the entrepreneurial Jasmin and a muscular bloke from Bradford called Wesley. Is a tiny company a start-up? Start-up is an irritating term, isn't it? I was sceptical from the offset but down at heel and in need of money. No income is unfortunately not sustainable.

Training for the role consisted of three days spent wearing headphones and watching motivational videos where a middle-aged American woman in a trouser suit shouted at a crowd of disproportionately overweight people. The gist was that they could be anything they wanted to if they put their minds to it. At one point, she started talking about how great her husband was in bed, which didn't seem relevant at all.

After the training, I still had no idea what my job entailed. I'd also never used an Apple Mac before and had to do that awful thing where you ask a question you should know the answer to, then immediately afterwards have another question that you should definitely know the answer to. When this happened – three times – I sat staring at my screen for ten to fifteen minutes in hope that my first question had been forgotten, plucking up the courage to ask something else, while Jasmin emitted silent exasperation. This was long enough for a tight knot to form in my stomach and beads of sweat to start forming on my temples.

When my duties became apparent, I longed for the training days of headphones and the loud American woman. Jasmin gave me a script which confirmed that this was a cold calling gig. Ring people up that you don't know, ask them if they want any number of the dreadful commission-only sales positions, then try to book them in for a superfluous telephone interview. On the script, there was some nonsense about building rapport with the strangers you were badgering using the acronym, FORM. The idea was to ask people questions about their family, occupation and recreational preferences before delivering your message ("do you want a shit job?") I was unconvinced by the method. Does a conversation about any of these topics make a commission-only door-to-door sales role seem more attractive? If a man I didn't know rang me and asked me about my family, I would think, who the hell is this guy? hang up and consider changing the locks on my doors.

I gingerly made my first call and a man from Eastbourne picked up. Through gritted teeth, I asked some introductory questions. He was oddly receptive and after we'd discussed his golf handicap for a few minutes I bit the bullet and asked if he was interested in selling massage equipment on a commission-only basis. To my astonishment, he said yes and I booked him in for a telephone interview. That was easy, I thought. Maybe there is something in the FORM method after all? I was pleased but unnerved. Something about saying the average earnings are £35k but top reps are getting £100k didn't sit well. It seemed a tad unrealistic. How many vibrating neck supports would you have to sell?

With that said, I cannot deny the buzz of adding the man from Eastbourne to the interview spreadsheet. I got a high-five from both Jasmin and Wesley and started thinking about the possible £40 commission I'd get if he landed the job. Awesome. All I have to do is loosen my morals ever so slightly and I could become rich! Had I found my calling in cold calling?

After two weeks, I realised that no, I had not. Although the man from Eastbourne had passed his telephone interview with flying colours and I'd got my commission, it had been a false dawn. Most people were less enthusiastic about working in bad jobs and many hung up on me, even after I had established that they had two children and liked tennis. This was difficult. Jasmin and Wesley seemed to have a constant stream of people booked in for telephone interviews. How were they doing it?

Over the first few months I managed to just about scrape my targets, but I wasn't enjoying myself. Cold calling a hundred people a day isn't fun. Who knew? My enthusiasm was waning.

"Andy, a word," Jasmin asked one afternoon without looking up from her screen. I'd been pretending to work while mindlessly scrolling up and down the master spreadsheet in a bid to finally teach myself where M, S and T came in the alphabet without having to go through it in my head from the start. I'd also been clicking refresh on my phone to check the scores in a Finnish football game as I'd wagered £20 on HJK Helsinki to beat FC Haka. They were losing 1-0.

At hearing my name, I panicked before attempting to turn my phone off, in the process hitting the lever on my chair with my elbow, sinking me to the chair's lowest level.

"Come over here," Jasmin said.

Adjusting the chair's height in conjunction with wheeling it over proved impossible and I found myself at Jasmin's desk, sunk in the low chair with my long legs unsure where to sprawl.

"I need you to explain something," she said, typing furiously.

"What's the problem?" I asked. It could have been any number of things.

"How did Mr Akhbal pass his telephone interview last week?"

"He seemed like a good candidate," I said.

I had no idea who Mr Akhbal was.

"Andy, you have embarrassed me."

"How come?"

"For starters, Mr Akhbal can't drive and doesn't own a car." This was a prerequisite for the job.

"And he is currently under house arrest for a serious assault case, which was in the papers a few months ago."

"Really?"

"Yes. Did you not ask him any of the safeguarding questions?"

"I'm sure I did. I always do." I said, knowing that I rarely do. My voice was starting to sound like that horrible version of yourself that you hear back on recordings and think; I can't sound like that?

"I think you need to go out and meet some clients. If you can put a face to names, it will help your efficiency."

I was surprised by the outcome. Going to client meetings was regarded as a treat. Why was I getting rewarded for messing up? It dawned on me that this was comparable to the time that Edmund, the naughtiest kid in my school was given the lead role in Bugsy Malone. Give them responsibility with which they will thrive. I agreed to go to the meetings.

The first was with a man who sold AA breakdown cover outside a supermarket in Bradford. He was wearing a high visibility jacket.

"Hi, nice to meet you," I said. "Am I okay to ask you a few questions?"

"Like what?"

"Well, what kind of people do you think this job would appeal to? What should we be looking for?"

"I don't know."

"What are some perks of the job that I can tell candidates about?"

"There aren't any."

"I see. Can I stand with you and watch how it's done?"

"If you must."

I stood next to him.

"Not there."

I stood behind him.

I couldn't drive so Jasmin had arranged to pick me up three hours later. In this time, the man didn't get anybody to sign up for breakdown cover. It was a long three hours.

My second meeting was with a company that sold vacuum cleaners. I was sent on the road for this, my mentor a chain smoker sporting a sinister neck tattoo. He had recently left the army. He was, at least, more responsive to my questionnaire and seemed to like me although I got the impression that if I didn't agree with his political views, many of which were questionable, that could soon change. Our first appointment was at an elderly lady's house near Wakefield. As soon as we set foot in her house I knew something was awry. She'd been expecting someone to come and fix her vacuum cleaner, not tell her it was irreparable before flying into the hard sell. I was stood in her living room, clenching my teeth as the man unconvincingly tried to show her that the latest model could clean ceilings. I remember thinking; how have I ended up here? What decisions have I made in my life that have led to this?

As well as making me question where my life was going, the client meetings didn't improve my figures either. As time went on, it became embarrassing how far behind my colleagues I was. My failings were broadcast to the rest of the team (Wesley) in lurid green marker on a large whiteboard which was dissected every Monday at 8am. In a pseudo-cheery, American-style meeting, we were asked about our strengths and weaknesses then asked to set ourselves targets for the week ahead. The idea was to motivate the team and rally us, although I found it had the opposite effect, leaving my soul destroyed before breakfast.

"So Andy, really poor last week. How do you plan to improve?"

Maybe by not witnessing old ladies being fleeced in their living rooms?

"I suppose I'll make more calls? Be a bit more enthusiastic?"

"Yes! Let's do this, Andy!"

"Yes, let's," I replied.

"Oh, and I'll be listening in to all your calls this afternoon."

Fuck.

There are few things more degrading. I was reprimanded for not employing the FORM technique on a woman who couldn't speak because she was busy. What was I supposed to do?

"Sorry, I'm at the doctors. Can you call back in half an hour?"

"Tell me about your hobbies."

Jasmin gave me some pointers and I deduced that the route to success was: have few qualms about lying, refer to people as "yourself" instead of "you" and incorporate as many sporting analogies as possible into conversation – let's kick off, let's touch base, you're in pole position, by the end of play, the ball's in your court, a ball park figure, move the goalposts.

Two or three times a week, a man who ran a start-up in our block would strut into our office. He was my age if not younger with slicked-back hair. He wore an expensive trench coat regardless of the weather. It seemed that the purpose of his visits was to hug Jasmin then talk about how many hours he'd worked that week. It tended to be a lot of hours. I didn't warm to him. The kind of guy who absolutely loves Movember yet told people he thought the ice bucket challenge was a waste of water.

After six months, I found myself struggling to sleep and thought enough was probably enough. I started looking for new jobs on the internet, which is arguably less fun than selling breakdown cover in a supermarket. This led to daily calls from recruitment consultants, many of who were trying to FORM me. The method must have been in fashion. My entire life had become job sites and cold calls. How had this happened? I was nearly thirty. I sought advice from Louise who assured me, "it will pick up, just stick with it." There was a hidden message here though. No, I will not be the breadwinner whilst you sit at home playing FIFA and trying to write a book.

The inevitable happened when Jasmin invited me for a "chat" in the meeting room. I hate organised chats. I was asked via e-mail which was ominous as only she and I were in the office at the time, sitting four metres from one another. Why not chat there? I followed her to the room in silence.

"So, Andy, what do you think is the best step going forward?"

I considered my response. What should I say? If I had put a positive spin it and said things like, "Bad month. Numbers game. Enthusiastic. I'll kick on!" I might have kept my job.

I couldn't do it.

"It's not for me, is it?"

"I don't think so."

"Okay. Bye."

I walked out feeling both relieved and depressed, a rare emotional cocktail. When I was out on the street I realised that I'd left my cycling gloves in the office but didn't go back to get them. Instead, I went to the bookies and lost some money then sat in Leeds City Square looking at the pigeons wandering around, bobbing their heads. At least I'm not a pigeon, I thought, trying to cheer myself up. It must be pretty shit being a pigeon. And as for penguins, I don't think we have so much in common after all.

37

I wasn't too upset about it being the end of my road in recruitment – the ball had been in my court but I hadn't made the hard yards. I was getting on a bit though, leaving lingering questions about my purpose in this life. I did have a good distraction at least – I was going back to Hong Kong. I had assumed that when Louise and I left, we wouldn't return for several years but, in the event, we were back within months making me feel a little foolish about our grand farewell party. We were going back as my book was coming out and it was deemed desirable that I attended my own launch party.

Marvin said he'd put us up but Louise surprised me at the airport with news that she'd booked a hotel. This was not necessarily a selfless good deed.

"I'm not staying at Marvin's for five nights. He has sweaty rugby kit everywhere and goes out every night."

Fighting jetlag and anxiety, the launch party was a success. Marvin had done a wonderful job of getting a crowd together and it was overwhelmingly well-attended by old friends, football teammates and colleagues from our time in Hong Kong. I managed to stay sober enough not to mess up the speech and felt a touch embarrassed by, but nonetheless enjoyed, being the centre of attention for a while. Seeing my name in lights, albeit in blurred letters via a shaky overhead projector, went some way to easing my existential crisis. Who needs work anyway? I'll just write books forever. A solid plan? Will Louise support me while I get going?

I'd been nervous about the launch for a while but these apprehensions were outmuscled by something else taking up a permanent residency in the back of my mind. I was planning to propose to Louise. On our final evening, we took the ferry from Wan Chai across Hong Kong harbour. I wanted to go to our favourite restaurant in Hong Kong, a steakhouse offering splendid views of the Victoria Harbour, but amid the chaos of the last few days my phone had broken so I hadn't booked a table.

"Sorry sir, we are fully booked."

Had he not seen my face on the billboard last year? Did being a celebrity mean nothing to him? I pulled a pained expression.

"Please?"

He gathered this was important and flashed me a grin.

"I'll see what I can do. Come back in an hour."

We went to a nearby bar to kill some time. Like a man on a stag do I frantically gulped down my pint, swiftly ordering a second.

"What are you acting so weird, Andy?"

"What are you talking about? I'm fine. You're the weird one."

I was reasonably confident that Louise would say yes. After all, the alternative would have been pretty offensive given that we'd been knocking around together for nearly a decade. Why was I so worried?

We returned to the restaurant by which point I was a nervous wreck. The waiter led us to an outdoor table where we sat with picturesque views of the city skyline shimmering in the water.

"I'm just, um, going to the toilet," I said to Louise, banging my knee on the table and heading inside. I ordered a bottle of champagne, before returning to sit down, forehead sweating.

"So, have you enjoyed the trip, Andy?" Louise asked.

"Sure, whatever."

"Oh..."

The waiter returned with the champagne, again taking a little longer than I'd hoped.

"What's this for?" Louise said, sensing something was up.

I took a deep breath, kneeled on the floor, pulled the small box out of my sock, opened it and held the ring out in front of her.

She started to cry. Was this a good thing? Had I misjudged this? My knee was hurting. Why is that Chinese lady on the next table staring at me? My mind was sprinting.

"So, um. Will you marry me?"
Time stopped.
The Chinese lady started crying. What was her game?
Louise started crying too.
Then she smiled.

2017

Louise's train arrived at nine thirty which was an annoying time. I'd been looking forward to having two large bottles of Heineken and watching the friendly between England and Germany. As I was putting my shoes on, Lukas Podolski scored a screamer. It was tipping it down outside so I scurried to the car, coat pulled over head. I'd recently passed my driving test at the third time of asking, which was a huge relief although driving was causing new problems. While I was enjoying the freedom of the open road, Louise and I had recently had a weekend-ruining bust-up because I'd pranged the car on the side of a static bus and neglected to tell her about it.

"What the fuck have you done to the car?"

"Well..."

A bunch of hooligans had set alight to our neighbour's wheelie bin a couple of weeks previously and I'd considered blaming them for the damaged car before thinking better of it. The neighbours – a thirty-something couple – had since got a replacement bin but the man was still aggrieved by the vandalism.

"Hello mate, can I have a word?" he said, one morning as I was leaving for work.

For fuck's sake.

"Sure."

"I'm sure you're aware that we've been through a lot with our bins recently and I couldn't help but notice that you've put your own rubbish in our bin. Can you not do that again? Please."

"I don't think it was me, was it?"

"Well, I found a letter with your name and address in it so I think it was somehow."

Had he been rummaging through the bins?

"Well, I guess I can't argue with that," I said, straining to smile.

"Nothing gets past me, mate. I used to be a marine."

"Right. Sorry."

Passive aggressive veteran aside, I was enjoying life in our new neighbourhood where, with the help of our parents, we'd bought our first home. Fortunately, Louise understands money, mortgages and stamp duty much better than I do and took the reins, but there was still considerable stress along the way. For months, Saturdays were spent slogging around house after house meeting doppelganger couples who'd give us frosty smiles in kitchens as estate agents with gelled hair gushed about north facing gardens. Bundles of cash flittered away as we battled with bidding wars, family feuds and surveys littered with red ink but, after all this – and I'm aware everyone goes through this – we moved into a lovely little terraced house in January.

Buying a new home was not the only adult thing going on. We were also planning the wedding. More stress, more smiling folk after your cash and more bundles of cash flittered away. Less structurally flawed fireplaces at least. After a while, you begin to stop caring about cash.

"We need to transfer hundreds of pounds to a harpist you say? Sure, what are her bank details."

School, college, gap year, university, crap jobs, piss around abroad, crap jobs, okay jobs, buy a house, marriage. Not the most leftfield story for someone born into a middle-class family in 1980s England, is it? Is it bestseller material?

I arrived at Horsforth train station a few minutes early. Two police cars were parked up and a man in a shirt was stood with his hands on his head, getting soaked. I considered what crime he might have committed and sat, listening to Radio 1. An excitable DJ was introducing a "sick banger."

The train pulled in and Louise got off, wheeling a suitcase and carrying too many bags for an overnight stay in London.

"How was your trip?" I asked, starting the car and pulling out of the car park.

"Good, thanks," she said. "Can you stop a second?"

"You still don't trust my driving, do you?"

"Just stop, please."

I stopped.

"So," she said, "I've got something to tell you."

Oh God, what fresh hell was this?

She rummaged in her handbag and pulled out a white, plastic stick. I looked down at it.

Pregnant.

The Thing Is by Andrew Carter

The Thing Is by Andrew Carter

FICTION PUBLISHED BY PROVERSE

Those who enjoy **The Thing Is** may also enjoy the following novels, novellas and short story collections (listed separately).

A Misted Mirror, by Gillian Jones. 2011.

A Painted Moment, by Jennifer Ching. 2010.

Adam's Franchise, by Lawrence Gray. 2016.

An Imitation of Life. 2nd ed, by Laura Solomon. 2013.

Article 109, by Peter Gregoire. 2012.

**Bao Bao's odyssey: from Mao's Shanghai
        to capitalist Hong Kong**, by Paul Ting. 2012.

Black Tortoise Winter, by Jan Pearson. 2016.

Bright Lights and White Nights, by Andrew Carter. 2015.

cemetery – miss you, by Jason S Polley. 2011.

Cop Show Heaven, by Lawrence Gray. 2015.

Cry of the Flying Rhino, by Ivy Ngeow, 2017.

Curveball, by Gustav Preller, 2016.

Death Has a Thousand Doors, by Patricia W. Grey. 2011.

Enoch's Muse, by Sergio Monteiro.
        Scheduled, November 2018.

Hilary and David, by Laura Solomon. 2011.

Hong Kong Hollow, by Dragoş Ilca. 2017.

Instant messages, by Laura Solomon. 2010.

Man's Last Song, by James Tam. 2013.

Mila the Magician, by Zhang Jian (Catherine Chin). 2014.
(English/Chinese bilingual edition).

Mishpacha – family, by Rebecca Tomasis. 2010.

Paranoia (the walk and talk with Angela),
by Caleb Kavon. 2012.

Red Bird Summer, by Jan Pearson. 2014.

Revenge From Beyond, by Dennis Wong. 2011.

The Day They Came, by Gérard Louis Breissan. 2012.

The Devil You Know, by Peter Gregoire. 2014.

**The Monkey in Me: Confusion, Love and Hope
Under a Chinese Sky**, by Caleb Kavon. 2009.

The Perilous Passage of Princess Petunia Peasant,
by Victor E. Apps. 2014. (Young adult fiction.)

The Reluctant Terrorist: in Search of the Jizo,
by Caleb Kavon. 2011.

The Village in the Mountains, by David Diskin. 2012.

Three Wishes in Bardo by C. S. Feng.
Scheduled, November 2018.

Tiger Autumn, by Jan Pearson. 2015.

Tightrope! A Bohemian tale, by Olga Walló.
Translated from Czech by Johanna Pokorny, Veronika
Revická & others.   Edited by Gillian Bickley & Olga
Walló,
with Verner Bickley. 2010.

University Days, by Laura Solomon. 2014.

Vera Magpie, by Laura Solomon. 2013.

SHORT STORY COLLECTIONS

Beyond Brightness, by Sanja Särman.
    November 2016.

Odds and Sods, by Lawrence Gray. 2013.

The Shingle Bar Sea Monster and other stories,
    by Laura Solomon. 2012.

The Snow Bridge and other Stories,
    by Philip Chatting. 2015.

Under the Shade of the Feijoa Trees and other stories,
    by Hayley Ann Solomon. Scheduled, April 2019.

FICTION – CHINESE LANGUAGE

The Monkey in Me, by Caleb Kavon.
    Translated by Chapman Chen. 2010.

Tightrope! A Bohemian Tale, by Olga Walló.
    Translated by Chapman Chen. 2011.
    Chinese translation supported by the Ministry of
Culture of the Czech Republic.

~~~

FIND OUT MORE ABOUT OUR AUTHORS BOOKS PRIZES AND EVENTS

Visit our website:
http://www.proversepublishing.com

Visit our distributor's website: <www.chineseupress.com>

Follow us on Twitter
Follow news and conversation: <twitter.com/Proversebooks>
OR
Copy and paste the following to your browser window and follow the instructions:
https://twitter.com/#!/ProverseBooks
"Like" us on www.facebook.com/ProversePress

Request our free E-Newsletter
Send your request to info@proversepublishing.com.

Availability
Most books are available in Hong Kong and world-wide from our Hong Kong based Distributor,
The Chinese University Press of Hong Kong,
The Chinese University of Hong Kong, Shatin, NT,
Hong Kong SAR, China.
Email: cup-bus@cuhk.edu.hk
Website: <www.chineseupress.com>.
All titles are available from Proverse Hong Kong
http://www.proversepublishing.com
and the Proverse Hong Kong UK-based Distributor.

We have **stock-holding retailers** in Hong Kong,
Singapore (Select Books),
Canada (Elizabeth Campbell Books),
Andorra (Llibreria La Puça, La Llibreria).
Orders can be made from bookshops in the UK and elsewhere.

Ebooks
Most of our titles are available also as Ebooks.

40728330R00157

Made in the USA
Columbia, SC
14 December 2018